JASON MEYER
MARK
FOR YOU

the**good**book
COMPANY

Mark For You
© Jason Meyer, 2022

Published by:
The Good Book Company

thegoodbook.com | thegoodbook.co.uk
thegoodbook.com.au | thegoodbook.co.nz | thegoodbook.co.in

ISBN: 9781784982973

Cover design by Ben Woodcraft | Printed in India

CONTENTS

SERIES PREFACE

Each volume of the *God's Word For You* series takes you to the heart of a book of the Bible, and applies its truths to your heart.

The central aim of each title is to be:

- Bible centered
- Christ glorifying
- Relevantly applied
- Easily readable

You can use *Mark For You:*

To read. You can simply read from cover to cover, as a book that explains and explores the themes, encouragements and challenges of this part of Scripture.

To feed. You can work through this book as part of your own personal regular devotions, or use it alongside a sermon or Bible-study series at your church. Each chapter is divided into two (or occasionally three) shorter sections, with questions for reflection at the end of each.

To lead. You can use this as a resource to help you teach God's word to others, both in small-group and whole-church settings. You'll find tricky verses or concepts explained using ordinary language, and helpful themes and illustrations along with suggested applications.

These books are not commentaries. They assume no understanding of the original Bible languages, nor a high level of biblical knowledge. Verse references are marked in **bold** so that you can refer to them easily. Any words that are used rarely or differently in everyday language outside the church are marked in **gray** when they first appear, and are explained in a glossary toward the back. There, you'll also find details of resources you can use alongside this one, in both personal and church life.

Our prayer is that as you read, you'll be struck not by the contents of this book, but by the book it's helping you open up; and that you'll praise not the author of this book, but the one he is pointing you to.

Carl Laferton, Series Editor

FOREWORD

In certain evangelical circles, reading the Pauline epistles is prized over reading and studying the Gospels. Some mistakenly think that the really deep theology should be mined from Paul's letters. They consider the Gospels to be just a necessary introduction, sort of like an anteroom before one enters the great room of a house. I am thankful that many evangelicals are pushing back against this idea today. Many scholars are bringing out of the treasure house of the Gospels things both new and old (Matthew 13:51–52), and young students are entranced with the vision of Jesus as he is portrayed in the greatest story ever told. Some are awaking from their scholarly slumbers, realizing that it makes no sense to depreciate the fourfold story of our Lord and Savior.

One reason that the Gospels are overlooked or minimized is because they are narratives—stories that record what Jesus Christ did and said. Now, we would think that such stories would delight and enthrall readers, because we all know there is nothing like reading a good story. And yet we may end up reading the Gospel stories at a superficial level, so that once we are familiar with the basic account, we want to move on. But these stories are also carefully structured—and in a profoundly theological way—and there are riches for readers that are missed on a surface reading.

If some are prone to skate over the Gospels, that is particularly true with the Gospel of Mark. After all, it is the shortest of the Gospels. Matthew's Gospel contains great discourses (long teaching sections) that are missing in Mark. Luke, in his Gospel, also tells the story in a distinctive manner, adding many stories and unforgettable parables that aren't in Mark and Matthew. Readers are also drawn to the ineffable beauty of the portrait of Jesus painted in the Gospel of John.

Where does that leave us with Mark? A careful reader will see the stunning craftsmanship and structure of this Gospel. The theology of the book is conveyed through the narrative, so that as we read the story, we discover who Jesus is and what his words and deeds mean for our lives today.

And that brings me to Jason Meyer's expository guide. This book is characterized by clarity and faithfulness, so that here readers encounter Jesus just as he is presented by Mark. I was struck repeatedly by the lucidity of Meyer's presentation, and he uses illustrations and stories from the modern world to unpack Mark's meaning. And that is not all. The theology of the Gospel is beautifully presented in this volume. This book is relatively brief, but the theology dug out of Mark is profound and life-changing, taking us back 2,000 years to the most momentous events in all of history. I think of the words Augustine heard in a garden around 1,600 years ago and now apply them to this wonderful resource: "Take up and read" (*Tolle lege*).

Thomas R. Schreiner
February 2022

INTRODUCTION TO MARK

Church history has not always been kind to the **Gospel*** of Mark. It has sometimes been seen as the least important Gospel simply because it is the shortest. Some have further cast doubt on its value by regarding it as a kind of *Cliff's Notes* version or an abridged form of Matthew's Gospel (Augustine of Hippo, *The Harmony of the Gospels*, p 78).

Perhaps I picked up on these negative vibes and allowed them to color my view of Mark's Gospel. I still remember the first time I taught through it. I had done a lot of my doctoral work in Paul's letters. Then I got a job as a Bible professor, and I taught a New Testament Survey class. I decided to start with the Gospel of Mark because many people think it was the first Gospel to be written. I entered that study with low expectations and a somewhat impatient eagerness to get through Mark so that I could get to the longer Gospels.

But I was wrong, and my life was changed. If I have a first love now in Scripture, it is this Gospel and the Jesus who stands forth from its pages.

I quickly discovered that Mark is not an abridged version. In fact, when the Gospel writers share a story in common, Mark often gives the longest account. Mark gives us extra color in certain stories, which helps them come alive. But these detailed additions do not make the overall story feel long.

Mark's Gospel is fast-paced and action-packed. Mark uses the word "immediately" 41 times. The action comes fast, and the conflict escalates quickly. Mark devotes more time and attention to stories about Jesus than to the teaching of Jesus. But make no mistake: the teaching is there. What Jesus says is often the climax of the story. It's just that Mark does not record lengthy sections of Jesus' teaching all in one go.

Mark begins with a burst of speed right out of the gate as he declares that Jesus is the divine "Son of God" (Mark 1:1). There are no infancy narratives about the birth of Jesus (Matthew 1:18 – 2:18;

* Words in **gray** are defined in the Glossary (page 255).

Luke 1:5 – 2:21). No genealogies (Matthew 1:1-17; Luke 3:23-38). No explanations of how he carefully compiled this account of Jesus (Luke 1:1-4). Mark does not meander with his message. He narrates this story in such a way that in town after town and story after story the message sounds: *The Son of God has come!* There is a trumpet blast at the beginning (1:1-11) and end (15:39) and at all points in between to show that Jesus is the divine Son of God (3:11; 5:7; 9:7; 12:1-11; 13:32; 14:61-62).

> The message does not meander. But mystery keeps on building.

But in the midst of this consistent message, there is a mystery that keeps building. Conflict and confusion abound because people struggle mightily to understand the mystery of how the powerful Son of God (as he's shown to be in Mark 1 – 8) could also be the Suffering Servant (as we see increasingly in Mark 8 – 16). The mystery and the suspense build up a head of steam as the Son gets closer and closer to **Calvary**. Indeed, it is only at the cross that someone finally puts both pieces together and confesses that the crucified Christ is the divine Son of God (Mark 15:39).

The Gospels are certainly intended to speak to everyone, but each Gospel writer had a more specific target audience in mind. The Gospel of Mark is especially focused on Roman **Gentiles**. Mark explains things from **Hebrew** culture that Roman Gentiles would not understand. Therefore, it is significant that the climax of the Gospel shows a Roman centurion testifying to the truth that the crucified Jesus is the Son of God.

The Main Attraction

Rather than devote space at the beginning to a detailed introduction of the historical background of Mark, I will take a page out of Mark's playbook and move immediately to the main attraction of Mark: Jesus! Mark portrays Jesus in a way that is stunningly compelling.

His unrivaled power and wisdom leave one with a sense of awe, but the portrayal of his unparalleled heart touches us even more deeply. Consider Mark 6:34 as an example:

"When [Jesus] went ashore he saw a great crowd, and he had compassion on them, because they were like sheep without a shepherd."

The word for "compassion" here is a wonderful and picturesque Greek word: *splanchnizomai*. That word will not mean anything unless you have a medical background and know the word splanchnology (i.e. the study of the gut). Do you see the stunning truth about Jesus? Sometimes people talk about having "a gut feeling." It means you feel something from deep within you. In the same way, Jesus did not have some superficial pity for the people. Seeing their needs stirred him way down in the depths of his being. It is hard to remain unmoved when we see Jesus so moved to compassion.

In the **incarnation**, we see not only the power of God and the wisdom of God but the heart of God. Jesus pours out his love on many different people in story after story all the way to the crescendo of the cross. It was there that God poured out his **wrath** on Jesus so that he could pour out his love on us through Jesus.

Basic Outline of Mark

1. **Introduction** (1:1-13; *Mark For You* ch. 1)

   Jesus' Baptism (1:1-11)

   Jesus' Temptation (1:12-13)

2. **Jesus in Galilee** (1:14 – 8:21; *Mark For You* ch. 2 – 6)

   Beginning Ministry (1:14-45)

   Growing Controversy (2:1 – 3:6)

   The Clear Divide Between Insiders and Outsiders (3:7 – 4:34)

   Signs and Responses (4:35 – 8:21)

3. **The Journey to Jerusalem** (8:22 – 10:52; *Mark For You* ch. 7 – 9)

Two-Stage Healing of Blindness (8:22-26)

Peter's Confession: Partial Sight (8:27-30)

First Passion Prediction (8:31-38)

The Transfiguration and Remaining Blindness (9:1-13)

Belief and Unbelief (9:14-29)

Second Passion Prediction (9:30-50)

Blindness of the Pharisees and the Disciples (10:1-16)

Blindness of the Rich Man and the Disciples (10:17-31)

Third Passion Prediction (10:32-45)

Healing of the Blind Man and Discipleship (10:46-52)

4. **Jesus in Jerusalem** (11:1 – 15:39; *Mark For You* ch. 10 – 14)

Jesus and the Jerusalem Temple (11:1 – 13:37)

Jesus and the Temple of His Body (14:1 – 15:39)

5. **Conclusion: Burial and Resurrection** (15:40 – 16:8; *Mark For You* ch. 14)

1. INTRODUCING THE SON OF GOD

The first 13 verses are like the opening of a symphony. A well-composed symphony will sound the note or theme that the rest of the musical score will develop and explore. Mark's opening note is his own confession of faith: his belief that Jesus is the Son of God. But Mark is not content to sound this note in isolation. His introduction consists of four stunning testimonies announcing that Jesus is the divine Son of God. This method of sharing multiple testimonies creates an echo effect that builds in volume until it climaxes with the crescendo of God the Father's testimony at the **baptism** of Christ.

But the introduction also sounds a note of cosmic conflict and drama. Satan comes to tempt Jesus—and the Son of God cannot save sinners if he becomes a sinner.

The Testimony of Mark

With great speed, Mark gets right to the point: "The beginning of the gospel of Jesus Christ, the Son of God" (**v 1**).* The Gospel of Mark is all about the "gospel." In the ancient world, the word "gospel" or "good news" would most often be used of the declaration of a military victory (e.g. 1 Samuel 31:9). But this gospel is defined in relation to the person of Jesus. The good news of salvation is not first and foremost a proposition but a person. Jesus is the embodiment of the good news.

The word "beginning" helps create the effect of bursting off the

---

* All Mark verse references being looked at in each chapter part are in **bold**.

starting blocks. But it does not mean merely first in sequence. It also means "origin." So it has the echo of "creation." The first book of the Bible opens in the same way: "In the beginning, God created the heavens and the earth" (Genesis 1:1). The gospel of Jesus Christ is nothing less than a new creation. It is the unprecedented moment when the Creator of the world steps onto the stage of the world he made. The *beginning of the good news* is wrapped up in the mind-splitting, jaw-dropping identity of Jesus, the eternal Son of God, who has come in the flesh as the promised **Messiah**.

But Mark doesn't want you to take his word for it. He is not claiming to speak an opinion based on his own authority. He is claiming to speak truth from God. Mark now will show how God has spoken through the prophets in a way that perfectly accords with this testimony.

The Testimony of the Prophets

Mark **1:2-3** is a mixed quotation from three places: Exodus 23:20, Malachi 3:1; and Isaiah 40:3. Exodus 23:20 took place centuries before Jesus, when God had delivered the Israelites from Egypt (the exodus). God declared that he was going to send a messenger before them. So, Mark **1:2-3** is the first of many times in Mark that we hear the overtones of the exodus deliverance—portraying the deliverance Jesus brings as a new exodus.

This new deliverance was foretold by the prophets Malachi and Isaiah, who are also being quoted here. Malachi 3:1 warns that God will once again send a messenger. This time he will prepare the way before the dreaded day of judgment, which he calls the "day of the Lord" (Malachi 4:5). Isaiah 40 speaks of preparation as well. The word of God comes to God's people in exile and points to a voice crying in the wilderness, which will prepare the way of the Lord.

Mark stitches these three texts together because they highlight the careful preparation that must precede the coming of the Messiah. The key to understanding this verse is to look at the various personal pronouns. There is a first person ("I," "my"), a second person ("you," your"), and a third person ("him"). The "I" is a reference to God as the one who sends the messenger (Mark **1:2**). The "you" and "your" have to be references to the people. The third person ("make straight paths for *him*") is explicitly identified as "the Lord" (**v 3**). God is sending someone to prepare the way for the Lord to come. So the prophets testify to the divine identity of Jesus: he is "the Lord" in these prophecies.

This prophecy of the forerunner had already been fulfilled. God gave John the Baptist the task of getting people ready for the greatest moment in human history.

The Testimony of John the Baptist

So, third, Mark gives us the testimony of John the Baptist (**v 4-8**). John prepares people to receive the Messiah by a baptism of **repentance**. This method of preparation highlights the true problem with the people (sin against God) and the solution for the people (repentance).

Mark's portrayal of John also includes where he does this: in the wilderness and the Jordan River (**v 4-5**). The Jordan was a significant landmark. It was not just a river; it was a *border* between the wilderness and the promised land. The people crossed it when they first reached the **promised land** after escaping Egypt and wandering in the wilderness. Now the Jews are receiving a call to leave their place of spiritual exile and enter the wilderness as the place of preparation from which God will deliver them into a new "promised land."

John was not the first person to make this call:

"Even in the first century, Jewish prophets led followers to reenact the crossing of the Jordan River in hopes of anticipating Israel's liberation from the Roman Empire."
(David Rhoads and Donald Michie, *Mark as Story*, p 69)

But the deliverance John points to is not deliverance from the Romans. Earthly powers pale in comparison with the enslaving and condemning power of sin. Unlike other so-called prophets, John called people to the Jordan to point them to a spiritual problem, not a political one.

Mark now helps the reader see the true identity of John (**Mark 1:6**). He gives a physical description of what John wore (camel's hair, leather belt) and what he ate (locusts, wild honey). The point of the description is to identify John as a prophet like Elijah in terms drawn from 2 Kings:

> "[The king] said to [his messengers], 'What kind of man was he who came to meet you and told you these things?' They answered him, 'He wore a garment of hair, with a belt of leather about his waist.' And he said, 'It is Elijah the Tishbite.'"
>
> (2 Kings 1:7-8)

Imagine a movie on the American Civil War. The camera moves to a person, and there is a still shot of his features. He is tall, with a dark beard and a tall, black top hat. The movie does not need to have anyone break in and say, "By the way, that is Abraham Lincoln." Everyone recognizes him by his distinctive dress. In the same way, everyone can see that John wears the distinctive dress of Elijah—so he is a prophet like Elijah.

Mark finally gives the microphone to John so he can give his testimony about Jesus (Mark **1:7**). John is the voice crying in the wilderness from Isaiah 40:3, and his message also comes from Isaiah 40. His preaching prepares the Jews for the startling fact that the Mighty God is coming (Isaiah 40:10). John is not the Messiah. In fact, John says he is not even worthy to do the most menial task of a servant. The Jews regarded unfastening someone's sandals as a task reserved for slaves. Jewish instructions say that a disciple should do everything for his teacher that a slave would do—except this one thing (Morna Hooker, *The Gospel According to St. Mark*, p 38).

John again highlights how much greater the Messiah is by contrasting himself with him. "I baptize you with water; but he will baptize you with the Holy Spirit" (Mark **1:8**). The distinguishing mark of John's **ministry** is his connection to water, which is why he is often called John *the Baptist*. The defining mark of the Messiah's ministry will be his connection to the Holy Spirit. What a contrast! No one can bestow the Spirit in the Old Testament except God. Who could be so identified with the Spirit that he has control to command the Spirit? The Messiah must be God incarnate!

The Testimony of God

Fourth, we have the testimony of God himself (**v 9-11**). The baptism of Jesus is an epic event—the opening overture of his ministry. It is such a familiar story that many people miss the scandal of it. You should stop in your tracks and ask, "Wait a minute—why?" This was a baptism of repentance. Jesus was not a sinner, and he did not need to repent! What could Jesus possibly be doing in that water? Jesus is identifying with the need of the people that he has come to save. In Christian baptism, going under the water means dying with Jesus, and coming up out of the water means rising to newness of life with Jesus. But before we could identify with Jesus in our baptism, he had to identify with us and all that we had done as sinners in his baptism.

The passing reference to geography (**v 9**) **foreshadows** the rejection of Jesus that will take place later. Jesus came from Nazareth. This place was something of a byword for unworthiness (see Nathanael's quip in John 1:46). The Mighty One of Isaiah 40 came from an obscure, lowly place that people mocked.

Another surprising aspect of the story is the word Mark chooses for what happens to the heavens. Matthew and Luke say that the heavens were opened, but Mark says they were "torn open" (Mark **1:10**). The tearing or rending of the heavens was the fulfillment of Isaiah's prayer: "Oh that you would rend the heavens and come down" (Isaiah 64:1). This irreversible tear is good news indeed. Some people use the phrase "All hell is breaking loose." The picture here is so much better. Mark is saying that all *heaven* is breaking loose (Paul Minear, *The Gospel According to Mark*, p 50).

Another reason why Mark uses the word "torn" is to connect what happens here with the end of the story. The story begins with the tearing of the heavens; it ends with the tearing of the temple curtain (Mark 15:38). This curtain had been a symbol of humanity's separation from God. So, first the heavens are torn, and God comes to us. Then the temple curtain is torn so that we can go to God. The sacrifice of Christ has now torn open the way to God.

Next the Holy Spirit descends upon Jesus. The Spirit does not have a physical form, but here he descends in a dove-like way (**1:10**). I think the point of this detail is to convey that the descent was not the swooping attack of an eagle but the gentle hovering of a dove. This is a picture of the new creation because the same Spirit once hovered over the chaos of waters at the beginning of time (Genesis 1:2). The coming of the incarnate God and the gentle hovering presence of the Holy Spirit signal the arrival of the new creation.

The Father testifies that Jesus is the divine Son of God, but his declaration goes further: Jesus is also the promised Suffering Servant. Where do we see those two things? God the Father uses the language of two texts: Psalm 2:7 ("I will tell of the decree: The LORD said to me, 'You are my Son'") and Isaiah 42:1 ("Behold, *my servant,* whom I uphold; my chosen, *in whom my soul delights*"—my emphasis). Jesus is the Son of God from Psalm 2 and also the servant of God from Isaiah 42: the servant who would later be described as suffering to bear the sins of others (Isaiah 53). The Father's testimony provides the structural framework for all of Mark. The powerful Son of God (Mark 1 – 8) is also the Suffering Servant (Mark 8 – 16). Throughout Mark, people struggle mightily to put those two aspects of Jesus' identity together. But the Father does it seamlessly. His testimony highlights how he is going to address his rebellious world: the divine Son has come to be the suffering servant.

> The Father's testimony provides the framework for all of Mark.

The beloved Son reference comes from the story of the command to sacrifice Isaac: "Take your son, your only son Isaac, whom you love"

(Genesis 22:2). Jesus' sacrifice would take place in the same region as the sacrifice of Isaac (Mount Moriah is later identified as Jerusalem: see Genesis 22:2 and 2 Chronicles 3:1). So this language seems to further establish how the Son will suffer as a sacrifice.

The identification of Jesus as the Servant of Isaiah 42 is significant for another reason. The very next phrase of Isaiah 42:1 says this about the Servant: "I have put my Spirit upon him; he will bring forth justice to the nations."

The author, the prophets, John the Baptist, and God the Father all testify to Jesus' true identity. They tell the crystal-clear truth that the divine Son has come into the world. But the response of the Father is unique: Jesus is his beloved Son. The Father's words do not make that relationship; they only highlight the loving relationship that has always existed.

As the prophets had already announced, the people were to respond with repentance when he came. But even as John preached repentance, Jesus identified himself with sinners through baptism. The divine Son came to be a sacrifice for sinners. There is no gospel apart from the suffering and death of the Messiah. There is no salvation without his **substitutionary** sacrifice.

God the Father doesn't need to repent and believe, because he has always truly known and truly loved the Son. We, on the other hand, have walked in both ignorance and rebellion. We must repent and believe that Jesus is the Son of God in order to receive the benefit of what he has done.

Once we have done so, our testimony about the Son becomes similar to the Father's. The Father delights in the Son, and everyone who believes does the same. So the Father's confession of delight in the Son sets the stage for the rest of Mark, as we are invited to delight in everything we see Jesus saying and doing in the rest of the story. There is no one like him. There is no one worth more and nothing that can satisfy like him. Nothing else comes close to Jesus Christ.

Questions for reflection

1. How do you think you would have responded if you had been part of the crowd at Jesus' baptism?

2. How would you sum up Mark's message in these first eleven verses?

3. How could these verses help you explain to a non-Christian friend what you believe about Jesus and why?

PART TWO

Mark **1:12-13** continues to set the stage for Jesus' public ministry. Jesus follows the movements of Israel in the exodus and relives their experiences. Just like Israel after their escape from Egypt, he is super-naturally led into the wilderness to face temptation.

The Gospel of Mark forces us to consider not only the person and work of Christ but the person and work of Satan. We must beware of either underestimating or overestimating the influence of the devil.

Underestimating the devil is deadly. One of his greatest tricks is to get people to ignore him altogether and even to doubt his existence. He does some of his best work in the shadows. The greatest deception is one in which you can't even detect the deception until it is too late.

Overestimating the devil—seeing him everywhere and blaming him for everything—is also a mistake. The devil is not God—not even close. He is not almighty. He is not all-knowing. He is not omnipresent (able to be everywhere at once). He needs a well-organized army of demons to do his dirty work because he is limited.

But he is a mastermind. He reminds me of what Sherlock Holmes says about Professor Moriarty—he is the "organizer of half that is evil and of nearly all that is undetected in this great city" (Arthur Conan Doyle, "The Final Problem"). The devil, too, stands behind a web of crime without always being directly detected.

Of the two mistakes we could make, my guess is that we are much more likely to veer toward the first and underestimate him. The scope of his power and impact is startling. Moriarty is like a common shoplifter compared to Satan. The "whole world lies in the power of the evil one" (1 John 5:19). The devil offers Jesus all the kingdoms of the world because they have been delivered to him and he can give them to whomever he wills (Luke 4:5-6). The devil is "the father of lies" (John 8:44), but he is not lying about the **fallen** world belonging to him at some level. The Bible calls this age the "present evil age" (Galatians 1:4) because the evil one is the "god of this world"

(2 Corinthians 4:4). When was it delivered to him? The answer is that Adam (the first man) was the first ruler of the world as God's **vice-regent** (Genesis 1:26). Satan deceived Adam and Eve, and the world was plunged into the present evil age with Satan as the new ruler (John 12:31; 14:30; 16:11).

Jesus has come to dethrone him. "The reason the Son of God appeared was to destroy the works of the devil" (1 John 3:8). In a sense, the temptation narrative is the first offensive in that mission. But we cannot read this story as if Jesus were on his own. The temptation narrative is a triumph of the **Trinity**.

Mark does not say, *After the baptism, Jesus went out into the wilderness*. That is technically true. But Mark is highlighting how he got there. It was on foot, but it was also the Father's plan and by the Spirit's power. The word choice here is so strong and so emphatic for what the Spirit does. The verb translated as "sent" means "cast out" or "drive out." It is the word used when Jesus casts out demons. Mark **1:12** places stress on the propelling power of the Spirit.

Mark highlights the fact that Jesus was not acting independently but submissively and obediently, as the beloved Son who always obeys the Father. He never went rogue—never. The trinitarian picture present at the baptism continues now in the temptation. The Father planned it, the Spirit empowered Jesus in it, and Jesus submitted to it.

Echoes of Temptation

Verse 13 is like walking into an echo chamber. Have you ever had that experience? You say "echo," and you hear the reverberation back many times: "Echo, echo, echo." I believe there are three key echoes from the Old Testament here. Of course, you don't have to make these three connections for this text to make sense. Mark was writing for Gentiles, who may have completely missed the Old Testament references. But part of their **discipleship** would have been to read all the Scriptures as pointing to Jesus.

In this regard, reading the Bible can be a little bit like a New Orleans barbecue sauce that I enjoy making. This sauce has a multi-layered depth of flavor. You can taste many different flavors in one sauce. Similarly, the more of these Scriptural connections we make, the richer and deeper and more satisfying any verse becomes to our spiritual palette. We can keep coming back to the Bible again and again because there is always more to see.

> Reading the Bible is like tasting a multi-layered sauce.

The first echo takes us back to Israel's wandering in the wilderness. The combination of the two words "wilderness" and "forty" cannot help but bring back to mind the wandering of Israel in the wilderness for forty years. Remember that Jesus submitted to a baptism of repentance for sin because he was identifying with the people he came to save. His very name means "the Lord saves" because "he will save his people from their sins" (Matthew 1:21). The identification with the people here takes the form of Jesus as the new Israel.

The addition of temptation makes the connection even stronger between Israel and Jesus. Israel was also called God's "son" (Exodus 4:22). Israel was also tested in the wilderness; but Israel was disobedient.

With the reference to Satan, the second echo also takes us back, this time past Israel all the way to the temptation of Adam and Eve. Jesus, the last Adam, will obey where the first Adam failed. That is why the temptation takes place in the wilderness and not a garden paradise. Adam's failure got humanity cast out of paradise, but Jesus left the heavenly paradise to seek us in the wilderness—in order to bring us back to paradise.

The temptation Jesus faced was greater in every way than the one Adam and Eve faced. Trust is not difficult in paradise because all the provisions needed to sustain life are present. Adam and Eve could eat from all the trees except one. The wilderness, however, is life-threatening because the things needed to sustain life are missing. How can you trust God to provide for you when you cannot see any means of provision around you?

Satan and the wild animals stand on one side as threats to Jesus, while the angels are helps to Jesus. They minister to him. This is not as odd as it sounds at first if you have ears tuned to biblical history. Think back to the story of Elijah, when he faced a difficult time in the wilderness in 1 Kings 19:1-8. Jezebel threatened his life so he went a day's journey into the wilderness. He sat down in dejection and asked the Lord that he might die. He slept, and then an angel came and woke him up and strengthened him with food and water.

The Father's Shelter

Our third and last echo is seen in the combination of the wild animals and the angels. I believe that Mark brings both into the picture because he is connecting Jesus' experience to dwelling in the shelter of his Father. This is an echo of Psalm 91:11-13, the one place that brings angels and wild animals together in regard to times of distress:

"For he will command his angels concerning you
   to guard you in all your ways.
 On their hands they will bear you up,
   lest you strike your foot against a stone.
 You will tread on the lion and the adder;
   the young lion and the serpent you will trample underfoot."

At the start of the same psalm, we read:

"He who dwells in the shelter of the Most High
   will abide in the shadow of the Almighty.
 I will say to the LORD, 'My refuge and my fortress,
   my God, in whom I trust.'" (v 1-2)

This is certainly true of Jesus. With danger all around, Jesus made the Father his dwelling place and, in the heat of the desert, he rested in the shadow of the Almighty. God delivered him from the devil and the wild animals. Jesus is the Genesis 3:15 Savior, who trampled the tempter and **serpent** underfoot.

Jesus was tempted in every way as we are, yet without sin (Hebrews 4:15). When I was a professor, people would tell me that they could not relate to Jesus because he never sinned. What does he really know of the power of temptation if he never gave in to it?

Author Paul Tripp has the best word picture in answer to this confusion. He asks us to imagine a strong man bending an iron bar at a fair.

"The first bar is thin and weak, and he bends it to a ninety-degree angle and it breaks. The second bar is much thicker and stronger and even though the strong man exerts all his strength, it bends until the ends touch, but never breaks. Which bar endured more pressure? The second! It absorbed the full force of the man's strength and didn't break. On earth, Jesus was like that second bar. Because he never gave in, because he did not run away, because he never went where temptation would lead, but stood strong until that moment of temptation was over, and he endured the full power of temptation. Christ endured stress, pain, suffering, and sacrifice of an intensity that we will never face because he did not break. He stood strong against sin for us. He endured everything the world could throw against him." (*Instruments in the Redeemer's Hands*)

Here is what happens when we catch the echo of Psalm 91: we can be certain of the answer to the question "How did Jesus withstand all that the fallen world could throw at him?" The answer is love! The loving relationship between the Father and Son on display earlier (Mark **1:10-11**) is still on display here (**v 12-13**). Jesus is revealed to be the beloved Son at his baptism, and the Father still loves him as he sends him into the wilderness. Jesus loves the Father and trusts him. The Father and the Son share a love and a delight that cannot be broken by anything—no wilderness, no wild animals, and no devil! This exactly fulfils the end of the psalm: "Because he holds fast to me in love, I will deliver him" (Psalm 91:14).

This was not the last time Jesus faced Satan's temptation. It would happen again in the Garden of Gethsemane. Once again it was love for the Father that drove Jesus forward.

> "I will no longer talk much with you, for the ruler of this world is coming. He has no claim on me, but I do as the Father has commanded me, *so that the world may know that I love the Father.* Rise, let us go from here." (John 14:30-31, my emphasis)

The Father's delight in and acceptance of Jesus is what enabled Jesus to endure the threats and terrors of the temptation. Adam and Eve failed to trust God's character and instead trusted Satan's words. But the beloved Son knows the character of both the Father and Satan. The Father is perfectly and purely true and trustworthy; Satan has no truth in him. The Son defends the character of the Father. He said, "Not what I will, but what you will" (Mark 14:36). And he went to the cross for us and our salvation, and to vindicate the Father's character and glory!

Every time we have sinned we have essentially said, "God, not your will but mine be done." Jesus, the Savior for sinners, said, "Not what I will, but what you will." The Father and Son are in perfect harmony and alignment with no interruption. Obedience should be the glory of humanity. Now for the first time we see what we were supposed to be like. Jesus can fully sympathize because he understands temptation, but he can also fully save because he overcame temptation.

Questions for reflection

1. Do you think you take the devil too seriously or not seriously enough? How does this passage correct your view?

2. What does Mark 1:1-13 show us about the relationships between Father, Son, and Holy Spirit?

3. What particular temptations do you face at the moment? How could what you have read help or challenge you when you are tempted to sin?

2. WHAT JESUS CAME FOR

We turn now to the first of the three main movements in Mark: Jesus' ministry in and around Galilee. This is the canvas upon which Mark will paint sign after sign showing that Jesus is the divine Son of God.

1:14-45 is a snapshot of Jesus' ministry in Galilee. He preaches, calls disciples, casts out demons, and heals the sick. But these verses are structured in such a way to show the priority of preaching over healing. Casting out demons and healing the sick function as the proof of the message of Jesus' preaching. When the disciples want Jesus to return to his healing ministry, he declares that they are taking him off mission. He has come out of heaven in order to preach the gospel, not merely to heal the sick.

Preaching the Gospel

Mark **1:14-15** announces Jesus' victory over temptation: there would be no good news for Jesus to proclaim if he had given in to temptation in verses 12-13. But these verses also prepare us for what's ahead. Many texts in Mark record Jesus' preaching without specifying the substance of the preaching (e.g. 1:38-39; 2:2). That is because Mark has already given a summary of his message in these verses.

At one level, **1:14** simply lets the reader know that John's work is complete and the time has come for the beginning of Jesus' ministry. Mark will describe the details of what happened to John later (Mark 6:17-29). Here he simply says that John "was arrested" (**1:14**). This word is significant because it shows the way the ministries of the two men were linked at a deeper level. The term translated "arrested" really means "handed over." This word will show up three more times in Mark—but with reference to Jesus (9:31; 10:33; 14:41). John was handed over, and Jesus will be as well. In other words, there is already a foreboding shadow that passes over the preaching of Jesus. If the forerunner is rejected, what will become of the Messiah?

"The gospel of God" (**1:14**) is the glad tidings that God has come to save. Jesus' claim that "the time is fulfilled" (**v 15**) highlights the fact that his preaching fulfills Isaiah's prophecies. Isaiah spoke of a voice crying in the wilderness who would prepare the way (Isaiah 40:3). He then described a herald of good news who says, "Behold, the Lord God comes with might" (v 10). This end-time herald would come in the power of the Spirit as the anointed one and bring good news for the poor, the brokenhearted, the captives, and the prisoners (61:1).

Isaiah's prophecies are fulfilled in Jesus, who preaches the good news of salvation and that God's reign has come. It was of Jesus that Isaiah was speaking when he said:

"How beautiful upon the mountains
  are the feet of him who brings good news,
who publishes peace, who brings good news of happiness,
  who publishes salvation,
  who says to Zion, 'Your God reigns.'" (52:7)

Many expectations had developed since Isaiah's time concerning what the coming of the kingdom would look like. Many thought of the kingdom of God as something that would come and make right all the wrongs—vanquish evil, tear down the rulers of the earth from their thrones, banish sickness. Everywhere we turn in Mark, we will see people that reject Jesus because he does not conform to their expectations of who the Messiah should be and the kingdom he should bring.

> The kingdom is not a place but a climactic event.

When people hear the term "kingdom," many instinctively think of a place. But the Bible presents the kingdom not as a place but as a climactic event when God intervenes in human affairs. Jesus is sharing the glad tidings that the King has come, which means that the kingdom has come. His teaching will show that the kingdom is hidden and seems small in the present time (Mark 4:26, 30-31), but it will come in its fullness and power in the future (4:28-29, 32; 9:1; 14:25). People can "enter" the kingdom (10:14-15), but it takes a miracle (v 23-27). Some receive the kingdom, and others reject it.

Jesus is a herald of this kingdom. In the ancient world, a herald would go into enemy territory in advance of an approaching army and warn of destruction unless the people there accepted the terms of peace (Jason Meyer, *Preaching*, p 23). That is what Jesus is doing when he calls people to repent and believe. Repentance means a change of mind and a change of direction: turning from rebellion and submitting to the terms of surrender. When we repent, there is a profound moment of realizing that rebellion against the King has been the pattern of our life. We confess that we have tried to be our own king. Faith then receives the terms of peace that have been extended and accepts Jesus as Lord. A good definition of faith is reliance. When we repent and believe, we turn from our rebellion to rely completely upon what God has done to save us.

The Bible also recognizes that repentance and faith have counterfeit expressions. Faith is dead if it is mere intellectual assent with no accompanying evidence or works (James 2:14-26). As for repentance, sometimes people mistake it for the tears that accompany it—as in this story about a drunk old man from Mark Twain's *The Adventures of Huckleberry Finn*:

> "After supper [the judge] talked to him about temperance and such things till the old man cried, and said he'd been a fool, and fooled away his life; but now he was a-going to turn over a new leaf … The judge said it was the holiest time on record, or something like that. Then they tucked the old man into a

beautiful room, which was the spare room, and in the night some time he got powerful thirsty and clumb out on to the porch-roof and slid down a stanchion and traded his new coat for a jug of forty-rod, and clumb back again and had a good old time; and towards daylight he crawled out again, drunk as a fiddler." (quoted in David Garland, *The Gospel of Mark*, p 65)

Repentance is easier said than done. How can we possibly change the core of who we are? How can such a deep work happen? Can we just decide to repent and believe? Repentance and faith happen within us, but they do not originate from us. The Bible says that both repentance (2 Timothy 2:25) and faith (Ephesians 2:8-9) are gifts that God must grant.

Authority to Call Disciples

Mark **1:16-20** contains two calling narratives (**v 16-17, 19-20**). They are very similar in structure. Jesus takes the initiative in both narratives. He sees (**v 16, 19**) two sets of brothers, and he calls them (**v 17, 20**). In the first calling narrative, Jesus commands Simon (aka Peter) and Andrew to follow him. In the second, it simply says he "called" James and John.

An understanding of discipleship in the ancient world will help recover the shock value of this narrative. Normally, a disciple would ask a teacher if they could learn the **Torah** from him. But in this case, it is the other way around. Not only that, but Jesus did not ask. He commanded. In this sense he is more like a prophet than a normal teacher. But here the surprise goes further. Prophets did not call people to follow themselves but God. Yet Jesus *commanded* people to "follow *me*" (my emphasis). Jesus is more than a prophet. He is the Lord and King.

Jesus' use of the phrase "I will make you become fishers of men" is often overlooked as a proof of his deity (Mark **1:17**). Jesus did not invent the imagery of fishers of men as a clever play on words. The imagery comes from the prophets. "Behold, I am sending for many fishers, declares the LORD, and they shall catch them" (Jeremiah 16:16). Jesus' use of this **metaphor** is a claim to **deity** because God himself is the one who sends for the fishers. Jesus was doing something that only God does because Jesus is God.

Both sets of men "immediately" "left" something and "followed him" (Mark **1:18, 20**). Simon and Andrew left their nets, while James and John left their father Zebedee. Notice that following Jesus has a high cost. This text says that there must be a leaving before the following. Here following Jesus means leaving the family and the family business.

This is not a light thing to do! Following Jesus as Lord means relinquishing every worldly claim. It should radically impact how we relate to everything—family, job, money, food, and anything else we call "ours." Jesus says, "Seek first the kingdom of God and his righteousness" (Matthew 6:33). His rule and reign must rise above all the rest. Discipleship turns our world upside down because we relinquish every worldly claim. But it turns our world right-side up in another sense because we put the right things first.

Consider what church tradition tells us about the later life of these four men. Simon Peter was crucified upside down, Andrew was crucified in Greece, James was beheaded, and John was exiled. Of course, they did not know this when they first followed Christ. But they did know what to put first. We, too, have no guarantee about what our earthly future will look like when we follow Christ—but we do know our eternal future.

I grew up with sheep and sheepdogs. I loved the way our sheepdog would do his work of herding the sheep. He always had one eye on the sheep, but the other eye was always on his master. It was so inspiring to watch. He was in his glory! In the same way, men and women are in their glory when they have their eye on the Master in this way—always ready to obey. By contrast, in our sin, we cannot be compared to sheepdogs but to stiff-necked animals that are stubborn and slow to move or obey (see Exodus 32:9). Even as Christians seeking to obey

God, we often hesitate or resist. But the disciples' obedience here is total and immediate.

The language of discipleship has been changed in recent years. Contemporary preaching on discipleship tends to call for a commitment to Christ. But older generations heard a call not to "commit to Christ" but to "surrender to Christ." The word "surrender" gives all control to Christ. The word "commitment" leaves the control with the disciple to determine how committed or uncommitted they are.

But disciples do not take credit for their discipleship. Jesus gets the glory because his command contains the power to create the thing he is calling for. Here in Mark, the command "follow me" (Mark **1:17**) is the key to the whole story. In fact, it is another overlooked proof of Jesus' deity. Jesus does not coax these men or reason with them or try to persuade them. He just says, "Follow me," and they follow.

The simplicity of the formula "follow me" plus "they followed" shows the reader the sheer power of the Creator at work. In the creation narrative, God said, "'Let there be light,' and there was light" (Genesis 1:3). It is a word of command, not a word of appeal. "One begins to see that becoming a disciple of Jesus is more of a gift than an achievement" (Christopher Marshall, *Faith As a Theme*, p 136). When the Creator calls, creation obeys.

Questions for reflection

1. What does the phrase "the kingdom of God" mean? What does it look like in your life?

2. When is following Jesus particularly hard for you? Why is it worth it?

3. Practically speaking, what do you think is the difference between "surrendering" and "committing" to Christ?

PART TWO

Authority to Teach

The next part of the narrative showcases more of the Creator's words of command in the way he teaches and the way he casts out demons. The shift in scene is significant. The move from the seashore to the synagogue, and from the fishermen to the scribes, is a move from the margins of Jewish society to the center.

Jesus teaches in the **synagogue**, and his authority in teaching leaves the people awestruck because it is in such a stark contrast with that of the scribes (Mark **1:21**). There is a constant refrain in Mark of conflict with the scribes over the question of authority (see **1:22**; 2:6, 10; 3:15, 22; 11:27-29, 33). Jesus' teaching was independent of the traditions of the scribes, and so they saw Jesus as a direct threat to their power and control over the people.

The scribes were experts in the interpretation of the law. Their in-terpretations existed in an oral tradition which served as a kind of second law (Mark 7:5-13). Scribes taught by quoting other **rabbis** in a rapid-fire way—*Rabbi Hillel says... but Rabbi Gamaliel says... but Rabbi Eleazar says...* and so on. They spoke with derivative authority. Imagine the shock of someone coming with such direct authority as Jesus: "Truly, Truly I say to you..." Jesus did not quote the authorities; he spoke as the authority.

Yet the amazement of the crowd fell short of faith.

Authority to Cast Out Demons

Demonic possession is the satanic counterfeit of the indwelling of the Holy Spirit. The Spirit comes to indwell believers and makes them more fully human—holy and flourishing as God designed us to be. But demons enter into someone to take control of them in order to steal, kill, and destroy (see Mark 9:20-22). So it must have come as a bit of a shock to find an **unclean** spirit in what was supposed to be sacred space at a sacred time—in the synagogue on the **Sabbath** (**1:23**).

The demon speaks direct words of confrontation (**v 24**). The phrase "What have you to do with us?" is used by someone who is being attacked without provocation (see Judges 11:12; 2 Samuel 19:22; 1 Kings 17:18). "The demon seems to be suggesting that by his teaching there, Jesus had invaded the territory of this spirit" (Ben Witherington, *Mark*, p 91). The demon is saying, *Why are you bringing this conflict to us?* The plural "us" is probably a recognition that Jesus has come against the whole host of demons—not just this individual demon. The whole satanic realm is under attack because the rightful king has come to reclaim what has been lost.

The demon's attempt to identify Jesus—"I know who you are" (Mark **1:24**)—is a hostile yet feeble attempt to confront the Lord of glory, who has all authority. It should probably be read as a naming ritual—an attempt to get control of the situation and power over the person by using their correct name. Jewish **exorcists** of Jesus' day believed that they could use the names of higher spirits as magical incantations to get rid of the lower spirit. This demon is trying to do a similar thing.

But Jesus simply tells the spirit to be silent and gives it a command to come out (**v 25**). The word for "be silent" is the same word Jesus will use when rebuking the wind and the waves in the stilling of the storm (Mark 4:35-41). It is also used for muzzling an ox (1 Corinthians 9:9; 1 Timothy 5:18). "Be muzzled" is just a way of saying, *Shut up— not another word.* Jesus has authority over demons just as a farmer has authority over livestock. He does not derive his power from anywhere else. It belongs to him.

The demon was powerless before the command of the Creator. He convulsed the man, let out a loud, chilling demonic shriek, and then did exactly what Jesus commanded—he came out (Mark **1:26**).

Biblical scholar E.F. Kirschner has written a dissertation on casting out demons in the ancient literature. His conclusions (quoted in R.T.

France, *The Gospel of Mark*, p 100) help recover for us the astonishment that the crowd must have felt. He notes frequent references to the concept of casting out demons and techniques for casting out demons, but almost no narratives or examples in which they were actually cast out. It was all theory and no practice.

> No category except "divine" can explain what Jesus does and says.

So no one in the 1st century would have heard this account of Jesus' authority over demons and said, "This is interesting, but it's what we would expect of any remarkable religious person." They would have been astonished—as we are meant to be. Astonishment is not the same as people repenting and believing. It just means that Jesus blew apart all of their categories for who he could be. We will find that no category except "divine" can explain what Jesus does and says.

For now, the crowd simply asks, "What is this?" And Jesus' fame spreads throughout the region (**v 27-28**).

Authority to Heal

Modern readers hear about the healing of a fever in **verses 29-31** and we struggle to be impressed. But people in Jesus' day did not have medicine to keep a fever from rising, and so fever was a deadly killer. We forget how many lives aspirin has spared!

The Old Testament sometimes presents fever as a divine punishment (Leviticus 26:16; Deuteronomy 28:22), and the rabbis regarded fever as a heavenly fire that only God could put out (see David Garland, *The Gospel of Mark*, p 72). So the healing of this fever is yet another proof of Jesus' deity. Jesus can extinguish what no one else can.

The news traveled so fast that by evening many had come to be healed or have demons cast out (Mark **1:32**). Mark says that it was as if "the whole city was gathered together at the door" (**v 33**). There was a tidal wave of need—and Jesus had more than enough compassion and power to meet it. "And he healed many who were sick with various diseases, and cast out many demons" (**v 34**). There is no question here of people earning Jesus' compassion by their religious performance. All we need to bring to him is our need.

Jesus did not permit the demons to speak because they knew him (**v 34**). He does not need the demons to proclaim his name. He certainly does not want them on his public-relations team! He has come to plunder their kingdom. So he forces them to remain silent.

The Priority of Preaching over Healing

The deity of Jesus can be seen not only in his unique power over disease in healing but also in his unique intimacy with the Father in prayer. Unlike the **Pharisees**, who wanted everyone to see them praying, Jesus would often withdraw to desolate places to pray—as he does here in **verse 35**. The place of prayer did not matter as much as the person being prayed to. Have you ever wanted to spend time with someone and didn't want anything to get in the way? Jesus wanted to get alone with his Father. You don't suddenly slip away to do something you do not like. You don't slip away to take out the trash or to do your taxes. You slip away from the hustle and bustle and pressure to do something you love—something that restores and strengthens. Jesus slipped away to pray because he prized his time with his Father.

But Simon Peter and the other disciples pursued him (**v 36**). The word Mark uses for "searched" has strong overtones of urgency and haste. The urgency of the search seems to carry over also into the urgency of the comment, which is best read as a mild rebuke: "Everyone is looking for you" (**v 37**). In other words, Peter was saying, *What are you doing out here? You are needed back there!*

The term "looking for" (also translated "seeking") often has a negative connotation in Mark's Gospel. The first two occurrences concern intrusions that would obstruct his mission (**v 37** and 3:32); the next two uses of the word testify to unbelief (the Pharisees seeking a sign to test him, 8:11-12); five occurrences are all references to people seeking to kill Jesus (11:18; 12:12; 14:1; 14:11; 14:55); and the last occurrence is a reference to the women looking for his dead body in the tomb (16:6). It seems that "seekers" always get Jesus wrong in the Gospel of Mark!

The disciples seemed to be caught up in the unprecedented results of Jesus' healing ministry. The whole city was at the door. It would be a mistake to move on and not make the most of this moment.

But Jesus' response shows that they do not understand his mission. Ultimately, he has not come to heal but to preach. In fact, Jesus declares that is why he came out (**1:38**). He is not talking about the reason he left the house. He is talking about the reason he left heaven and came to earth. In other words, the disciples, like the crowds, don't understand their main need. It is not healing. It is not exorcism. These things are secondary. Their main need is salvation. That is why Jesus came to preach the good news. The disciples don't see the real need, so they don't understand his mission.

The Son is carrying out the plan of the Father. Jesus left heaven in order to preach and purchase the good news. Healing and preaching are not competing activities. Healing and casting out demons are signs of the kingdom confirming the message that the King has come.

The Healing of the Man with Leprosy

In Jesus' times, few people were seen as more repulsive than those suffering from leprosy. Leprosy was a skin condition, and it was obvious to the sight. This disease was a social death sentence, because the sufferer had to cry out "unclean" and live alone outside the community (Leviticus 13:45-46). By Jesus' day, the rabbis had specified that those with leprosy had to remain 100 cubits away from others if they were upwind and 4 cubits away if downwind. (A cubit is the distance between elbow and fingertip, about 1.5 feet or 46 cm.) If a person came into contact with someone who had leprosy, they were also declared unclean and would have to go through an elaborate cleansing ritual to regain the status of being "clean" again.

But the man in these verses dares to come close to Jesus. He draws near because he believes Jesus can heal him (Mark **1:41**).

This faith is remarkable because every Jew knew that only God is able to heal leprosy. Take, for example, the story of Naaman the Syrian in 2 Kings 5. He was a mighty man in the Syrian army, but he had leprosy. The king of Syria, hearing that there was a prophet of God in Israel, sent a letter to the king of Israel asking him to heal Naaman of his leprosy. The king's response is telling: "He tore his clothes and said, *Am I God*, to kill and to make alive, that this man sends word to me to cure a man of his leprosy?" (2 Kings 5:7, my emphasis).

This man in Mark has faith that Jesus can do what only God can do. He does not go to Jesus as a prophet who may intercede with God for him (which is what Naaman was looking for); he goes directly to Jesus as God. The man does not doubt the ability of Jesus to heal; he only wonders whether he will be *willing* to heal.

Jesus was moved with pity or compassion (Mark **1:41**). This is the wonderful Greek word *splanchnizomai*, which comes from a word meaning "guts"—which is why the King James Version sometimes translates it as "the bowels of compassion." Jesus is portrayed as compassionate to the core. The man with leprosy would have turned the stomachs of others with disgust, but he turned the stomach of Jesus with love.

Jesus revealed his compassionate heart before he revealed his unparalleled power. "He stretched out his hand and touched him" (**v 41**). This was probably the first human touch the man had received in years. Jesus says, "Be clean." And once again the command of the Creator creates what that for which it calls. "Immediately the leprosy left him, and he was made clean" (**v 42**).

Jesus charged him to be silent, to show himself to the priest, and to offer the sacrifice Moses had commanded for cleansing (**v 43-44**).

The fact that Jesus sent him to the priests shows not only Jesus' high regard for the Law of Moses but also his great compassion for the man. The man would need the consecration of the priests to be reinstated into society. Jesus did not want him to remain in social isolation.

Jesus commands silence to prevent precisely what happens in **verse 45**. Because the healed man spreads the news, Jesus is in such demand that he cannot openly enter a town (**v 45**). The leper and Jesus have effectively traded places. Healed of leprosy, the man can now return to society, while Jesus has to start staying away from towns. Still, people come to him "from every quarter," desperate to hear and see him.

Questions for reflection

1. What is your overall impression of Jesus in this passage?

2. What emphasis do preaching and prayer for healing receive in your church or in your own faith? Do you think anything should change?

3. "All we need to bring to Jesus is our need." How do you respond to this? What needs will you bring to Jesus today?

3. A MAN OF AUTHORITY

This next section of Mark features a series of five controversies. The same pattern is present in each one: (1) Jesus does something surprising, (2) the scribes challenge it, and (3) Jesus responds in a way that silences the scribes. These conflicts build to a climax in which Jesus turns the tables on them. In the final conflict, Jesus confronts them with a direct question and becomes angry because they refuse to answer. They respond with a plot to murder him.

Jesus and the Paralyzed Man

Jesus is back in Capernaum (**2:1**), probably in the house of Simon Peter's mother-in-law. The crowds have assembled again and filled the house to overflowing (**v 2**). Mark tells us that Jesus is preaching the word (**v 2**). The content of his preaching is not spelled out because Mark gave a summary earlier (1:15).

Suddenly, we are introduced to four men carrying a paralyzed man. They cannot get into the house through the door to see Jesus so they climb onto the roof.

A typical house in 1st-century Israel had a flat roof constructed of timbers laid parallel to each other. Sticks were laid crosswise over the timbers. Then reeds, branches, and thistles were laid upon that layer. Finally, the whole thing was overlaid with about a foot of dirt, which was packed down to resist water.

Mark reports that they "unroofed the roof" (a literal translation) and dug an opening. Can you imagine the scene? Everyone in the house would hear the digging and the tearing of the branches. Debris would fall on the people gathered inside the house. A beam of light would come bursting into the house as the man was lowered down.

Mark does not narrate the crowd's response as they experience this interruption. We do not know how the owner of the house responded. In today's society, this might be a lawsuit waiting to happen! But we know how Jesus responded. He did not look at these events and see property damage. He saw "their faith" (**2:5**). In the Gospel of Mark, faith can never be reduced to intellectual assent. The faith of these four men is on display in their attitude towards Jesus. They are single-minded. Their mission is to get their friend to Jesus because they know he alone is the answer to their friend's problems.

But when you come to Jesus, you always get more than you bargained for. Jesus looks beyond the obvious need to the ultimate need. Paralysis will not send you to hell—sin will. Jesus declares that the sins of the paralyzed man are forgiven (**v 5**). The reader once again is confronted with the question of the relationship between the message of Jesus and the miracles of Jesus.

> With Jesus, you get more than you bargained for.

We focus first on forgiveness. Jesus *knows* the sins of this man, and he *forgives* them. Both of these things are proof that Jesus is God. Who else knows all of the sins of someone else? It is also stunning because the forgiveness of Jesus implies that he saw these sins as being against him in a personal sense. If I am walking down the street and I see two people fighting and one punches the other on the nose, it would make no sense to say to the one who threw the punch, "I forgive you." They would both look at me like I was crazy. They did not sin against me. The one sinned against would have to do the forgiving.

Though our sin may hurt others, all sin is first and foremost against God. Every confession of sin at some level must say, "Against you, you only, have I sinned and done what is evil in your sight" (Psalm 51:4).

But the paralyzed man received even more than forgiveness. Jesus gave him a new family status when he addressed him as "son." He has become part of the family of God. He has gone from being a child of wrath to a child of God.

We will discover the same truth in Mark 5, when Jesus stops to heal a woman who has been bleeding for many years. She receives more than healing; she receives a family. Jesus calls her "daughter" and declares that her faith has saved her. These stunning declarations are stirring reminders that **adoption** is an even greater gift than forgiveness. A family declaration is greater than a **forensic** declaration. Forgiveness says, "You are not guilty; you are free to go." Adoption says, "You are free to stay here forever."

Mark reports that there were scribes "sitting there" (**2:6**). He seems to imply that it is standing room only in this crowded house, but the scribes were sitting. They probably claimed the places of honor and took the posture of a tribunal here to judge the ministry of Jesus. And they rendered a silent judgment in their hearts: blasphemy!

The irony is thick at this point. The scribes are both right and wrong at the same time. Here is their logic:

- We know God alone can forgive sins.

- Jesus claims to forgive sins.

- Therefore, Jesus is making himself out to be God.

- This is blasphemy.

They got the question right ("who can forgive sins but God alone?"), but the conclusion wrong ("he is blaspheming").

Blasphemy is a frequent charge against Jesus in the Gospels. The clearest definition comes in John's Gospel: "You, being a man, make yourself God" (John 10:33). The scribes understand the awesome audacity of this claim. But they do not see the sting in the tail of their conclusion. If Jesus is God and they say he is not, then they are the ones committing blasphemy. In fact, Jesus provides two compelling proofs of his deity in the rest of the story.

First, he demonstrates that he knows their hearts. Mark makes it abundantly clear that the scribes did not say these things out loud. The scribes were "questioning in their hearts" (Mark **2:6**), and Jesus perceived "in his spirit" (**v 8**) that they had these questions "within themselves" (**v 8**), so he asked them point blank why the questions arose "in your hearts" (**v 8**). Jesus sees not as man sees. "Man looks on the outward appearance, but the LORD looks on the heart" (1 Samuel 16:7).

Second, he heals the paralyzed man in order to show that, as God, he has the authority to forgive sins. Jesus clearly makes this point prior to the healing by posing a question. He does not ask which is easier to do (forgive or heal), but which is easier to say. Forgiveness is easier to claim because it is invisible and internal. It is impossible to see from the outside. But physical healing is visible and external. It would be immediately evident to everyone if Jesus' word of healing failed.

Jesus turns to the paralyzed man and says, "Rise, take up your bed and walk" (Mark **2:11**). The man cannot help but immediately obey the command of the Creator (**v 12**). The crowd responds with amazement, and they glorify God, saying, "We never saw anything like this!" (**v 12**). The crowd knows Jesus can do what they have never seen anyone else do. That is the clue to his identity. Jesus does not persuade the man to dig deep and do what he could already do. The man's legs are dead. He has no ability to obey Jesus' command. But that is the point: Jesus can heal the paralyzed man because, as God, he has the power of the Creator. Dead legs live because Jesus spoke living legs into being.

How do the miracles of Jesus relate to the message of Jesus? The miracles are not the point; they are pointers. Jesus can do what no one else can do because he is God. The miracles confirm the message: *Behold your God! He has come.* And this story in particular demonstrates that Jesus did not come merely to show the power of God but to bring the salvation of God. The man left carrying his bed, but he no longer carried the burden of his sins on his back.

Jesus performed the healing so that everyone would know that he had "authority to forgive sins" (**v 10**). Jesus does not use the word "ability" (can he do it?) but "authority" (has he been authorized to do it?). He is the divine Son, who does not act independently. He goes forth with the Father's authority to accomplish the Father's plan.

Verse 10 is the first time in Mark that Jesus uses the title "Son of Man." There is one place in the Old Testament that contains that title and the idea of authority: Daniel 7:13-14. The Septuagint, a Greek translation of the Old Testament which Mark would have known, uses here the word "authority" where our English Bibles use the word "dominion":

"I saw in the night visions,
and behold, with the clouds of heaven
   there came one like a son of man,
and he came to the Ancient of Days
   and was presented before him.
And to him was given dominion [authority]
   and glory and a kingdom,
that all peoples, nations, and languages
   should serve him;
his dominion is an everlasting dominion,
   which shall not pass away,
and his kingdom one
   that shall not be destroyed."

The Old Testament connects the Son of Man and authority. But does it say anything about a paralyzed person and forgiveness? Hopefully, by this point in Mark you are learning to say, "I bet Isaiah has something to say about that." Isaiah 33:22 says that "the LORD is our king; he will save us." The spoils of his victory will be divided and "even the lame" will partake (v 23). "And no inhabitant will say, 'I am sick'; the people who dwell there will be forgiven their iniquity" (v 24). Isaiah also says that God will come to save (35:4), and, as a result, "then shall the lame man leap like a deer" (35:6). It is no accident, then, that Jesus heals a lame man.

People are supposed to see Jesus—claiming to be the Son of Man with authority from God—forgiving a lame man, and causing them to suddenly cry out, *Behold our God! He has come to save*. But although there is amazement and astonishment, we see no repentance or faith from this crowd. If they really believed that Jesus could forgive sins, then they too would be tearing the roof open to beg him for forgiveness. But they don't.

This story implicitly pleads with us not to be like the scribes or the crowd and fall short of faith. We should be like the paralyzed man and his friends. First, learn the lesson of this man: Jesus goes beyond our obvious need to our ultimate need. We need forgiveness and adoption into God's family more than we need anything else or anyone else. This story is a stirring reminder that Jesus is both willing and able to forgive.

The lesson the paralyzed man learned also can help make sense of seemingly senseless tragedies. It is easy for us to shake our fist at God during tragedy and say, "I see no reason for this, God!" Perhaps the paralyzed man did this too. But the great **theologian** J.C. Ryle comments on the blessedness of this man's brokenness:

"Who can doubt that to the end of his days this man would thank God for this paralysis? Without it he would probably have lived and died in ignorance, and never seen Christ at all. Without it, he might have kept his sheep on the green hills of Galilee all his life long, and never been brought to Christ, and never heard the blessed words, 'your sins are forgiven.' That paralysis was indeed a blessing. Who can tell but it was the beginning of eternal life to his soul?"

(*The Gospel of Mark*, p 20-21)

Second, be like the four friends. We all know people that need Jesus. We are not their Savior, but we can help bring them to him. Faith-filled parenthood or friendship means having a single-minded mission to bring people to Jesus. That applies if you are a mother or a missionary. Christians cannot play the Holy Spirit. We cannot place the burden of saving others on ourselves. But we can act in accord with the conviction that says, "I will let no obstacle stand in my way as I attempt to bring this person to Jesus."

Questions for reflection

1. How do the friends of the paralyzed man show faith?

2. Do you ever find yourself trying to be the savior for others instead of bringing them to the Savior? How can you be more like the friends?

3. How aware are you of your need for Jesus? How does the story of the paralyzed man help you?

PART TWO

Jesus and the Tax Collectors

The story of Jesus and the tax collectors begins with a very important distinction between the crowd and a disciple. The crowd came to him (**Mark 2:13**), but disciples follow him (**v 14**).

Both the crowd and the disciples hear the teaching of Jesus. But only disciples follow Jesus. The crowd comes and goes, but a disciple follows Jesus as a permanent way of life.

What accounts for the difference? The call of Christ. Jesus *teaches* the crowds, but he *calls* his disciples. Mark does not present any other psychological or situational indicator of why disciples follow Jesus. He just says, "Follow me," and they follow. Once again, Mark wants the reader to see that becoming a disciple is a gift of **grace**.

But this call narrative is different in that Levi is not a fisherman, but a despised tax collector (**v 14**).

The scribes regarded this as scandalous. It all came down to how one drew the dividing lines of Jewish society in terms of who was in God's kingdom and who was out. Peter, Andrew, James, and John were all fishermen. They would have been surprising choices for disciples to be sure, but not scandalous ones. But a tax collector was a traitor. They were working for the oppressors of their own people. Jewish literature lumps tax collectors with thieves and murderers. They were disqualified as witnesses in court, expelled from the synagogue, and seen as a disgrace to their family. In fact, they were so hated and despised that all the rabbis were agreed it was morally ok for a Jew to lie to a tax collector (see James R. Edwards, *The Gospel of Mark*, p 83).

The fact that so many outcasts had gathered in one place reveals something of the scope of the scandal. This would have been too much for any self-respecting scribe to overlook. It was bad enough to call one tax collector to follow you, but this looked like a moral pandemic—there were "many tax collectors and sinners." They did not have a loose association to Jesus; they were defined as his followers (**v 15**). The scribes saw a wicked feast.

In truth, though, this feast is a celebration of salvation. The party-goers are not here merely because they are friends of Levi; they are here because they are followers of Christ. Mark tells us that there "were many who followed him" (**v 15**). These outcasts and outsiders have known rejection, but now know acceptance in the Messiah.

The scribes question the disciples: "Why does he eat with tax collectors and sinners?" (**v 16**). Their category of "sinners" needs some elaboration. These were people who were complete outsiders as defined by the law plus the tradition of the **elders**. They did not occasionally transgress the traditions and teachings of the scribes but stood outside it as a way of life. The Jewish system of religion regarded them as hopelessly lost.

The scribes would say that tax collectors and sinners are morally unclean, just as those with leprosy are ritually unclean. Therefore, they conclude that eating with morally unclean people will make Jesus ritually unclean. The scribes are acting like ritual-purity police, and they blow the purity whistle on Jesus. He stands unclean and condemned according to their traditions.

> They blow the purity whistle on Jesus.

But Jesus says he is the spiritual doctor (**v 17**). When he says, "I came not to call the righteous, but sinners," he is certainly not claiming that some people are righteous on their own and do not need a Savior. He is taking the scribes' perspective and turning it against them. The scribes clearly see the tax collectors and sinners as spiritually sick—and they think that Jesus, by joining them, is catching their contagion. But what if Jesus is not joining them as someone who is sick, but ministering to them as someone who heals the sick?

Jesus constantly turns conventional categories upside down. The scribes look as if they are the insiders, while the tax collectors and sinners are the outsiders. In the mind of the scribes, Jesus sides with the wrong side. But who has the right to define who is inside and outside the kingdom of God? This is the central point in all of the five controversies in this section. It all comes down to the word "authority."

The root characteristic of Jesus is that he has authority—he is authorized by God to do all that he does. He has authority to forgive sins and thus he can eat with forgiven sinners. He teaches as one who has authority (Mark 1:22). He always thinks, says, and does the things of God. The scribes are those without authority (v 22) because they do not teach the things of God but the "commandments of men" (7:6-7). They perceive themselves to be "righteous" and "well" as those in "no need" of a doctor or Savior. The irony is that they need a doctor just as much as the tax collectors.

A seismic shift has taken place. The Messiah has come. He preaches the need to repent and believe the gospel (1:15). Those who reject his preaching, like the scribes, are actually on the outside of the kingdom, while those who receive it enter the kingdom.

Jim Marshall was a gifted defensive end for the Minnesota Vikings in the National Football League. Unfortunately, he is mainly known for an infamous mistake. The opposing team fumbled the ball, and he picked it up and ran all the way to the end zone. He thought he had scored a touchdown for his team. The problem is that he ran the wrong way. Instead of scoring six points for his team, he gave the opposing team two points.

The scribes are the Jim Marshalls of Jesus' day. They think they are close to scoring a touchdown and getting into the kingdom of God. They think they are further ahead than anyone else. Jesus is trying to help them see that they are actually running the wrong way.

The people in Jesus' day who seemed to be most attracted to Jesus were those who knew they were sinful and needed a Savior. The people who seemed most repulsed by Jesus were the respectable religious elite. We have sometimes reversed that in the history of the church. The respectable religious (scrupulous) elite are often the most comfortable in church. The down-and-out can often feel the most uncomfortable in church. They may believe that going to church would just make them feel worse. The church of Jesus should herald the heart of Jesus longing to receive sinners into his family. Those who come to him he will not cast out (John 6:37). But no Pharisee should feel smugly comfortable in church.

Jesus and Fasting

The third controversy story (Mark **2:18-22**) follows the same framework: scandal, challenge, answer. This challenge comes from the people, not the scribes. They notice an inconsistency. They see the disciples of John and the Pharisees fasting, but not Jesus' disciples (**v 18**).

Jesus could have responded in a multitude of ways. He could have challenged the heart behind the fasting of the Pharisees. On another occasion he called them hypocrites for fasting in public because they wanted to be seen by others (Matthew 6:16-18). He could also have challenged the fact that the prescribed fasts of the Pharisees went beyond the Bible. The only prescribed fast in the Old Testament was fasting on the **Day of Atonement** (Leviticus 16:29, 31). Later fasts became traditional during the time of the prophets (Zechariah 7:5; 8:19). The Jews of Jesus' day fasted to commemorate and mourn the great disasters of old. The Pharisees also fasted every Monday and Thursday. For them, fasting had become part of a religious perfor-mance—a badge to wear to show they were really serious about their religious practices. Jesus could have criticized this. But he chose to go to something much bigger.

He begins with a sketch of a wedding as a time of celebration and feasting. It is not a fitting time for fasting (Mark **2:19**). Since Jesus is here, people should be celebrating. But Jesus says a time will come when fasting will be fitting. The bridegroom will be taken away (**v 20**). These words strongly foreshadow the death of Jesus.

The second and third pictures are very similar to each other: patching a garment (**v 21**) and putting wine into a wineskin (**v 22**).

Both pictures contain a contrast between the old and new and a warning not to mix them together. No one fixes an old garment with a new patch of cloth because the patch will shrink and cause a worse tear in the old garment. No one will put new wine into an old wine-skin because the new wine will expand and break the old skins.

The point of these two **parables** about the old and the new is quite clear. The teaching and practices of the Pharisees and scribes represent the old traditions. They have added many things to the Bible. These man-made rules and man-made traditions have become stiff and brittle. Jesus cannot be added to their traditions; he is like new wine that will bust their traditions wide open.

The new wine and the new patch represent the fresh teaching of Jesus—everything must be recalibrated now that the times of fulfillment have come. The religious traditions of the Pharisees are like a religious straitjacket which Jesus will tear apart. People must be prepared to follow Jesus and break free from man-made tradition.

But there is something else happening here. Jesus is saying that the people have the question all wrong because their entire orientation is off. They are asking how Jesus relates to fasting when they should be asking how fasting relates to Jesus.

Fasting must be recalibrated with the coming of Christ. While he is with his disciples, they cannot fast. When he is taken away, then they will fast. There is something explosive about Jesus using the **analogy** of the bridegroom. The Bible pictures the people of God as the bride of God. The book of Hosea portrays God's rebellious people as unfaithful, always wandering away from God. But Isaiah announces a new work as God himself will come as the husband for his unfaithful bride (Isaiah 54:5-8).

Jesus' analogy should have called to mind this ancient hope that God would show up on the scene and draw back his disobedient bride with everlasting love and great compassion. The bridegroom has come. The ancient promise has been fulfilled. Should God's people look sad and gloomy? Jesus has modeled this fulfilment-of-prophecy approach at the feast with forgiven tax collectors and sinners in Mark **2:15-17**. This is a time for feasting, not fasting.

The coming of Christ to save shows that Christians should be characterized by *joy*. Joy is an essential part of Christianity, not icing on the cake. It is not jewelry to dress up Christianity as an accessory; it is an essential part of the body of Christianity.

What honors the Lord? What brings the Lord Jesus glory? It is when the church of Jesus Christ, as the bride of Christ, says, *There is nothing I would rather do than spend eternity with you.* We are more than the friends of the bridegroom. The New Testament clearly shows that we are the bride (2 Corinthians 11:2; Ephesians 5:23; Revelation 19:7-9).

Fasting dishonors God if we regard it as a work that will win Christ to be our bridegroom. No amount of fasting, praying, or obeying can make us acceptable to God or earn his favor. Fasting honors God as part of our communion with Christ, not our union. We will fast from anything that gets in the way of our relationship with him. We say, *This much I love you: I will gladly give up anything that causes my love to grow cold for you.* And fasting dishonors God when we forget that fasting has an expiration date. When the bridegroom returns, the wedding feast of the Lamb will begin, and the time of fasting will be no more (Isaiah 25:6-9).

Questions for reflection

1. How do you see yourself? Are you inside or outside the kingdom? Why?

2. How does the way you see Jesus and yourself impact the way you view others? Where does our tendency to look down on others come from? Why is it so tempting to think we are better than others at times?

3. Can you think of any traditions or practices that we add to the Bible that are disconnected from Christ?

PART THREE

Jesus and the Sabbath

Mark **2:23-28** highlights the fourth consecutive scandal that Jesus faces. Jesus is going through the grain fields on the Sabbath, and his disciples begin to pluck heads of grain (**v 23**). Old Testament law established this means of provision for hunger: "If you go into your neighbor's standing grain, you may pluck the ears with your hand, but you shall not put a sickle to your neighbor's standing grain" (Deuteronomy 23:25). This command was designed as provision for people who lacked food. So the disciples do not have to work for food on this day. God has already provided the food for them to enjoy. They did not plant the crops or prepare the field; the food is left there for them by the command of God.

But the Pharisees challenge this as a scandalous breach of the law on the Sabbath (Mark **2:24**). Here, there are a couple of troubling little details. The first is that it seems as if the Pharisees swooped in out of nowhere. No one reported this story to the Pharisees; they had to be there watching and waiting. They were spying on Jesus and waiting for a reason to accuse him. They are the Sabbath police, the purity police. They are hair-trigger critics. Finally they see a Sabbath infraction. Like referees in the National Football League, they throw the flag, stop the game, and call a personal foul.

They charge the disciples with doing work that would be unlawful on the Sabbath. How would the disciples' actions have qualified as "work"? In the traditions of the Pharisees, it was lawful to eat heads of grain, but not to pluck heads of grain because that would count as threshing, a type of work forbidden on the Sabbath. But the Pharisees were not reading Deuteronomy 23 rightly. The whole point was that the disciples did not have to do work to get the grain because God had ensured that it would be left for them.

It is important to understand why the Pharisees had expanded the written law with their own traditions. Centuries earlier, the Israelites had gone into exile from the promised land because they broke the law of God. Now they were back in the land, but they were still in captivity to the Romans. They were waiting for the Messiah. The Pharisees believed that if Israel kept the law and became obedient enough, the Messiah would come. If they didn't keep the law, they would go into exile again. So the Pharisees decided to be extra careful. They did not want people to break the written law, so they added further restrictions, like a fence to keep the people away from any breach.

Jesus could have challenged the man-made restrictions to the Sabbath. He could have challenged the ruling on the field by the Pharisee referees by making the case that plucking did not equal threshing. But instead he followed the same line of argument he had begun when he said that something new had come that would burst their old wineskins.

He declares that they are in error in three areas: in regard to (1) the Bible (**v 25-26**), (2) the Sabbath (**v 27**), and (3) the Son of Man (**v 28**). Jesus takes them to Bible school in **verses 25-26** by going to 1 Samuel 21:1-6. The priests would bake bread on the Sabbath and place twelve loaves on a table in the **tabernacle**. This bread was called "the bread of the Presence." The priests (and only the priests) were allowed to eat it later in the week. But Scripture has a story about **David** and his companions when they were hungry. David ate the bread that only the priests could eat. Because they were with him, his companions were able to eat as well. Jesus' situation has much in common with David's. In both cases, something unlawful happens that is not judged by God as a sin. In both cases, the leader's authority enables the companions to eat something that may be technically unlawful.

Jesus also corrects the way the Pharisees approach the Sabbath. They believe the Sabbath should be served. Jesus says that the Sabbath was made to serve humanity, not the other way around (Mark **2:27**). However, the key error the Pharisees keep making is that they do not rightly recognize who Jesus is, and so their conclusions are completely off. They ask how Jesus relates to the Sabbath when they should be asking how the Sabbath relates to Jesus. Jesus makes the claim that "the Son of Man is Lord even of the Sabbath" (**v 28**).

Jesus is great David's greater son. David had authority over the Israelites as the anointed king. Jesus is Lord not only over the people but over the Sabbath. Jesus is the fixed point of reference to which everything else must relate. Everything revolves around him, not the other way around.

This text represents another installment in the exposition of Jesus' true authority as God. The Pharisees do not understand that they are bringing a Sabbath question to the Maker of the Sabbath, and thus the Lord of the Sabbath. Jesus is the one who created the world and then rested. He gave the Sabbath as a blessing for humanity, not as a burden to crush humanity.

The real irony in this story is that the Pharisees are doing something unlawful with the Sabbath. They are working on the Sabbath by turning the Sabbath into a work. They think of the Sabbath as a way to earn God's blessing and acceptance. But the Sabbath is not a work that we bring to God so he can be impressed with how well we are resting. The Sabbath is not the point; it is a pointer. The original Sabbath provision of rest points to Jesus' greater provision of rest.

It would be a foolish thing to have a relationship with someone's shadow and not the person. The rest that Jesus gives is superior to the shadow that is Sabbath rest. Sabbath rest had to happen every week, and it needed to be repeated. But God rested on the seventh day—not because he was tired but because his work was finished. The same is true of the work of redemption. When Jesus said, "It is finished," it meant his work was complete. You cannot add to the work of Christ on the cross. We can now rest in the finished work of Christ.

Jesus and Healing on the Sabbath

Mark **3:1-6** is the climax of the five conflicts. This time Jesus brings the challenge to the religious leaders.

Sometimes we become so familiar with reading the Gospels that we miss the audacity of what is really happening. One almost feels sorry for the scribes and Pharisees at this point. Imagine the audacity of trying to ambush God incarnate. It is mission impossible.

Jesus enters the synagogue, and there is a man with a withered hand (**v 1**). The Pharisees also spot him. They wonder if Jesus will heal this man on the Sabbath. They watch him like a hawk because they will have grounds for accusing Jesus if he heals the man. The principle they use to judge whether healing "work" should be done on the Sabbath is minimal: any danger to life takes precedence over the Sabbath.

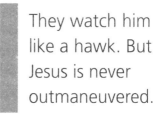

They watch him like a hawk. But Jesus is never outmaneuvered.

They look at this man and know that his life is not in danger. So they lie in wait. But Jesus is never outmaneuvered. This time he brings the challenge directly to them.

Jesus commands the man with the withered hand to come to him (**v 3**). He poses a piercing question about whether or not it is "lawful" to "do good" on the Sabbath. This question gets to the heart of what the law is. The law is the expression of doing good and condemning evil. It is hard to imagine the law condemning doing good.

This question is not hard to answer unless the listeners' hearts are hard. Here is God incarnate standing before them, calling upon them to choose life and choose what is good. Their response is shocking.

They say nothing (**v 4**). Jesus has exposed them for the frauds that they are. They don't care about people. They lack compassion. They don't have hearts that are set on doing good or saving life. Their motive for following the rules is not love. The Sabbath has been turned into a competition to see who can do nothing best. The Sabbath loses all meaning when it is disconnected from God's heart to bless his people.

Jesus looks at them in anger (**v 5**). In their hardness of heart, the experts in the law have totally missed the law and are looking for ways to accuse the lawgiver. In doing good and saving life, Jesus is embodying the law and the heart of God in his own person.

Bible scholar Rikk Watts says it exactly right:

"The Torah, which offered life and good, is perverted to keep a man crippled, to turn the synagogue into a house of bondage, and so it makes them mortal foes of the one who himself gives the life and does the good that the Torah promised."

("Mark," in *Commentary on the New Testament use of the Old Testament*, p 144)

The irony once again is that the Pharisees are rejecting the author of life. To reject him is to reject life and choose death. And they are literally choosing death because now they start plotting to put him to death (**v 6**).

The Pharisees had no political power to carry out capital punishment and so they had to make an unlikely alliance with the Herodians—the supporters of King Herod. This was a group who wanted to keep things the way they were. They wanted to keep the peace because they were the people in power. If there were too much political unrest, the Romans might come and destroy them. The Herodians were living for the here and now. The Pharisees did not believe the Herodians were authorized to rule; they were waiting for the Messiah to take care of them and deal with the Romans. But the Herodians didn't want the Messiah. The only thing the two groups could agree on was the need to get rid of Jesus. They would come back together at a later time to trap Jesus in his words (Mark 12:13).

The other irony is how the Pharisees respond to Jesus' question. Is it lawful to do harm and kill? You would think the answer is "Of course not." But doing harm and killing is exactly what they are doing—even on the Sabbath. They may refuse to answer, but the secret thoughts and plots of their hearts give them away once again.

Questions for reflection

1. What does it mean that Jesus is Lord of the Sabbath?

2. What tends to interrupt your rest in Christ? How can you walk in greater rest in the days to come?

3. Are there areas in your life about which Jesus would be angry? Who could you pray about this with?

4. OUTSIDERS AND INSIDERS

What makes someone an outsider to or an insider in God's kingdom? The next section of Mark develops that theme with narrative (**3:7-35**) and teaching (**4:1-34**).

Outsiders: Jesus' Ministry to the Crowds

In **3:7** Jesus withdraws again to the sea of Galilee. Mark sketches the extent of Jesus' ministry and its geographical reach. People are coming from everywhere. They come from the northwest part of the province (Tyre and Sidon) and the eastern part (the **Decapolis** and areas beyond the Jordan). They even come from Idumea, beyond Israel in the south.

Jesus' influence is unparalleled. There are so many people that even when he tries to withdraw, he cannot get away. He needs to take measures like having a boat ready to escape into because otherwise the crowd would crush him. The crowds are so great because he has healed many (**v 10**). Jesus has come to preach the gospel, but the greatest attraction seems to be his healing ministry.

The crowds are also large because Jesus is casting out demons (**v 11**). Mark presents these encounters as no contest. Jesus is stronger. There is barely even a struggle. The demons immediately fall down before him and confess his identity. There is such strong irony at work here: those who are most opposed to his kingdom are the ones who most immediately fall before him. To know Jesus is to bow before him.

Mark notes once again that Jesus commands the demons to be silent. Jesus does not want the demons to proclaim his name because he does not want to be seen to be in league with them in any way. The scribes will nevertheless make this accusation later (**v 22**).

Another reason Jesus commands the demons to be silent is that he wants people to confess that he is the Son of God. Mark opens this Gospel that way (1:1) and he ends it that way, with the confession by the Roman centurion (15:39). People can only see Jesus' true identity and confess it by the power of the Holy Spirit. So Jesus does not want his name confessed by a demon using a body as a human puppet.

Insiders: Jesus' Ministry to the Disciples

The crowds are attracted to Jesus, but **3:13-19** bears witness to the deeper work of cultivating disciples. This stands out as Jesus' special focus.

Discipleship involves life together. The crowds learn by hearing Jesus; the disciples learn by living with Jesus. This is intensive—24 hours a day, seven days a week. Sometimes it is easy to forget that we have a similar opportunity. Jesus promised he would be with us always, even to the end of the age (Matthew 28:20). Jesus is with us, and we must learn to cultivate our fellowship with him.

This call to commune with Jesus can be heard as a burden—we start thinking about all that we need to do to maintain fellowship with Jesus. But Scripture confronts this self-centered focus. Note here that Jesus called "those whom he desired" (Mark **3:13**), and they came to him. Once again, the ultimate explanation for anyone coming to Jesus as a disciple is not that we first desire him but that he desires us. "Behold," he says in Revelation 3:20, "I stand at the door and knock. If anyone hears my voice and opens the door I will come in to him and eat with him, and he with me." He reminds us that he is

> Jesus is pursuing us. He wants to be with us.

pursuing us. He wants to be with us. He takes the initiative to knock, and we open the door.

We should feel a deep measure of conviction over those times when we have effectively told Jesus to go away because we have to answer emails or go to the store or spend time on social media. I remember when I first became a Christian how eagerly I would answer every call and every prompting from the Lord. I knew those promptings—which seemed like interruptions in my day—were actually invitations to fellowship with Jesus. What about you? What are the distractions and the subtle shifts that cause you to put Jesus off and displace him from the place of pre-eminence in your life?

Discipleship also involves being empowered by Jesus. He sends the twelve disciples out to do the work of ministry as apprentices with his authority. They are now called "apostles"—the word means "sent ones." They are sent out to do what he has been doing: preaching and casting out demons (Mark **3:14-15**).

Verses 16-19 list the names of the apostles. Mark does not share many details about each individual. His purpose seems to be to highlight their names and show that there are twelve of them. The number twelve is highly significant because it represents the people of God who were formed into the twelve tribes of Israel. So this list shows that Jesus is making a new start. He is calling a true Israel to follow him, starting with twelve men.

The True Family of God

Mark **3:20-35** is our first opportunity to see one of Mark's sandwiches. A sandwich is a literary technique in which an author begins with one story and ends with that same story (or a corresponding one), but something else is sandwiched in between them. The middle story helps interpret the story at the beginning and end. Here we begin and end with a story about Jesus' family, while sandwiched between is the story of Jesus' conflict with the scribes.

- Jesus' family responds to Jesus (**v 20-21**)

  - The scribes respond to Jesus (**v 22**)

  - Jesus responds to the scribes (**v 23-30**)

- Jesus responds to his family (**v 31-35**)

The sandwich structure shows that "his family" (**v 21**) is a reference to Jesus' mother and brothers (**v 31-35**). They set out to "seize him," saying, "He is out of his mind" (**v 21**). Those closest to Jesus try to control him because they think he has gone crazy. This is a startling reminder that proximity to Jesus is not enough; allegiance to Jesus is what matters.

It is striking that they want to silence Jesus, given that Jesus has just silenced the demons. The word "seize" is a stunning word in Mark. Three times it refers to Jesus seizing the hand of someone he heals (1:31; 5:41; 9:27), but it most frequently occurs in contexts where people are hostile toward Jesus. Eight times it refers to what people who are openly against Jesus try to do (**3:21**; 6:17; 12:12; 14:1, 44, 46, 49, 51). Yet here it is his own family who seek to seize him.

The scribes, meanwhile, think that Jesus is demon-possessed (**3:22**). Mark repeats the phrase "were saying" from **verse 21** to show the correspondence between Jesus' family and the scribes. Both are trying to restrain him.

The scribes cannot deny that the work of Jesus is supernatural. There could only be two supernatural sources: God or Satan. They say the work of Jesus comes from Satan: "... for they were saying, 'He has an unclean spirit'" (**v 30**).

Beelzebul seems to mean "Baal the prince." The chief rival to faith in **Yahweh** in the Old Testament was Baal religion. Often biblical writers refer to foreign "gods" as demons (Psalm 96:5; 1 Corinthians 10:20). Thus Beelzebul would be the ruler of evil spirits. In Mark **3:22-23** Jesus equates Satan with Beelzebul as the "prince of demons" (see also Matthew 9:34; 10:25; 12:24; Luke 11:15).

Jesus demonstrates the folly of their interpretation of his powers by showing its flawed logic (Mark **3:23-26**). How could Jesus be extending Satan's kingdom if he is casting out demons? Everyone knows that a civil war in Satan's kingdom would not build it but weaken it. Jesus then shows that he is waging a heavenly war, not a civil war (**v 27**). God's kingdom is being built, and Satan's kingdom is being plundered. Someone stronger has come—God himself. Satan (the strong man) has been bound, and now his house is being plundered.

Why does Jesus use this image? Isaiah 49:24-26 has already used it to speak about the mission of the Servant of the Lord:

"Can the prey be taken from the mighty,
   or the captives of a tyrant be rescued?
For thus says the LORD:
'Even the captives of the mighty shall be taken,
   and the prey of the tyrant be rescued,
for I will contend with those who contend with you,
   and I will save your children …
Then all flesh shall know
   that I am the LORD your Savior,
   and your Redeemer, the Mighty One of Jacob.'"

Remember that the first miracle in Mark is an **exorcism** (1:25-26). Jesus is the King, the Mightier One, and the demons cannot stand against him. The ruler of the demons is powerless to bind Jesus; instead Jesus binds him and plunders his house.

In **3:28-30** Jesus shows the grave implications of the scribes' interpretation. This is not a momentary mistake but an eternal sin—a blasphemy against the Holy Spirit, which cannot be forgiven. The scribes are saying that Jesus is motivated by evil rather than good; by Satan rather than by God; by an unclean spirit rather than by the Holy Spirit. In this sense, they are the people Isaiah warned about: "Woe to those who call evil good and good evil, who put darkness for light and light for darkness" (Isaiah 5:20). This is a stunning irony. The official, recognized spiritual leaders in Israel are so blind that they cannot tell the difference between the work of God and the work of Satan. They have zero discernment. They are unfit to lead God's people. The irony of this story is that the scribes who accuse Jesus have themselves become aligned with Satan in opposing Jesus.

There is a fork in the road here. One path leads to life and the other to death. The scribes have charged Jesus with blasphemy (Mark 2:7), and now Jesus charges them with blasphemy (**3:28**). No neutrality is possible. Someone is blaspheming—either Jesus or the Jewish leaders. Which side will the reader take?

A note on this "eternal sin" (**v 29**). People with a tender conscience often ask if they have committed the unforgiveable sin. But there is no record in Scripture of someone who has genuinely repented and sought forgiveness being rejected and denied. In fact, this passage has good news: all other blasphemies can and will be forgiven (**v 28**).

Anyone who is worried that they have committed this sin has *not* committed it—because that very anxiety itself shows a sensitivity to repentance and seeking forgiveness. The eternal sin is perpetual unbelief that refuses to call what Jesus does good, and calls it evil instead. In that state, forgiveness can never come, because forgiveness is only found by embracing Jesus as the Son of God.

Mark now takes us to the final part of the sandwich (**v 31-35**). Once again Jesus' family "sent to him" and "called him" (**v 31**). The crowd relayed the message that his family was "seeking" him (**v 32**). In the culture of Jesus' day, it was widely understood that your family had a claim on you. That is the clear sense of the word "seek" in Mark. It usually describes an attempt to gain control over Jesus; the family assumes they have rights over him.

Jesus turns their request on its head. He looked at those who sit at his feet in a posture of discipleship. They are his true family (**v 34**). In other words, his physical family (standing outside) does not have a claim over him. Rather, *he* has a claim over his true family (his disciples). His family is not the lord of him; he is the Lord of the true family of God. Jesus defines the family of God as those who do the will of God (**v 35**). Mark keeps highlighting the fact that there are insiders and outsiders, and their place is defined by their response to Jesus.

By the time Mark was written, Jesus' family was highly regarded in the church. Jesus' brother, James, had assumed leadership of the Jerusalem church; his mother, Mary, was also held in honor. One **commentator** drives the implication home for today:

> "If Mark is willing to put such people to the test, surely no one
> can presume to be 'in' with Jesus apart from faith and commit-
> ment." (James R. Edwards, *The Gospel of Mark*, p 125)

We cannot confuse baptism, **confirmation**, a Christian background, or church attendance with following Jesus. No one can lay a claim upon Jesus and gain any kind of acceptance into his family through anything other than Jesus himself (John 1:12-13). That means the family of God is open to all who call upon the name of the Lord.

The way the scribes treated Jesus is a warning for the family of God. Do you expect to be treated better than Jesus? We often expect that everyone will speak well of us as followers of Christ and be at peace with us. But in fact, some of the most frequent and painful opposition or persecution might come from those in closest relationship to us—like our physical family. Jesus says we should expect that, in Matthew 10:35-39. These were not hypothetical words for the first followers of Christ. They were not abstract. They described real life then, and they still describe real life for many Christians today.

Questions for reflection

1. How does Jesus view discipleship? How can this inform your own perspective and practice of following Jesus?

2. "Proximity to Jesus is not enough; allegiance to Jesus is what matters." What do you think allegiance to Jesus looks like today?

3. Are there areas in your life where you are minimizing or dismissing Jesus' words or authority—aspects that are not yet surrendered to him?

PART TWO

Mark **3:7-35** has drawn the divide between insiders and outsiders with three narratives. Now Mark explains it with teaching (**4:1-34**). It turns out that this divide is divinely intended, and Jesus' parables are like a litmus test to expose what is already there.

Mark **4:1-20** is the second sandwich in Mark. Here Mark begins and ends with the parable of the sower (**v 1-9, 13-20**). The filling of the sandwich is Jesus' teaching on the purpose of parables (**v 10-12**). The rest of the chapter consists of four more parables (**v 21-32**), and it concludes with a summary of Jesus' strategy. The crowds, as outsiders, get only parables, but Jesus explains everything privately to the disciples as insiders (**v 33-34**).

The Parable of the Sower

The crowds are so large that they sit on the lake shore and Jesus teaches them from a boat (**v 1-2**). Certain places along the Sea of Galilee were like a natural amphitheater which would allow a human voice to be projected effortlessly to several thousand people on shore (James R. Edwards, *The Gospel of Mark*, p 126).

Once again Mark directs our attention to the crowds. It would be easy to conflate success in the ministry with the size of the crowd. But external appearances are deceiving. Jesus, however, can look at a great throng of people and see what is truly happening in their hearts. In fact, there is a great connection between **verse 1** and the parable Jesus is about to tell. The crowds are beside the sea on the "land," which here is literally the "soil" (**v 1**). Then he gives a parable in which that same word "soil" shows up several times—and the various soils of the parable represent the people in the crowd.

A parable (**v 2**) is a type of teaching that is something like a riddle. Some inside knowledge is required to crack the code the parable uses to compare physical and spiritual realities. When you know what the symbols in the parable mean, you will know its overall message.

"Listen! Behold, a sower went out to sow" (**v 3**). In the symbolic world of this parable, there is a sower and seed. The sower sows the seed broadly—he does not select the best ground and then only cast the seed there. The same type of seed goes to four different types of soils. The seed is the same, but the results are vastly different.

The first kind of soil is a path. It is obvious that this parable is not attempting to describe actual sowing techniques. No one would sow seed on the path—it is so packed down by people walking on it that the seed will not sink down at all. In the parable, the seed stays on the surface and the birds come and eat the seed (**v 4**).

The second kind of soil is rocky ground. Picture a layer of topsoil with a layer of rocks underneath. The problem here is that the soil is shallow. Jesus stresses the shallowness of the soil twice (**v 5**). The plant immediately springs up, but it does not have a root system sufficient to sustain it. When the sun rises, the plant is scorched and it withers away (**v 6**).

The third type of soil has the right depth, but it is crowded with competing thorns. The thorns grow up and choke the seed, with the result that there is no grain (**v 7**).

The same kind of seed is sown into three different soils and all have the same unhappy ending: no harvest. The only happy ending comes with the fourth type of soil.

The "good soil" produces a harvest. Jesus presents the extent of the harvest in terms of "thirtyfold" or "sixtyfold" or a "hundredfold" (**v 8**). These numbers indicate how many heads of grain are produced per seed. One seed is able to produce 30 or 60 or 100 heads of grain. These numbers are not normal yields. Some scholars calculate that the average yield in Jesus' day would have been one seed producing 7.5 heads of grain. After no yield from three out of the four soils, this is an extravagant yield. It is a sign of God's phenomenal blessing.

The Purpose of the Parables

Notice the change in scene as we come to the middle of the sandwich (**v 10-12**). Jesus is no longer in the boat teaching the crowds. He is now alone with "those around him" and his twelve disciples (**v 10**). This same phrase ("those around him") occurred in the previous story (3:34) to describe the disciples who were inside the house as his true family, while his physical family remained on the outside.

In other words, the insiders are asking him about the meaning of the parable. Jesus reminds them of the blessing of being on the inside: the secrets of the kingdom of God are given to them (**v 11**).

The secrets of the kingdom of God are a kind of insider knowledge given directly from God. A secret is not necessarily hard to understand; but it must be revealed in order to be known. For example, a teacher may give a surprise quiz that is not announced ahead of time. If the teacher tells half of the students there will be a surprise quiz tomorrow, then it would be a secret that half of the class knows.

> Outsiders get the parables. Insiders get something extra.

Jesus reveals the secrets of the kingdom to his disciples as his true family. The outsiders do not receive insider information; they only receive the parables (**v 11**). In fact, Jesus uses parables with this explicit purpose in mind. The parables create two categories of people: insiders and outsiders. The outsiders get only the parables. The insiders hear the same parables as the outsiders, but they are given something extra— how to interpret them.

Once again, it's something of a shock to observe who populates these two groups. People might assume that serious and devoted Jews like the Pharisees and scribes would be insiders and that common people (especially tax collectors and sinners) would be on the outside. But the reverse is true.

These verses show that the disciples of Jesus are directly dependent upon Jesus. He alone can reveal the secrets of the kingdom. Jesus is the Son of God, and, as such, he is the only one who really knows the plan and purpose and work of God. What God is up to is not immediately clear to everyone. Not everyone can see God's reign and rule at work in what Jesus is doing. Jesus has to disclose it—they are all dependent upon him for this revelation.

Why is the kingdom of God not immediately obvious to everyone? **Verse 12** gives the answer. All the hearers will see and hear, but only the insiders will perceive and understand. That is the point of quoting Isaiah 6.

The division of people into insiders and outsiders is not an unintended consequence of the parables but their very purpose. The phrase "so that" signals an intent, not just a result (**v 12**). Jesus knows what he is doing. He is fulfilling Isaiah 6:9-10:

"They may indeed see but not perceive,
   and may indeed hear but not understand,
   lest they should turn and be forgiven." (Mark 4:12)

This is why Jesus uses parables. People see but do not perceive. They hear but do not understand. The intended effect is that they do not turn and are not forgiven. All four types of soils receive the word, but only one of the four soils sees and perceives, hears and understands. Only one group turns and receives forgiveness.

This is a straightforward reading of the text, but it does introduce perplexing interpretive problems. We will tackle those interpretive issues after completing the rest of the sandwich.

The Meaning of the Parable

Jesus supplies the insiders with the information necessary to break the code of the parables (**v 13-20**). The sower is Jesus. The seed is the word preached (**v 14**). Mark highlights once again that Jesus has a sowing ministry of preaching, not mere healing. In fact, this parable has a verbal connection with Mark 1:38. Jesus tells his disciples that they and he need to go to the next towns so he can preach there because "that is why I came out" (1:38). The word "came out" or "went out" is the same in both texts in the Greek (1:38; **4:3**). Jesus left heaven to sow the word all through Galilee—and beyond.

He also explains the symbolism further. The four types of soils represent four different types of hearts of those who hear the word. The first soil represents a hardened heart—so hardened that the word has no effect. Satan comes and snatches the seed away (**v 15**).

This soil belongs to the hardest-hearted hearers like the scribes and Pharisees. They immediately reject the teaching of Jesus. There is no initial acceptance—only hard-hearted opposition.

The next two types of soils refer to the crowd. It looks at first glance as if they are receiving the word, but it does not produce a harvest.

Some in the crowd have shallow hearts with "no root in themselves" (**v 17**). They receive the word joyfully but not deeply (**v 16**). This shallow reception of the word means that they "endure for a while" (**v 17**), but when trials come, they fall away and stop following Jesus.

Others have crowded hearts. Their hearts are full of "the cares of the world and the deceitfulness of riches and the desires for other things" (**v 19**). These things choke the word, and these hearers do not become followers of Christ. An idolatrous heart will strangle the word and choke it to death. This is a warning against worldliness. When the word and the things of the world come into conflict, which one will win? The world will win in the hearts of those who are counterfeit Christians.

The disciples are different. There is a fourth type of heart. The word will win over the things of this world in the hearts of true followers of Christ. The fourth type of hearer hears the word and accepts it. The language changes here to a present tense conveying a continuous process: it could be translated "the ones who are hearing the word, accepting the word, and bearing fruit" (**v 20**). These three things basically define what a disciple is. All four kinds of hearers hear Jesus' words and three initially accept them. But only this type of hearer endures in their embrace of the word, and the word produces a harvest. The harvest is stated in various percentages. For some the yield or return is 30, 60, or 100 (**v 20**). The first three groups do not hear with true faith, but this fourth group does.

Questions for reflection

1. What types of heart do you see in the people around you?

2. What does this parable tell you about the work of God in people's lives?

3. How does this encourage you to persevere with sharing the gospel?

PART THREE

Now we must return to some of the perplexing interpretive problems of **verses 10-12**. Why do some people have good hearts? Are they born with them? Do some people just work harder to become more spiritually sensitive? The middle of the sandwich answers the question conclusively. God has to change the heart before it can receive the word. He has to take out the hard heart of stone and put in the heart of flesh. This heart change is the defining difference between the disciples and the crowd.

The parables are a little like a metal detector. It lets out a sound when it passes over metal underground. The parables are a heart detector for insiders and outsiders. The parables pass over those with hard, shallow, or crowded hearts and there is no sound. But when an insider hears the parable, it makes an impact in their heart. They have to know more. They do not want to leave Jesus. They ask questions because they have a deeper thirst and a greater hunger.

Jesus preaches parables to bring this unseen division into the light so it can be clearly seen.

One perplexing issue is that of why Jesus would not want people to turn and be forgiven (**v 12**). Jesus uses a negative purpose statement meaning "in order that something would not happen." We use these types of statements in everyday language when trying to avoid an unwanted result: "I am not going to speed so that I don't get a speeding ticket." But why would Jesus not want people to turn and receive forgiveness? The answer is that he is turning some people over to judgment.

Isaiah 6:9-10 shows up at least four other times in the New Testament with this same sense (Matthew 13:14-15; Luke 8:10; John 12:39-40; Acts 28:26-27). That is why the context of Isaiah 6 is so important. God declared judgment upon Israel for their idolatry. Why the reference to ears and eyes that don't hear or see? God was communicating that this was poetic justice. They had become as blind and deaf and mute as the idols they worshipped (Isaiah 44:18-20). The psalmist gives the same warning:

"Their idols are silver and gold,
   the work of human hands.
They have mouths, but do not speak;
   eyes, but do not see.
They have ears, but do not hear;
   noses, but do not smell.
They have hands, but do not feel;
   feet, but do not walk;
   and they do not make a sound in their throat.
Those who make them become like them;
   so do all who trust in them." (Psalm 115:4-8)

The Lord had handed them over to this: "They know not, nor do they discern, for he has shut their eyes, so that they cannot see, and their hearts, so that they cannot understand" (Isaiah 44:18; see 29:10).

The right response to Jesus' words is not resignation and fatalism. The good news of the gospel goes out into all the world. The only way that any hearts will receive it is if the Lord opens people's hearts as he did for Lydia (Acts 16:14). If he has opened your heart, then receive the word today. Have you heard his voice through his word? Receive it with haste. Do not push it away or put it off. The Bible speaks today and says, "Today, if you hear his voice, do not harden your hearts" (Hebrews 4:7).

If you are a Christian, the Bible's message is full of hope and help. That is why Jesus keeps referring to "ears to hear" (Mark **4:9**). If you have been given ears to hear, then use them! God does not see for us or believe for us or hear for us or obey for us, but he does do the decisive work that enables us to see or believe or hear or obey. Once he fixed our broken eyes and ears and hearts, then he says, *I have given you new eyes; use them.*

Parables of the Kingdom

When I was about 13, my brother and I would take some glass bottles down to an old landfill near our house. We would throw a bottle in the air and hit it with our baseball bat. There was an amazing explosion of glass. It was fun until we learned that you cannot control where the glass flies. We got cut a few times before we learned our lesson.

Jesus' four parables in this section are similar. He takes contemporary expectations of what the kingdom will look like, and then he throws them up in the air and shatters them with his verbal bat. Jesus' parables shatter all false expectations about the kingdom of God

The Lamp and the Measure

The lamp in the parable in **4:21-23** is a reference to Jesus. The original language makes that point even more clearly. Translated literally, the text tells us that the lamp is not "brought in" but "comes in." Jesus' opponents (and even his family) want to limit his influence. In effect, they want to hide him under a basket or a bed. But the light of the world has come into the darkness in order to occupy an elevated place and spread the light.

The preaching of Jesus brings the hidden things into the light. The light will expose what is hidden in darkness, and it will also reveal the children of light. The family of God has the gift of ears that hear (**v 23**).

The flip side of this command is a warning. The disciples are to use care in how they hear. The measure they use for listening will be like a boomerang and come back upon them. If someone listens well and receives the truth, they will receive even more (**v 24-25**). If someone listens poorly and rejects or shows no interest in the truth, even the little they have will be taken from them (**v 25**). The parable of the sower has given an example of this principle: Satan snatches away the seed that is given to those with hard hearts (**v 15**).

The Growing Seed and the Mustard Seed

The next pair of parables highlights the growth of the seed. The first parable focuses on the hidden power of the seed and the process of growth. Even though it looks as if nothing is happening for a long time (it is hidden and under the surface), the miracle of growth is happening (**v 27**). The seed has the power to be productive even while we sleep or rise. The earth produces fruit "by itself" (**v 28**). All the farmer does is harvest it (**v 29**).

This teaching would shatter misconceptions about the kingdom. No one had imagined that the coming of the kingdom would be hidden and happen under the surface. People expected it to be big and obvious and overpowering. They also expected it to come as a result of their hard work of obedience to God. But in fact it is God himself who brings the growth.

The second parable (**v 30-32**) is also surprising. Jesus compares the kingdom to a small seed. No one had expected that the kingdom of God would look so feeble at first. But the point of the parable is that the kingdom has a deceptively small beginning but an epic ending. This text almost certainly contains an allusion to Ezekiel 17:22-24, where God promises to plant a tree. That promise features a reversal of expectations. Rather than starting with a lofty cedar tree, God is going to begin with a tender twig. God will plant it, and it will grow and bear branches and produce fruit, and in the shade of its branches every kind of bird will dwell and nest. Similarly, the parable of the mustard seed shows that the kingdom will have a small start but will conclude with a large ending. Jesus' teaching has sometimes been called "the already / not yet." The kingdom has already come, but it is not yet here in its fullness.

Christ came the first time in such a hidden way. He was born in a manger, not a king's palace. The first coming was deceptively small in his birth and death. But he rose from the dead. He ascended to the throne of the Majesty on high. He sent the Spirit to continue his work in the world. He will come again on the clouds of heaven with all the angels as the reapers at the final harvest. That second coming will be big and obvious and overpowering.

The Pattern of the Parables

Mark concludes with a return to the insider/outsider theme. Once again we hear that the crowd only receive parables, while the disciples privately receive more revelation and explanation (Mark **4:33-34**).

The parables test our spiritual appetites. Peter tells us that we should long for the milk of the word so that we can grow up into salvation (1 Peter 2:2). Jesus shares big truths about the kingdom. The disciples need to grow into these truths. It is the most natural thing in the world for a baby to grow when there is proper nutrition.

> We do not just read the Bible; it reads us.

The Bible is an amazing book. We do not just read it; it reads us. It is a discerner of the thoughts and intentions of the heart (Hebrews 4:12). How are you responding to God's revelation? Do you hunger for more so that you grow more, or are you content with low levels of Bible intake? Christians need to recover the wonder and privilege of revelation. 20th-century minister Martyn Lloyd-Jones said it well:

"Ah, we have been looking at a great and wonderful and glorious mystery. I know of nothing, as I have emphasised repeatedly, more wonderful for us to contemplate and consider. Do you not feel your minds being expanded and stretched? Do you not feel that it is a great privilege to be allowed to look into such wondrous mysteries and glorious truths? God has given us His word that we might do so, not that we might skip over it lightly, but that we might delve into it and try to grasp what has happened." (*Great Doctrines of the Bible*, p 287-288)

Does reading the Bible feel like a precious privilege or a dry duty?

Don't skip over his word lightly, but dive deeper. It is hard work. But as pastor John Piper once said:

"Raking is easy, but all you get is leaves; digging is hard, but you might find diamonds." (*Future Grace*, p 10)

Questions for reflection

1. Is there any way in which you are hardening your heart to God's word? What would a soft and receptive heart look like for you?

2. How do you respond to the idea that God turns some people over to judgment? How will this inform your prayers for your loved ones who don't believe?

3. Do you need any help in diving deeper into the Bible? From where could you seek this help?

5. WHAT NO ONE ELSE CAN DO

We now begin a long section of signs and responses in which we continue to see the division between outsiders and insiders (Mark 4:35 – 8:21). Jesus' signs conclusively prove his identity. There are some signs that many people can see and others that Jesus gives to the disciples in private settings. This dynamic is on display in the rhythm of the bread miracles for the crowds (6:30-44; 8:1-10) and the boat miracles for the disciples (4:35-41; 6:45-51). The cycle culminates with bread in the boat (8:10-21).

The First Boat Miracle

The calming of the storm is the first of the private miracles. There are two wrong ways to read this story. Some try to explain away the miracle: perhaps Jesus actually said, *What a dreadful storm! It must be over soon*, and his disciples misunderstood his words and took them as the cause of the sudden calm (H.E.G. Paulus, quoted in David Garland, *The Gospel of Mark*, p 194). I disagree with this, but I want to call attention to this interpretation because something crucial is being recognized here that **evangelicals** sometimes skip over: the physical reality of the storm. The other wrong approach fails to recognize this and immediately spiritualizes the story. We read about a physical storm that Jesus stilled for the disciples, and we make it about Jesus stilling our storms of suffering today. But this passage is not first and foremost about us but about Jesus. Only after we see what the text says about him can we see what it has to say to us and about us.

In **4:40**, Jesus says to the disciples, "'Why are you so afraid? Have you still no faith?'" That question is an interpretive key. Faith is the major theme of the story.

Mark describes the situation in **verses 35-37**. These verses build the bridge between the previous text and this one. Remember that the crowd was so large that Jesus taught them from a boat while they gathered on the shore (v 1-2). Mark has shown Jesus' public teaching with a full day of parables and then his private explanations to the disciples at other times (v 10, 34). Now evening has come, and he wants to go to the other side of the lake. They set off in the boat.

In **verse 37** comes the crisis moment: a windstorm arises, and waves are breaking into the boat. But Jesus is asleep (**v 38**). The disciples fear for their lives, but Jesus seems oblivious to the danger.

Fear replaces faith and causes a crisis question: "And they woke him and said to him, 'Teacher, do you not care that we are perishing?'" (**v 37**). The way they frame the question is important; it's not well translated in most English Bible versions. There are different ways to frame a question in the original language. You could ask a question that does not imply any answer, or a question that implies a negative answer or a positive answer. For example, Paul asks a series of questions in 1 Corinthians 12:29-30 that imply a negative answer. "Are all apostles? Are all prophets? Are all teachers?" The way the text is phrased in the Greek implies that the answer to all of these questions is "no." All are not apostles, all are not prophets, and so on.

Our text gives us an example of a positive question: "You do care that we are perishing, don't you?" (Mark **4:38**). The disciples trust Jesus, but suffering introduces **dissonance** into this trust. They believe Jesus cares, but this storm looks deadly, and he looks indifferent. How can they put these two facts together?

Suffering disrupts our trust too. We think God cares, but when suffering comes, it stretches our ability to see his care. It can seem as if he is sleeping. In the boat, it did not merely seem that Jesus was sleeping: he was!

But the fact that Jesus is sleeping makes two important points. First, sleep is proof of Jesus' humanity. Psalm 121 tells us that God does not slumber or sleep. Jesus is doing something that humans must do. He is not faking it with one eye open. He is really sleeping. Because he is fully human, he has to fully sleep.

That observation sets the stage for a second one. In the Old Testament, there is a frequent link between sleep and faith (Psalm 3:5; 4:8; Proverbs 3:23-26). Take Psalm 3 as an example. David is on the run. He describes how his enemies are pursuing and taunting him (v 1-2). But then he looks at what God is like (v 3-4), and as a result he is able to write verses 5-6:

"I lay down and slept;
   I woke again, for the LORD sustained me.
I will not be afraid of many thousands of people
   who have set themselves against me all around."

David slept because he had faith. The Lord was the one who sustained and protected him.

In the same way, Jesus can sleep in a storm because his Father sustains him. Jesus knows his Father has his eyes on him at all times. Jesus sleeping on a cushion is a faith-filled model for us to emulate. Our Father is a shield, a rock, a refuge, a very present help in times of tumult and trouble.

> Jesus is the model of faith. But he is also the object of faith.

But Jesus is far more than the model of faith; he is also the **object** of faith. He can be the model of faith because he is fully human; he can be the object of faith because he is fully divine—as we see once again in Mark **4:39-41**.

Only God can control the sea. This is quite a common idea in the Psalms. For example, Psalm 107 describes men who go to sea and there witness God's "wondrous works" (v 24). There is a great storm, which is entirely God's doing. The sailors are "at their wits' end" (v 27). They are in the same boat as the disciples—terrified! But they know that there is only one person who can help them:

"Then they cried to the LORD in their trouble,
   and he delivered them from their distress.
He made the storm be still,
   and the waves of the sea were hushed." (Psalm 107:28-29)

God is the one who calms storms. The disciples did not fully comprehend that they were crying out to the Lord himself in their distress. They woke Jesus, and he had no need to cry out to God to still the storm. "And he awoke and rebuked the wind and said to the sea, 'Peace! Be still!' And the wind ceased, and there was a great calm" (Mark **4:39**).

We know that they did not expect him to do this because of the next verse:

"And they were filled with great fear and said to one another,
   'Who then is this, that even the wind and the sea obey him?'"

(**v 41**)

The disciples should be glad like the sailors in Psalm 107:30 because their lives have been spared. Why are they more afraid now than when they thought they were going to perish? Fear is a frequent response to a supernatural sign in Mark. Jesus has just shattered their pre-existing categories. The disciples do not have it all put together at this point. They think Jesus is the Messiah. But they begin to wonder if he is more. Are they meeting their Maker in that boat?

Jesus and the Demon-Possessed Man

Mark structures the next story with three main movements, which reflect the way Jesus addresses three groups: demons (Mark **5:1-13**), the crowd (**v 14-17**), and a disciple (**v 18-20**). Each of the three movements features someone begging Jesus for something (**v 10, 12, 17, 18**).

In the opening part of the story, Mark highlights three things about this demon-possessed man. First, this person is totally unclean (**v 2**). He makes his home in an unclean place (the tombs), and an unclean spirit has made him its home. Second, no one has enough power to subdue or tame him (**v 3-4**). This unclean spirit has totally dehumanized the man; wild animals are normally what need to be tamed, not humans. Third, he is tormented (**v 5**). He cries out night and day. He cuts himself with stones. Demons hate God, but they cannot destroy or deface him, and so they try to destroy and disfigure the image of God wherever they can.

The next part of the story features a power encounter between Jesus and the demons (**v 6-8**). Instead of falling upon Jesus in attack, the man falls down before Jesus in fearful recognition that Jesus is stronger. The demon's question—"What have you to do with me?"—is the same one asked by the first demon we encountered in Mark's Gospel (1:24).

Jesus makes the demon tell him its name. The demon replies, "My name is Legion, for we are many" (**v 9**). A legion was the largest unit of troops in the Roman army—about 5,600 soldiers. This man has an entire army of demons living in him and tormenting him.

But they are no match for the almighty army of one, so they "beg" Jesus multiple times not to torment them or make them leave the region (**v 10**). They "beg" to be sent into the pigs (**v 12**). And they go down into the sea as the pigs drown (**v 13**).

The second movement of the story documents the response of the crowd (**v 14-17**). The herdsmen flee to tell the townspeople about what happened. The people come and immediately see that the demon-possessed man is clothed and in his right mind (**v 15**). They could not tame him, but Jesus has transformed him. Do they rejoice that Jesus has done what no one else could do?

No. The crowd responds the same way as the disciples in the previous story: with fear (**v 15**). What happens next is a tragedy. When they hear about the transformation of the man and the destruction of the pigs, they beg Jesus to leave (**v 17**). The demons beg to go into the pigs (**v 12**), but the crowd begs Jesus to go away (**v 17**). The crowd would rather have an army of evil spirits in their region than the Savior of the world. They conclude that being without Jesus would be better than being with him.

But Mark frequently demonstrates that disciples will respond differently to Jesus than the crowds. This man has the heart of a disciple and begs to be with Jesus (**v 18**). It's a compelling climax to the story. The demons beg that they might not leave the region (**v 10**). The crowd begs Jesus to leave the region (**v 17**). Only the man in his right mind begs for the right thing: to stay with Jesus (**v 18**).

Discipleship is being with Jesus (3:14). The man is sitting at Jesus' feet (**5:15**) like those that Jesus claims as his true family (3:34). The irony is that Jesus grants the request of the demons and the crowd but not of this man. Instead Jesus has a mission for him. Unlike his command to the man with leprosy in chapter 1, Jesus does not command this man to be silent, because this is not Jewish territory. He commands this Gentile to go to his people and tell them what the Lord has done for him (**5:19-20**).

The story of the demon-possessed man serves the same purpose as the story of the stilling of the storm. It is another demonstration of Jesus' deity. Jesus is the messianic warrior who comes to deliver his people from those who are stronger (Isaiah 49:24-26). He is the stronger one who plunders Satan's kingdom (Mark 3:27).

But he is a surprising Messiah. The Jews expected a second exodus redemption in which the Messiah would destroy their enemies. The first exodus had seen the Egyptian army drown in the sea. This time Israel assumed the Roman army would meet the same sort of fate. How surprising to see an army of demons drown in the sea instead.

But there is another Old Testament echo in this story. Isaiah has something to say about this man. God is ready to be found by those who do not seek him (Isaiah 65:1). He is ready to reveal himself to the rebellious, who sit among the tombs (Isaiah 65:4; Mark **5:3**) and eat pig's flesh (Isaiah 65:4). Now we know why Jesus told the disciples that he had to go to the other side of the lake, into Gentile territory.

He was going to say, "Here I am" to "a nation that was not called by [his] name" (Isaiah 65:1).

No one was strong enough to help this man. But Jesus can do what no one else can do. He does not tame us; he transforms us. He does not bind us; he sets us free. He is a great Savior who gives not only grace but mercy. Grace is the unmerited goodness and love of God given to those who have forfeited every claim upon him and his love, and who deserve nothing but judgment and condemnation. Mercy is the goodness and love of God toward those who are in misery or distress as the result of their sin. Jesus saves the guilty and shows mercy to those in misery. Jesus' mercy calls us to mission: to tell others how much the Lord has done for us and "how he has had mercy" on us (Mark **5:19-20**). We are meant to read this story of his glory and beg him not to leave our lives, but to stay.

Questions for reflection

1. How will the story of the calming of the storm change the way you pray for those who are suffering, or the way you pray when you yourself are suffering?

2. How can you express your faith in Jesus this week?

3. What great things has Jesus done for you? Who could you tell about those things?

PART TWO

The Daughter Sandwich

Mark constructs another sandwich in **5:21-43**. Jesus has returned from the region of the Gentiles, and he is in Jewish territory once again. And as always, there is a great crowd (**v 21**). A ruler of the synagogue comes in exactly the same way that the demon-possessed man did in the previous story. He falls at Jesus' feet (v 6, **22**) and cries out to him. It is hard to see in translation, but the two stories have exactly the same words; both Jairus and the demon "beg earnestly" (v 10, **23**).

Jairus begs earnestly because his "little daughter is at the point of death" (**v 23**). "Little" is a term of endearment—like when I call one of my teenage daughters "baby girl." This girl is not little in age: we learn later that she is twelve years old (**v 42**).

Mark hints at where this story is going. The request is that Jesus would lay his hands on her "so that she may be made well" (**v 23**). But it also says, "... and live" (**v 23**). So Jesus agrees to go to her (**v 24**).

Another Daughter

The middle of the sandwich comes next. The crowd is pressing in on Jesus (**v 24**). This significance of this detail will become more apparent in a moment. Mark alerts the reader to the presence of a woman who has had a flow of blood for twelve years (**v 25**). In the Old Testament, a woman was considered unclean during her menstrual cycle. But this woman's blood flows continuously, not just once a month. So this woman is like someone with leprosy: she is unclean all the time.

Mark gives a snapshot of her suffering. She "had suffered much" not just under the disease but under physicians trying to cure her (**v 26**). The end result of all this human "help" was that she went from bad to worse because she had ended up not just sick but poor.

She had run out of money and hope. Mark makes a connection between her and the demon-possessed man. In both cases, people tried to do what they could, but they could not help (v 3-4, **26**).

She heard the reports about Jesus, and she believed. As a result she "came up behind him in the crowd and touched his garment" (**v 27**). The natural way to read the story would be to regard this unclean woman is contagious. Her uncleanness would make Jesus unclean. But Jesus is greater. She believed that touching him would not make him unclean but make her well (**v 28**). She believed that he could do what no one else could do.

Her approach also says something about her sense of shame. She wants to touch the edge of his garment from behind and then make a quick getaway and return to the shadows. Her plan seems to work because she is immediately healed (**v 29**). But Jesus knows that a healing has happened, and he knows that she needs more than healing. So he asks a question: "Who touched my garments?" (**v 30**).

This is where the detail about the crowd in **verse 24** comes into play. The disciples' response to Jesus' question is a veiled rebuke (**v 31**). *Did you happen to notice the crowd, Jesus? They are all pressing in on you. Everyone touched you!* But they are blind to what Jesus is truly doing.

Jesus "looked around to see who had done it" (**v 32**). The woman knows she is known. She cannot stay hidden any longer. She falls down before Jesus, just like Jairus and the demon-possessed man (**v 33**). Why does Jesus draw her out? In his tenderness, he knows exactly what everyone needs, and he patterns his healings around that knowledge.

This woman was an outsider, always living in the shadows of society. So he forces her to come in front of everyone. Normally, Jesus moves people away privately (e.g. 7:33). But he does not want this to be private. The shackles of shame need to be broken. The demon-possessed man was set free to tell his testimony to others (**5:19-20**), and this woman needs to experience and do the same (**v 33**).

He then says a stunning thing to her. He calls her "daughter" (**v 34**). Jesus knows that she needs more than healing; she needs a family. He tells her that her faith has "made [her] well." The word for "made well" is also the word for "saved." She is healed both physically and spiritually.

The next verse also uses the word "daughter." Someone rushes up to Jairus to tell him that his daughter is dead. Mark wants the reader to feel the drama of the moment. If Jesus were a doctor, this could be an example of medical malpractice. A little girl was on the verge of death but Jesus stopped to heal a medical issue that was not life-threatening.

But here is the significance of the sandwich. We see someone pleading with Jesus, *Would you please come and heal my daughter, my little girl, the one that I love?* And Jesus, in the middle of the passage, gets interrupted and takes time to say, *Hey, I've got to stop for a moment and heal my daughter.* The woman is his. He sees her. He wants her to know—and he wants everyone else to know—that she is his daughter.

Faith brings more than the gift of healing: it brings the gift of identity. Jesus called the paralyzed man his son (2:5) and now he calls this woman his daughter. Salvation says more than "You are not guilty; you can go free." It says, "You are family; you can stay." If you are a Christian, you are a son or daughter of the King. The story of this woman is part of a much bigger story. Ever since the first sin, people have tried to hide from God in their shame, but God will graciously call them out and not let them hide. God draws us out not to expose us but to clothe us and call us as his own.

Little Girl, Arise

The other piece of bread in the sandwich concludes the story of Jairus' daughter. The messenger shares his verdict. The little girl is dead. There is nothing more that the Teacher can do. "Why trouble the Teacher any further?" (**v 35**).

But Jesus overhears this conversation. He cares not only about the life of this little girl but the faith of her father. He commands Jairus to have faith: "Do not fear, only believe" (**v 36**). He is saying, *I know you are afraid. You think that my delay meant death for your daughter, and now your last desperate hope is gone—no one can do anything now. But faith knows I can do what no one else can do. I do not make mistakes.* The original request was that he would lay his hands on her so that she would "live" (**v 23**). Jairus should believe that Jesus can still answer that request.

So Jesus takes an inner circle of disciples with him to Jairus's house (Peter, James, and John). Seeing people weeping and wailing loudly (**v 38**), he asks what looks like another dumb question. "Why are you making a commotion and weeping?" (**v 39**). It would be like going to a funeral and asking, "Why is everybody crying?"

But Jesus knew what he was asking. He claimed that "the child is not dead but sleeping" (**v 39**). Surely this must have sounded like an insult—as if they did not know the difference between sleep and death. They thought his words were ridiculous and laughed at him (**v 40**).

It is the laughter of unbelief. The crowd does not believe, so Jesus once again makes the divide clear between insiders and outsiders by putting them all outside (**v 40**). Jesus takes the child's mother and father, and Peter, James, and John to the child. And they witness Jesus do what no one else can do. He takes the little girl by the hand and says, "Talitha cumi," which means "Little girl, I say to you, arise" (**v 41**). *Talitha* means "little girl" and *cumi* means "get up.'" This is not the word for resurrection. This is the word for "wake up." It is similar to what I do with my daughters in the morning: "Honey, time to get up." That is what Jesus says here.

> "Honey, time to get up." That's what Jesus is saying.

Jesus reached into death and pulled this little girl out by the hand. Mark tells us that the girl got up and started walking "for she was twelve years of age" (**v 42**). This detail does more than describe why she is able to walk. Mark is stitching together the two stories. Jesus' daughter in the middle of the story had had a flow of blood for as long as Jairus's daughter had been alive.

"And they were immediately overcome with amazement"—which seems like an understatement! Yet Jesus is not done being tender and showing his love. He is acting like a true parent here, isn't he? "He strictly charged them that no one should know this, and told them to give her something to eat" (**v 43**). Jesus cares for every little detail of the girl's life. He tells her parents that in their amazement they should not forget to feed her.

The three stories in Mark 5 have a unified point: these are all declarations of Jesus' deity. As God, Jesus can do what no one else can do. He is stronger than demons, stronger than disease, stronger than death. And the strength of his love shines even brighter. Jesus will fight demons or death or disease with unstoppable force, but he treats his people with unspeakable tenderness as family.

The Gospel of Mark is a little like the movie *The NeverEnding Story*. In that movie, the characters come to realize that they are part of the story. We need to ask: Who am I like in the Gospel of Mark? Where am I in the story?

The people that run to Jesus in the Gospel of Mark are not the smug, self-righteous scribes and Pharisees or the hard-hearted crowds that listen to his teaching but then go away. They are those who know they are broken, so they cannot deny that they need a healer. They are those who go from bad to worse. They are those who know shame, fear, and guilt but find grace, freedom, peace, love, power, and mercy when they meet Jesus. They fall before his feet, and he fiercely and tenderly comes to the rescue, breaks the chains, calms the fears, and gives new life and identity.

Blessed are the broken because they come to Jesus. It is all over the place in Mark: those who have leprosy, who are mute, deaf or blind, the woman with the flow of blood, and the desperate dad. They beg Jesus to do what only he can do.

You are part of this story. So don't sit on the sidelines. Don't pretend to be strong and self-sufficient. Run to him. Rely upon him. Rest in him. Trust him to do what no one else can do.

Questions for reflection

1. Basing your answer on this story, why might it be a blessing to be broken?

2. Jesus' mercy makes us part of the family of God. How does this truth change you?

3. How can you build others up in their identity in Christ?

PART THREE

The Unbelief of Nazareth

The contrast between the stories of faith in Mark 5 and the story of unbelief that begins Mark 6 could not be more different or more tragic. **6:1-6** tells the story of how the most famous alumnus of Nazareth was welcomed—or rather, not welcomed—home.

Jesus leaves the Sea of Galilee and travels 25 miles southwest to his hometown of Nazareth. He goes to the synagogue and begins to teach. In Luke's Gospel, when Jesus teaches at the synagogue in Nazareth, he turns to a text in Isaiah 61 about the coming of the Messiah. He says, "Today this Scripture has been fulfilled in your hearing" (Luke 4:21). We don't know whether this was the same occasion as that in Mark 6 or a different one but, either way, the inhabitants of Nazareth would have heard Jesus' claim to be the Messiah.

The reader already has a hint of how this homecoming reception might go. Mark has already told us that Jesus' family made the trip to Capernaum as unbelievers—they thought he was crazy (Mark 3:21). Here, in Nazareth, people get so angry that they try to throw him off a cliff.

They begin with astonishment and end with offense. Jesus' wisdom and the reports of his mighty works fill them with amazement (**6:2**). But they feel the dissonance between what he does and where he came from (**v 3**). They think they know him because they know his occupation and his family. His humble origin makes it unlikely that he could be a great person or have great wisdom. The common carpenter trade didn't produce a lot of brilliant philosophers or powerful generals. Jesus is surely nothing special.

Jesus quotes a proverb to them about a prophet being dishonored only in his hometown and among his relatives and household. His point is not that this *even* happens in his hometown, but *especially* there. People in Nazareth are so aware of Jesus' humanity that they cannot fathom his deity. This paradox is right at the heart of Mark's Gospel.

The Nazarenes' question is the latest of several similar ones: "What is this?" (1:27), "Who then is this?" (4:41), "Where did this man get these things?" (**6:2**).

It should come as no surprise that Jesus would be despised and rejected by men. He is the Suffering Servant of Isaiah 53. The Gospel of Mark presents two images of the Son. Sometimes we see the "royal" image of the Son (his glorious divine identity), and at other times we see the "servant" image of the Son (his humble earthly origins). But we don't have to choose between them. Jesus is both. That is what people repeatedly fail to understand.

The same thing is true today. Many are willing to acknowledge the historical Jesus of Nazareth. But people in Nazareth and people today are wrong when they see only a carpenter, only a son of Mary, and only a Nazarene. They miss that he is truly man and truly God.

Mark tells us that Jesus "could do no mighty work there, except that he laid his hands on a few sick people and healed them" (Mark **6:5**). This wording can make it seem that Jesus is limited and powerless unless people have faith—like in the movie *Elf,* where Santa's sleigh can't fly without Christmas cheer. Some people think that the Jesus "faith-meter" needs to be full in order for him to heal. But that is not the case at all.

Matthew makes it very clear that the real issue is the unbelief of the people. "And he did not do many mighty works there, because of their unbelief" (Matthew 13:58). The limitation came from their unbelief, not some inability of Jesus. In all of the stories in Mark, people come to Jesus because they believe he can heal. Unbelief would prevent them from coming. One commentator says it just right:

> "The people of Nazareth already knew of Jesus' miracles (Mark
> 6:2) but refused to believe. Their cynicism prevented most
> from bringing their sick to him for healing. Only a handful did
> so, and he healed them. Doubt has trouble believing; unbelief
> obstinately refuses to believe."

> (David Garland, *The Gospel of Mark*, p 238)

Some people today are proud enough to think they can think their way to God, and they trust in their intellect. Others want God to prove himself to them with powerful signs. They stand back with arms folded like a judge and say, "Do enough for me to believe in you." But the weakness of the cross confounds the strong. The apparent foolishness of the cross confounds the wise. So this story, which began with people marveling at Jesus' teaching, ends with Jesus marveling at their lack of faith (Mark **6:6**).

The Sending of the Disciples

One of the great themes of this Gospel is Jesus' authority. The first few chapters give prominence to the conflict between heavenly authority and all other authorities. The authorities and rulers of the demonic realm are no match for heaven's champion as he comes and routs the demons—even a legion of them. We see a different picture when it comes to human authority. Human authorities are blind to the identity of Jesus. His family rejects him as crazy, the scribes reject him as demon-possessed, and his hometown takes great offense to him.

Right after the rejection in his hometown of Nazareth, Jesus sends out the disciples. This section has a foreboding quality about it. Indeed, this is the beginning of another one of Mark's sandwiches. He sends out the twelve here (**v 7-13**), and they return to him in **verse 30**. What happens in the middle? The beheading of John the Baptist (**v 14-29**). The middle of the sandwich foreshadows the rejection that Jesus and his messengers will receive.

Here we see Jesus give authority to his disciples a second time (see 3:14-15). They are given authority to preach, cast out demons, and heal—like a trial run for the mission that will take place after his death and resurrection.

The words "called" and "send" are the same terms used earlier when Jesus called the disciples and sent them (**6:7**; 3:13-14). They are also given identical authority to cast out demons or unclean spirits.

The new addition in this story is the detail that they were sent out two by two.

Certainly we can see the practical wisdom of this strategy: going in pairs would provide support, protection, and camaraderie. But there is also something deeper happening. Remember that this whole narrative is about getting the word out that the kingdom has come and it is time to repent. There is judgment coming, as in a court of law. Two by two would satisfy the biblical requirement that there be at least two witnesses in legal actions (Numbers 35:30; Deuteronomy 17:6, 19:15; 2 Corinthians 13:1; 1 Timothy 5:19).

Jesus commands the disciples to bring four things with them (Mark **6:8-9**)—the very same items which God commanded the Israelites to bring in their flight from Egypt in the exodus: cloak, belt, sandals, and staff in hand (Exodus 12:11).

The urgency and haste of this mission has overtones of judgment. God is about to act. He is going to reveal something every bit as important as the exodus. But this time the judgment will not fall on the Egyptians but upon the Israelites, if they do not repent.

> Jesus' disciples are an acted-out parable.

But what is also striking is what Jesus commands them not to take. They won't take bread, bags, money to purchase provisions, or an extra tunic (Mark **6:8-9**). They must be dependent upon the people to whom they minister. They are an acted-out parable: it will become evident very quickly if people are receiving or rejecting their message by whether they themselves are received or rejected.

This command is a unique prescription, not intended for all missions; other texts say to send Christians out in a manner worthy of God so that they do not need to accept anything from those who do not know God (3 John 6-7).

Shaking the dust off your feet (Mark **6:11**) is a prophetic gesture that communicates a massive and tragic irony. "Jews shook the dust from their feet when they returned to Israel from Gentile territory" (David Garland, *The Gospel of Mark*, p 242). The tables are turned here with this gesture. When they act out this gesture within the land of Israel they are saying that this place is not part of God's people—it is a **pagan** place and will be cut off from God unless people repent.

The story continues in the book of Acts with Paul and Barnabas. The Gentiles rejoiced and those ordained to eternal life believed, but the Jews persecuted Paul and Barnabas, and so they shook off the dust from their feet against the Jews (Acts 13:50-51).

The disciples continue the ministry of Jesus by doing what he does. They preach repentance (Mark **6:12**), and they heal and cast out demons (**v 13**). It is important to note that the preaching of the kingdom and the signs of the kingdom belong together. It is not enough to have the signs without the preaching. Nor should the preaching be separated from the signs. The signs confirm the authenticity of the message and take us deeper into it. For example, the gospel declares the victory of Jesus over Satan. Matthew, Mark, and Luke record numerous occasions when demons are cast out—which Jesus ultimately did at the cross (John 12:31-33; Colossians 2:14-15). The miracles point forward to that ultimate victory. Similarly, Jesus purchased our healing at the cross. In heaven, there will be no souls with any sickness. And the resurrection body will never get sick. The cross has purchased both. When God brings healing—either in Jesus' time on earth or today—it is a preview of the greater healing to come.

The Unbelief of Herod

Mark now narrates the meat of the sandwich. Remember that the two pieces of bread are the sending (Mark **6:7-12**) and returning of the disciples (**v 30**). The middle is the beheading of John the Baptist (**v 14-29**).

The disciples went out to call for repentance. John the Baptist preached the same message. It was not received well. We ought not to be naïve about the call for repentance and the cost of discipleship. But that is not all that this sandwich tells us. In **verse 30**, the disciples come back and report about all they have done and taught. They are on a ministry high. In the call for repentance, we should not be naïve about how strong the opposition will be—but we also should not be cynical about how powerful the gospel is to overcome that opposition.

Verses 14-29 are like an episode of *Keeping Up With the Herodians*. The Herod of this story is Herod Antipas. His father was Herod the Great, the Herod who tried to have the baby Jesus murdered. Palestine was divided into four regions after the death of Herod the Great, and his four sons each ruled one part. Herod Antipas ruled Galilee and Perea from 4 BC to AD 39.

Antipas persuaded Herodias, who was the wife of his half-brother Philip, to divorce her husband and marry him. John clearly and courageously declared that Herod's marriage was against the Jewish law: "If a man takes his brother's wife, it is impurity" (Leviticus 20:21; see Leviticus 18:16). Herod imprisoned John for this, but he also tried to protect him from Herodias, who wanted him dead. Herod was in quite a predicament. He could not have John running around preaching against him, but he also did not want to kill John because he feared him as a righteous and holy man (Mark **6:17-20**). When he heard John preach, "he was greatly perplexed, and yet he heard him gladly."

Herodias was cold and calculating, and she was looking for the right opportunity to act on her grudge against John. The opportunity came when Herod had a birthday party filled with drinking and dancing (**v 21-25**). Herodias' daughter danced for Herod and all his important dinner guests. She pleased him so much that he made a rash vow to give her whatever she wanted. She dutifully asked her mom what she should request, and Herodias told her to ask for the head of John.

Herod was played like a chessboard. He feared losing face with his guests more than he feared John losing his head. He ordered the execution, and the gruesome act was carried out (**v 26-28**). John's disciples risked their lives to come and get his body and bury it (**v 29**).

Now that Jesus is becoming well known, some are saying that he is actually John the Baptist, risen from the dead (**v 14-15**). Herod himself shares this high opinion of Jesus (**v 16**). But a high opinion of Jesus and hearing preaching gladly do not constitute **saving faith**. Herod fears man more than God and loves sin too much to let go and repent.

John is the photo negative of Herod in this story. He could not be bribed or threatened into saying less than God would have him say.

Repentance is not a popular message. We must face that fact today. It used to be that the church occupied the moral high ground. People believed that society would be better if everyone lived according to the church's moral code. But now, many people believe that the church and what it stands for are bad for society, and that those who preach repentance are bigoted and intolerant. As I said before, we should not be naïve about this opposition; but we should also not be cynical. There will be opposition, but the power of Jesus can overcome the opposition. The disciples came back and reported to Jesus all that they had done and taught (**v 30**). There were many ministry successes to celebrate.

Why does Mark include this section on Herod? It is important to remember how closely he connects the ministries of John and Jesus. There are only two passages in Mark that are not about Jesus and they are both about John (Mark 1:2-8; **6:14-29**). But they are really about Jesus because they foreshadow much about Jesus. Mark 1:2-8 presents John as the forerunner of Jesus' coming, and in **6:14-29** John is the forerunner of Jesus' death.

The parallels between Mark 6 and Mark 14 – 15 show us that John's death is preparing us for Jesus' death.

1. Both John and Jesus were killed by political tyrants who vacillated but, in the end, put them to death because of the fear of man.

2. Both deaths were the result of political conniving and manipulation.

3. Both men were righteous and innocent victims.

But there is one amazing difference. John died because of the sin of others; Jesus died for the sins of others. Jesus came into the world to save sinners—not those who deny they are sinners. The only hope is on the other side of repentance—getting out of denial so you can own your sin. That is the only hope, because there is a sacrifice for sin. There is no sacrifice for denial.

Questions for reflection

1. Where does unbelief show up in your life—even in partial, not full-blown, ways? What areas of your life do you need to bring to Jesus in faith?

2. When have you seen Jesus' authority and power on display? How could you pray for more of this?

3. Martin Luther said that the Christian life is not a single act of repentance but a life of repentance. Do you agree? What does ongoing repentance look like in your life?

6. ALL THINGS WELL

The First Bread Miracle

The feeding of the 5,000 (Mark **6:31-44**) is one of the most beloved stories in the Bible. The Gospel writers loved it too. It is the only miracle contained in all four Gospels.

Jesus is going to provide rest for his disciples (**v 31**). The crowds have become too crushing—coming and going so that Jesus and the disciples cannot even eat (**v 32**). So they go away in a boat to a desolate place to rest. But the crowds recognize them and run so that they beat them to the spot (**v 33**). When the disciples reach their secluded destination, they find a great crowd waiting for them.

Most of us would become greatly irritated and mumble under our breath about how hard it is to get a day off. But Jesus never sinned. When he saw the crowds, he did not erupt in anger but with compassion. "When he went ashore, he saw a great crowd, and he had compassion on them, because they were like sheep without a shepherd" (**v 34**). Here we see that wonderful Greek word once again: *splanchnizomai*. Seeing the people stirred Jesus to the core with compassion.

"The LORD is my shepherd; I shall not want" (Psalm 23:1). This passage in Mark 6 is the fulfillment of that ancient hope. The message of this text is good news for those who know they are harassed and helpless. Jesus is the long-awaited Shepherd, who satisfies his sheep—providing both spiritual food and physical food.

Jesus first provides the guidance and teaching they need. The text says, "And he began to teach them many things" (Mark **6:34**). He teaches them at length—so much so that it becomes late in the day. The remote nature of the place and the lateness of the day create another problem, which the disciples recognize (**v 35**). Their solution is to send the people away to find food (**v 36**). Bear in mind that the disciples have not eaten yet either (**v 31**). They have had their fill of ministry. They want the crowd to go away.

But Jesus says something shocking: "You give them something to eat" (**v 37**). John's Gospel tells us that this command was actually a test because Jesus already knew what he was going to do (John 6:6). The disciples immediately look to their physical resources. They point out that they don't have the kind of money it would take to purchase enough food. They would need 200 denarii—more than half a year's wages.

Jesus sends them to see how much food they do have (Mark **6:38**). They find five loaves and two fish. So Jesus organizes the people into groups of hundreds and fifties. He takes the five loaves and two fish, looks up to heaven and says a blessing, breaks the loaves, and gives them to the disciples to set before the people (**v 41**). The result is that all the people eat and are satisfied (**v 42**).

We have just seen how Herod threw a banquet for himself and the elites of Galilee, and the sinful party led to death. Jesus holds a banquet for what Herod would have regarded as the rabble of Galilee. This miraculous banquet of heavenly food leads to the sustaining of life and to satisfaction. More than half a year's wages would not have been enough to buy a little snack for this many people, yet Jesus filled the people with five loaves and two fish.

Each basket was a faith souvenir.

Mark also tells us that there were twelve baskets of food left over. Each of the twelve disciples had his own basket of leftovers as a physical reminder—a faith souvenir to mark this moment; Jesus can do what no one else can do. He can provide what no one else can.

This story contains four big and bold biblical echoes. First, Jesus is the greater Moses. Jesus feeds people with teaching from God and bread from heaven, just like Moses. He also organizes the people into sections so they can be fed in a more orderly way. This reflects Moses' instructions for the camp of Israel (Exodus 18:21, 25). The phrase "sheep without a shepherd" recalls Moses' prayer asking that God would appoint a successor for him so the people would not be left like sheep without a shepherd (Numbers 27:12–23). Jesus also provides rest in a desolate place, just as God, in the time of Moses, provided rest in the wilderness (see Psalm 95:7-11; Isaiah 63:14; Jeremiah 31:2; Hebrews 3 – 4).

Second, Jesus is also the greater **Elisha**. When Elisha asked his servant to feed all the prophets with just 20 loaves, he replied, "How can I set this before a hundred men?" (2 Kings 4:43). Elisha's response was "Thus says the LORD, 'They shall eat and have some left'" (v 43). And they did.

Third, Jesus is the fulfillment of Ezekiel 34. Ezekiel's prophecy brings a charge against the shepherds (the rulers) of Israel for not caring for their flock. The people were suffering "because there was no shepherd" (v 5). So God was going to come in judgment against those who should have been acting as shepherds, and he himself would come and seek out the lost sheep (v 11), providing food for them and making them lie down in rich pastures (v 14-15).

But God also said that he would send his servant David as a shepherd (v 23). Who exactly was coming to be the shepherd: God himself or David? The incarnation makes it clear that the answer is "yes." Jesus is the Son of God and the Son of David. He has come to shepherd his people.

Fourth, Jesus is the shepherd of Psalm 23. The people are not in want—he completely satisfies them (Psalm 23:1, Mark **6:42**). Jesus makes his sheep lie down in green pastures (Psalm 23:2, Mark **6:39**). This helps answer one of the questions that I always used to have when reading this text: why tell us that there was grass and why emphasize that it was green grass? Why is there grass if this is a wilderness? (Mark **6:31, 32, 35**). Psalm 23 is the key. The barren desert is green because the shepherd has found good pasture for his flock. He makes them lie down in green pastures here beside the lake (Psalm 23:2; Mark **6:32-33, 45**). Jesus has come to restore their weary souls with teaching that guides them into right paths (Psalm 23:3; Mark **6:34**). Truly, "The LORD is my shepherd; I shall not want."

The Second Boat Miracle

When the feeding of the 5,000 is over, Jesus goes up a mountain to pray alone (**v 45-47**). Jesus has to dismiss the crowd; they do not leave on their own this time (**v 45**). It also seems that the disciples are hesitant to leave; Jesus has to make them get into the boat (**v 45**). Presumably this is because anticipation that Jesus is the Messiah is building—John's version of the story tells us that Jesus withdrew because "they were about to come and take him by force to make him king" (John 6:15).

In Mark **6:47** the story is paused to highlight the separation between Jesus and the disciples. Jesus is praying alone, while the disciples are in the boat. They are making headway painfully, for the wind is against them (**v 48**). The word for "painfully" suggests a tormenting kind of strain; it's used elsewhere for the torment that comes from demon possession (Mark 5:7), childbirth (Revelation 12:2), and even hell (Revelation 14:10). This is a picture of suffering. It's the start of a pattern in Mark. It never goes well when the disciples are separated from Jesus. The same is true for us!

But there is hope. Mark does not simply tell us what is happening with the disciples. He explicitly tells us that Jesus sees it (Mark **6:48**). When Jesus sees things, he does not turn a blind eye to them. This is the very heart of our God on display. Jesus sees them struggling, and so he goes to them. But he does not come to the shore and wait for the boat to reach him. He goes out to them—without a boat. He walks on the sea. This is something only God does (Job 9:8).

But what in the world does the next phrase mean: "He meant to pass by them" (Mark **6:48**)? Commentators go all over the map on this one. Some even think that Jesus is playing games: *I am coming* *to you—just kidding, I am going to pass by you.* But this is no game. This is a fulfillment of the Old Testament. This is exactly what God did for both Moses and Elijah at Mount Sinai (or Horeb); he passed by them so they could see his glory (Exodus 33:19; 1 Kings 19:11). What God did for Moses and Elijah, Jesus is doing for the disciples.

Yet they do not understand his identity at all. Thinking he is a ghost, they respond with terror (Mark **6:49-50**). Jesus says: "Take heart, it is I. Do not be afraid" (**v 50**). Unfortunately, most translations obscure the meaning of the phrase *ego eimi*—"it is I." It can mean that. But it can also mean "I am"—the divine name. Once again, this is exactly what God did for Moses (Exodus 34:5-7). The whole story is a revelation of deity. Jesus is not saying, *Don't be afraid because you know me—I am not a ghost.* He is saying, *Do not fear because I am God!*

It's not surprising, then, that the wind ceases and the sea becomes calm when Jesus gets in the boat. One would think the disciples would immediately confess his true identity as the Lord of the wind and the sea. But they do not. Mark tells us, "And they were utterly astounded" (Mark **6:51**). This is not a positive pronouncement. Astonishment is not faith. In fact, Mark ends with the announcement that "their hearts were hardened" (**v 52**).

This response is exactly what happens in Job. God alone walks on the sea (Job 9:8), but the response three verses later is, "Behold, he passes by me, and I see him not; he moves on, but I do not perceive him" (v 11).

The disciples see the miracle but miss its whole point. Hardness of heart hinders people from perceiving that Jesus is God.

The last time Mark mentioned hardness of heart, it was that of outsiders—people who were angry with Jesus for healing a man on the Sabbath (Mark 3:5). So there is a building drama here. Are the disciples truly insiders? Do they have eyes that see and ears that hear? Jesus will ask them this very question later (8:17-21).

This story is a stirring reminder of how to read the Bible. Sometimes we read the Bible in order to commend ourselves to God—

we read so that God will see us. But reading the Bible worshipfully means reading it so that we will see God. Bible reading is not just a cerebral exercise in which we recover "the author's original intent." God is the divine author, and he intends to reveal himself. We should respond with worship, awe, and faith.

The Lord My Healer

Mark **6:53-56** contains many echoes of earlier miracles. First, this story reminds us of the story of the feeding of the 5,000. Jesus tried to get away with his disciples, but the people recognized him and ran to him (**v 31-33; 55**). Jesus did not turn any away but healed them (**v 55-56**). Second, the people brought the sick people on their beds. This reminds us of the story of the paralyzed man in Mark 2:1-12. Third, people implored Jesus that they might touch the fringe of his garment. This recalls the story of the woman with the flow of blood (5:27-28). Mark's point is that these brief stories scattered throughout Mark thus far are only a small-scale glimpse into the grand-scale healing grace of Jesus.

Conflict with the Pharisees

Some religious authorities now arrive to attack Jesus (**7:1**), including the scribes from Jerusalem who accused him of demonic possession in Mark 3:22. They are looking for ways to accuse him. Therefore, they ignore the healings which Jesus has just performed and latch on to an issue of ritual cleanness or uncleanness.

The Jews believed that "the shadow of a Gentile falling across a dish or plate made it unclean" (Donald English, *The Message of Mark*, p 143). Mark alerts the reader to how extensive this tradition of washing is for Jews: "The Pharisees and *all* the Jews do not eat unless they wash their hands properly" (**7:3**, my emphasis). This was not just a hygiene issue; it was a question of ritual purity. This tradition, although not part of the Old Testament law as such (except for priests and for food offered in the temple—see Exodus 30:17-21;

Numbers 18:8-13), had become so intertwined with Jewish religion that people believed that to be Jewish was to wash hands, cups, and vessels before eating. Mark specifically mentions the fact that they would wash after coming from the marketplace (Mark **7:4**)—which is where Jesus has just been performing miracles (**6:56**).

So the Pharisees and scribes believe Jesus is acting in an unclean way. "Why do your disciples not walk according to the tradition of the elders, but eat with defiled hands?" (**7:5**). They are basically saying that Jesus doesn't care about the holiness of God. Jesus is going to take that charge and turn it on its head.

Jesus' rebuke comes in three stages. First, he takes the charge that he has defiled hands and reverses it by saying that they actually have defiled hearts (**v 6**, quoting Isaiah 29:13). They are "hypocrites." This word can also mean "actor." The Pharisees are pretending to be someone they are not. Their ritual scrupulousness could look as if they are serious about drawing near to God, but Jesus says that their hearts are far from God. The motivation for their rule-keeping is not love for God but a desire to be seen by others. They're mere con artists.

Second, Jesus labels "the tradition of the elders" as Isaiah's "commandments of men." The Pharisees are pretending to be the mouthpiece of God, but they are only sharing manmade ideas and treating them as if they are commandments from God.

Third, Jesus gives an example of the way that insisting on their tradition actually causes others to break the commandments of God. The tradition of "Corban" is an example of a manmade commandment that breaks the fifth commandment (Exodus 20:12). They justify failing to care for their parents by saying that their money or possessions are "Corban"—devoted to God. They invoke God's name to avoid doing something which God himself commanded.

Don't miss the irony. The tradition of the elders added commands to the law of God in an attempt to put a fence around it—to make sure people couldn't get near breaking it. But in the end those traditions caused people to break the law. Jesus says they are leaving the commandment of God (Mark **7:8**), rejecting it (**v 9**), and making it void (**v 13**). Hypocrisy indeed!

Questions for reflection

1. Which of the four Old Testament echoes in the story of the feeding of the 5,000 do you find most helpful personally? Why?

2. What is your attitude toward Bible reading? How can you make sure you read God's word worshipfully?

3. How do people miss the point about Jesus today? What could you say to help them understand him better?

PART TWO

Inside and Outside

Responding to the Pharisees' charge of ritual impurity, Jesus now says that defilement is not an outside-to-inside issue, but an inside-to-outside issue (Mark **7:15**). In other words, there is nothing outside a person that can defile them by going inside, as the Pharisees claim (**v 15**). Rather, the things that come out of a person are what defile them.

The deeper meaning of this needs to be unpacked further. So Jesus leaves the people and enters the house (**v 17**). Once again, he leaves the outsiders outside, and he goes inside the house to speak to the insiders.

Yet even though Jesus takes the disciples inside, they cannot see inside the parable—they have to ask him about it (**v 17**). When they do, he asks them if them if they lack understanding like everyone else (**v 18**).

The problem is really their inability to understand the heart. Purity and holiness are first and foremost issues of the heart, not the stomach (**v 19**)—so food cannot defile people but only what is in their hearts. Mark translates the full implications of this principle: "Thus [Jesus] declared all foods clean" (**v 19**). In one sweeping sentence, all the dietary laws for what foods to eat or not to eat were dispensed with.

Jesus restates his point: "What comes out of a person is what defiles him" (**v 20**). He then provides a more extensive rationale that covers many of the Ten Commandments: "For from within, out of the heart of man, come evil thoughts, sexual immorality, theft [8th commandment], murder [6th commandment], adultery [7th commandment], coveting [10th commandment], wickedness, deceit, sensuality, envy, slander [9th commandment], pride, foolishness" (**v 21–22**). Then he summarizes his point: "All these evil things come from within, and they defile a person" (**v 23**).

Holiness is a matter of the heart, not the hands or the stomach. Jesus refers to the heart three times (**v 6, 19, 21**). The Pharisees are scrupulous with their hands and their cups and their lips but not with their hearts. The Pharisees think the disciples' hands are defiled, but Jesus gives them an x-ray that shows them that they are hypocrites with defiled hearts. Their insides are rotten—and that's what makes them outsiders when it comes to the kingdom.

Clean Gentiles

Mark 7 has raised the issue of whether hands or foods can be unclean. But underneath the surface, the much uglier question is whether there are unclean people. We are confronted with that very question now in this next story (**v 24-37**).

Once again, Jesus tries to escape from the crushing weight of the crowds and all of their needs. He leaves Gennesaret and travels to the region of Tyre—a Gentile region at least 20 miles from Capernaum. He has entered a house and is trying to keep his presence quiet (**v 24**). But he cannot remain hidden. People everywhere have heard of him (3:7-11).

A woman has a little daughter with an unclean spirit. She is a definite outsider. Even Jewish women did not approach Jewish rabbis. And Gentiles were not supposed to do so either—certainly not a Gentile woman who had a daughter with an unclean spirit! This woman has three strikes against her. What's more, Jesus is taking some time off. The situation does not look promising.

But she will not be stopped. The language of the request communicates persistence and urgency: "She kept begging him" (**7:26**). This is a gutsy move.

Jesus' response seems offensive at first glance (**v 27**). It looks like a racial insult. The Jewish people are the children. The Gentiles are the dogs. But this is not an insult. It is a parable. He is imagining a family meal. Jesus uses a form of the word for dogs which means "puppies." These are beloved pets. They will be fed. But they are not fed first.

There is an order to Jesus' mission. He came to show Israel that he is the fulfillment of all that God promised to Israel. After his resurrection, Jesus will send his disciples to make disciples of all the nations. But not yet—right now the Gentiles have to wait their turn.

She says, "Yes, Lord" (**v 28**). Wait a minute—she heard the parable and understood it? She is not hardened or blind or deaf. Stop the music. This woman is the first example of someone who actually understands a parable and responds rightly. No one else has really understood Jesus' mission. She understands it after hearing one sentence in the form of a parable. And she not only understands it—she does not argue against it.

She says, *I recognize that I do not have a place at the table until later because I am not from Israel. I accept that. But I see something else. This is a feast. There is more than enough for Israel. If I am a puppy in your story, I know that puppies also eat from the table when crumbs fall.* And she receives the answer to her request. The demon leaves her daughter. She gets what she asked for because of her response (**v 29-30**).

This Gentile woman is unique in Mark's story. She enters the world of the parable. She does not find the answer she wants there. But she refuses to leave. She stays and says, "Yes, Lord." Then she reasons from within the world of that parable and finds hope there.

What does this story have to teach us about what makes someone clean or unclean? In Jesus' time, this Gentile woman would have been regarded as an unclean dog. Yet this story turns the tables on all that. The inside makes someone clean. And she is clean because she is full of faith.

Jesus now takes a long journey (**v 31**). He goes north through Sidon and then southeast to the Decapolis on the eastern side of the Sea of Galilee. This is a 120-mile journey. It is not a direct route but more of a semi-circle. He is staying in Gentile territory.

Some people bring to him a man who is deaf and has a speech impediment. Jesus takes him aside from the crowd privately (**v 33**).

The scene is so personal. But what Jesus does is also perplexing. Why does he put his fingers into the man's ears (**v 33**)? Why does Jesus spit on his fingers and then touch the man's tongue? Jesus can just say the word and the man will be healed!

Here is the glorious, wonderful answer: Jesus is using sign language. It would not work very well if I came up to a deaf person and tried to explain something with loud words. They would not understand. Instead, Jesus takes the time to use touch to explain what he is going to do.

Behold, the tender mercy of the Almighty. Healing would have been mercy enough. But Jesus stoops down to minister to the special needs of this man. He sees the need, yes, but he also sees the man. He does not see a problem—he sees a person.

He looks up to heaven (**v 34**). Jesus doesn't do anything independently of his Father—he is the Son, always seeking the Father and always doing what the Father would have him do. Before he speaks, he does one other thing: he sighs (**v 34**). It seems he identifies with the pain of this man—all the sorrow and the struggle that comes from a life of not being able to hear or speak. Jesus is not indifferent or unfeeling. He sighs and feels the pain before bringing the healing and the joy. Here is power, love, and tender attention.

The man's ears are opened, and he speaks plainly and clearly (**v 35**). Literally, "the chain of his tongue was broken." The chain that has kept him in the bondage of silence is broken. Jesus came to bring liberty for every kind of captive.

Why doesn't Jesus want the report of this miracle to be shared (**v 36**)? He is addressing the inevitable misunderstanding of the people. They are still blind to who he is. They will share the report of the miracle and spread the wrong conclusions.

But the crowd cannot contain their joy and amazement and astonishment. It just keeps bubbling up and flowing forth. Mark says there is astonishment "beyond measure" (**v 37**). The amount of astonishment cannot be quantified! The crowd observes, "He has done all things well" (**v 37**). Jesus' resumé continues to grow. What can't this person do?

The people are really saying more than they know. The form of "he has done all things well" is closely linked to the Greek text of Genesis 1:31: "And God saw everything that he had made, and behold, it was very good." God created a world with no deafness or muteness or cancer—until sin entered in. But now the Creator has stepped onto the stage of the world he created, bringing a new creation. Wherever he goes, he is undoing the effects of the **Fall**. He does all things well because he is God. And wherever he goes, he is making all things new.

The Second Bread Miracle

As we near the end of the first half of this Gospel, Mark ties things together in a masterful way. We have seen a series of mighty miracles, which Jesus performed as signs showing that he is the supernatural Son of God—two involving boats and one involving bread. The next story, the feeding of the 4,000, adds another bread miracle (Mark **8:1-10**).

This story stresses the same points that the first bread miracle highlighted. First, the same heart of compassion is on display (6:34; **8:2**). Second, the disciples respond in a similar way. In the first bread miracle, the disciples came to Jesus and asked him to send the crowds away so that they could go and buy something to eat (6:35-36). This time, Jesus launches a pre-emptive strike and describes the problem himself (**8:3**). The disciples' memory should kick in at this point. *Oh, we have been here before. I know, I know… we will find out if anyone has any bread or fish, we'll bring them to you, and then you'll bless them, and the multitude will get fed, and we will pick up all the leftovers. We're ready.* But that is not what happens. His disciples disappointingly respond in the same way as the last time: "How can one feed these people with bread here in this desolate place?" (**v 4**).

Third, the feeding follows the same pattern. Jesus acts like a host and seats the people. Then he takes the loaves and the fish, gives thanks, breaks the food, and gives it to the disciples to set before the people (**v 6-7**; see 6:41).

Fourth, both stories also feature the same result. All the people eat and are satisfied (6:42; **8:8**); and the disciples pick up the leftovers (6:43-44; **8:8-9**).

The Unbelief of the Pharisees

Once again we have a sign that Jesus is the Son of God—which is why it is so jarring to immediately overhear the Pharisees' demand for a sign from heaven. They are seeking to test him (**v 11**).

Jesus sighs deeply, but it is not like he did with the deaf-and-mute man. Here he is not grieving with the Pharisees but grieving because of them and their unbelief (**v 12**).

Jesus refuses to play their game. He gave the crowd a sign out of compassion for their need, but he refuses to give the Pharisees a sign because their request does not come from a true place of need. No more sign is needed (**v 12**). Jesus does not want them to think that he is under their judgment; they are under his.

Bread in the Boat

Mark now brings this first half of his Gospel to a climax with a story of bread in the boat (**v 14-21**).

Jesus warns the disciples of the leaven (or yeast) of the Pharisees and the leaven of Herod (**v 15**). The disciples do not understand—they think he is commenting on their lack of physical bread. But in fact this "leaven" is the response to Jesus of unbelief.

We have just seen the Pharisees' unbelief. They demanded more signs, not because they were on the fence but because they were on the attack and trying to trap him. They were putting the Lord their God to the test, and they didn't even see it.

What about the leaven of Herod? We saw in 6:14 that Herod

believed that Jesus was John the Baptist risen from the dead. Herod's response looked better than that of the Pharisees at first glance. He heard of all the signs that Jesus was doing and thought he came from God. But he still came to the wrong conclusion. In the end, the responses of both Herod and the Pharisees were responses of unbelief. Both were rejecting the true identity of Jesus as the divine Son of God. The disciples must not respond like this.

To hammer this point home, in **8:17-21** Jesus asks some devastating questions that contain haunting allusions to Isaiah 6:10-12. Jesus is asking the disciples if they are really insiders. They have seen all the signs. But do they really have eyes that see or ears that hear? Those on the outside have physical eyes but do not see spiritual reality. Those on the outside have physical ears, but they don't hear spiritual reality. Those on the outside have physical hearts, but their spiritual hearts are hardened.

We have assumed so far that the disciples are insiders—those who are following Jesus because they have eyes to see. Now Jesus' confrontation puts a gigantic question mark over that assumption. Jesus asks them how they can still be so blind and deaf and hard after this string of stirring signs he has given.

> There is a gigantic question mark: are the disciples insiders?

It is easy to look at the disciples and feel a little smug. How could they keep forgetting the things that Jesus has done? But the question comes right back at us like a boomerang. You, too, have seen Jesus do all things well. Lame people leap, mute people speak, deaf people hear, those with leprosy are cleansed, women who are sick and unclean and ostracized are called "Daughter," dead little girls are raised up, demons are cast out, the wind and the waves cease, thousands of people are fed with five loaves and two fish, and Jesus walks on water. You could make a list of all the things you have seen the Lord do in your own life, too.

But what happens when the next hard thing comes? If you are anything like me, it is easy to panic and say, "What are we going to do? How could this ever work out? How could I possibly do anything about this?" Our initial impulse is to doubt and not trust, panic and not praise, and throw up our hands instead of getting down on our knees.

So the question this text has for us is the same one that Jesus had for his disciples. You have seen the signs. Do you not yet understand?

Questions for reflection

1. What would it look like to become more like Jesus in these stories?

2. Are there areas in your life where you find yourself doubting the power, wisdom, and goodness of the Lord Jesus? Where does the text hit home for you in this regard?

3. What does it mean for you to say that Jesus "has done all things well"?

7. THE STRUGGLE FOR SIGHT

We have come to the turning point in the Gospel of Mark. The next section (**8:22 – 10:52**), which follows Jesus and his disciples as they journey to Jerusalem, begins and ends with the healing of a blind man. These bookends are about physical blindness, but the stories in between are about spiritual blindness. This journey to Jerusalem is actually a struggle for sight.

The story of the blind man in **8:22-26** is only found in the Gospel of Mark. One detail stands out right away that troubles many people. Why did it take Jesus two attempts to heal this blindness? After spitting on his eyes and laying his hands on the blind man, Jesus asked him if he could see anything, and the man said, "I see people, but they look like trees, walking" (**v 24**). He saw but only partially. Then Jesus went to heal him a second time, and this time "he opened his eyes, his sight was restored, and he saw everything clearly" (**v 25**).

Did Jesus make a mistake or do something wrong the first time? No! The answer is quite simple: this healing is a parable, an object lesson. This blind man represents the disciples. They have partial spiritual sight, but also partial spiritual blindness.

Peter's Confession: Partial Sight

Verses 27-30 prove that the disciples do indeed partially see who Jesus is. Others are giving all the wrong answers: John the Baptist, Elijah, one of the prophets (**v 28**). But Peter gets it right! "You are **the Christ**" (**v 29**).

It seems that Peter has just answered Jesus' question from within the boat. *Do you get it yet, disciples? Can you see who I am yet?* (v 17). Peter answers, *Yes, we see clearly. You are the Christ.*

Jesus commands them to tell no one about him (**v 30**). He does so because they don't really understand yet. They are still partially blind. The next verses make this crystal clear.

The First Passion Prediction

Jesus clearly tells the disciples that he is going to suffer and die and rise again (**v 31**). Mark tells the reader that Jesus said it plainly (**v 32**). Jesus has only hinted about his death up to this point (for example, in Mark 2:20). Now he is explicit and emphatic.

Jesus uses the title "the Son of Man" (**8:31**). This is a title drawn from Daniel 7:13-14, where a mysterious figure, "one like a son of man," comes to the **Ancient of Days** and receives a kingdom. But surprisingly, Jesus says that the Son of Man is going to suffer. He will be rejected by the Jewish leaders and be murdered. Jesus is putting two Old Testament texts together. There is a Daniel 7 person who receives an everlasting kingdom and whom all the nations will serve, and there is an Isaiah 53 suffering servant who will be despised and re-jected and slaughtered. Jesus says that they are the same person: him. His kingdom will be established through his death and resurrection.

This is all too much for Peter (Mark **8:32**). He momentarily stops being a follower of the Messiah and starts trying to be a teacher of the Messiah: "And Peter took him aside and began to rebuke him." I imagine he said something like, *Messiahs do not die. You are sup-posed to go and defeat all of our enemies—not be killed by them. This is not the way it is supposed to work. You are wrong about yourself!* This is blindness. Peter has just declared that Jesus is the Messiah, yet in the next moment, he is telling Jesus that he does not understand what being the Messiah is all about.

At once, Jesus puts Peter back in his place. Seeing that he could lead all of his disciples astray, he says, "Get behind me, Satan" (**v 33**). Peter should go back to his proper place as a disciple—behind Jesus as a follower, not in front of him as his teacher.

Why does he call Peter "Satan"? Doesn't that seem a little harsh? I think the answer is fairly simple. Satan once offered Jesus a short cut—he could have all the kingdoms of the world, without going to the cross (Matthew 4:8-9; Luke 4:5-7). Peter's "teaching" is taking a page right out of that playbook.

Jesus explains the flaw with Peter's thinking: "For you are not setting your mind on the things of God, but on the things of man" (Mark **8:33**). Jesus knows he will not fit earthly expectations. The disciples are going to have to let go of worldly thinking in order to embrace the things of God—Jesus' death and resurrection.

This teaching is not just for the disciples but for the crowds as well (**v 34**). The cross is the point of contention, and so Jesus now clarifies: he is indeed a King who will one day come in glory (**v 38**), but he is also one who carries a cross.

This teaching would have come with the force of an electric shock. Not only would Jesus die on a cross, but those who followed him would also have to carry a cross. Jesus says that to be one of his followers, people must do three things (**v 34**): (1) say "no" to themselves ("deny himself"), (2) say "yes" to their death ("take up his cross"), and (3) follow Jesus.

We need to recover the scandal and the shock of the cross. Cicero, the Roman philosopher who died 50 years before the birth of Christ, wrote, "To bind a Roman citizen is a crime; to flog him is an abomination; to slay him is like killing a relative; to crucify him is—what? There is no fitting word that can possibly describe so horrible a deed" (*In Verrem* 2.5.165). Meanwhile, the Jews regarded the cross as a curse, because Deuteronomy 21:22-23 taught that those who are hung on a tree are cursed.

The message of the cross is just as counter cultural in our day. It seems so upside down. How is losing your life the way to save your life?

We are often told to "have it your way" and "follow your heart." This message cuts against that grain.

Jesus already taught that following your heart is a path that leads to death, not life. "For from within, *out of the heart of man,* come evil thoughts, sexual immorality, theft, murder, adultery, coveting, wickedness, deceit, sensuality, envy, slander, pride, foolishness" (Mark 7:21-23, my emphasis). We have to learn to say a profound no to some of our deepest longings. Proverbs 14:12 states this point with crystal clarity: "There is a way that seems right to a man, but its end is the way to death."

The world constantly pursues the things that seem right to them. You get ahead by getting more stuff—saying yes to what you want all the time. Self-denial seems like the path of loss, not gain. But let's say that you are so wildly successful in your quest to say yes to yourself that you end up gaining the whole world. Is it worth it to gain the world and lose your soul (Mark **8:36**)?

Don't miss the promise in this text. The cost of discipleship is connected to Jesus. Jesus calls us to lose our lives "for my sake" (**v 35**). We deny lesser things to get greater things. Jesus is saying, *As you deny yourself, you find your real self and eternal life in me.* All other ways are a dead end, but this path ends in life. Following Jesus is never mainly about what you lose but what you gain forever.

But there is a warning too. Following Jesus means not being ashamed of him and his words (**v 38**). If we have been ashamed of him in this life, he will be ashamed of us in the life to come—which will mean eternal death and separation from him.

The Transfiguration

Some have been tripped up by thinking that Jesus' promise in **9:1** is a reference to the second coming; but in fact it sets up the very next story. The phrase "some standing here" of **verse 1** is immediately fulfilled by "Peter, James, and John" of **verse 2**. These three disciples go up a mountain with Jesus. What they witness is the kingdom of God coming in power (**v 1**). The transfiguration is the moment when Peter, James, and John get to see the divine power and glory of our Lord Jesus Christ on display. Jesus' appearance changes, making his clothes more radiantly white than anyone on earth could bleach them (**v 2-3**).

The exodus is a really important backstory for the transfiguration. Moses went up a high mountain, God's glory came down in a cloud, and Moses heard God's voice. All of these details are here: (1) the high mountain, (2) God's glory in the cloud, (3) God speaking from the cloud, and (4) even Moses himself making an appearance. Even the reference to six days seems to be an intentional parallel (Mark **9:2**; Exodus 24:16). Mark is rarely so precise with chronology.

But there is also a stunning difference in the two stories. The transfiguration takes place on a different mountain— not Mount Sinai. Why? Because this is *not* Mount Sinai all over again. At Sinai, Moses saw the glory of God and even reflected it in his own face, as the moon

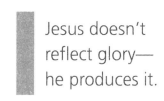

Jesus doesn't reflect glory— he produces it.

reflects the glory of the sun (Exodus 34:29). Jesus, however, is not like the moon but the sun itself—the *source* of the glory. The transfiguration shows that he is God. He produces the glory—it emanates from him. Jesus "is the radiance of the glory of God" (Hebrews 1:3).

People give many explanations for the presence of Moses and Elijah. There are some natural connections. Both Moses and Elijah had similar experiences on Mount Sinai, seeing the glory of God. There could also be a representative dimension: Moses represents the law and Elijah represents the prophets, which both testify to Jesus. One Old Testament Scripture mentions Moses and Elijah together with the coming of the Lord (Malachi 4:4-5). And Moses testified that a prophet like himself would come "and it is to him you shall listen" (Deuteronomy 18:15). The Father speaks these very words to the disciples: "Listen to him" (Mark **9:7**).

The transfiguration is the gift of sight, but Peter is blind to what he is seeing. He is the first to speak again (**v 5-6**). He proposes that they build three "tents" or dwelling places. Mark already tips his hand and reveals that this was not a good request for Peter to make: "... for he did not know what to say" (**v 6**). What was Peter missing? We are about to see clearly what he failed to see.

A cloud then overshadows them (**v 7**), and God the Father speaks. This is the second time that God the Father has spoken audibly in the Gospel of Mark. Let's compare the two.

"And a voice came from heaven, 'You are my beloved Son; with you I am well pleased.'" (1:11)

"And a voice came out of the cloud, 'This is my beloved Son; listen to him.'" (**9:7**)

Two big differences come to the fore. First, God the Father speaks directly to the Son at the baptism: "*You are* my beloved Son." At the transfiguration, the Father speaks to the disciples about the Son: "*This is* my beloved Son."

Second, the message at Jesus' baptism is a statement of identity. The message at the transfiguration is a statement plus a command. The Father makes the point as clear as possible: *This is my beloved Son—so—listen to him!*

These words are a direct rebuke. Peter's proposal would have lumped Jesus together with Moses and Elijah and put them on the same level. The rebuke is forceful: *Don't you dare put my Son in the same category as Moses and Elijah.* They reflected the glory of God. Jesus is the glory of God. They spoke from God; Jesus speaks as God. Listen to him because he is in a class by himself.

At Mount Sinai, God came down in the cloud and spoke. In the incarnation, God came all the way down and **took on flesh**. The voice of the incarnate God should be received as the voice of God.

The uniqueness of Jesus is further confirmed in the way the story ends: "And suddenly, looking around, they no longer saw anyone with them but Jesus only" (**v 8**). Jesus only! Moses and Elijah are no longer there. So listen to Jesus.

But the transfiguration is not just a warning against putting Jesus on the same level as others from the past. It is also a sneak peek at where all history is heading.

When Jesus was on earth, his deity was often "veiled in flesh," as the hymn writer Charles Wesley put it in "Hark the Herald Angels Sing." Mark has highlighted moments when Jesus' divine power was on display. But this was the one moment when his divine nature over-shadowed and outshone his human nature. It was a sneak peek at the second coming, the day when Jesus will come "in the glory of his Father with the holy angels" (**8:38**). Thus it is proof that Jesus' words can be trusted.

Peter wrote later about the transfiguration in 2 Peter 1:17-18. He was writing to people who were questioning whether Jesus would ever come again, and he says that the transfiguration confirms the words of the prophets (2 Peter 1:19). The transfiguration has made the prophecy of the second coming even more certain. Peter is able to say that he has not just read about it; he has seen it.

Questions for reflection

1. How does Jesus' definition of discipleship in 8:34-38 challenge you today?

2. Why is it important that the transfiguration is not a repeat of Moses' experience on Mount Sinai?

3. Does the second coming of Christ factor into your daily life? Or is it "out of sight, out of mind"? How can you live in the light of the second coming more?

PART TWO

Still Blind

Mark **9:9** is the ninth and final time that Jesus commands silence in the Gospel of Mark. But this is the only time he lets us know that this command to be silent was only temporary. The disciples were to tell no one what they had seen "until the Son of Man had risen from the dead."

Jesus is saying that until the dots of his death and resurrection are connected, none of the rest of the picture will make sense. The resurrection is the crucial vantage point from which he can be understood. The disciples can't understand until that happens.

How does the resurrection connect the dots with regard to suffering? *Rising* from the dead can only come after *being* dead. It is a package deal! Death and resurrection. We are back to what Jesus said in Mark 8:31—he must suffer and be killed and after three days rise again.

You may remember what happened last time. Peter opened his mouth and rebuked Jesus and got rebuked in return. Will he do better this time? Have the disciples learned their lesson?

No. Their blindness has not been removed. They don't understand what he means (**9:10**). But this time they conceal their blindness rather than blurting it out. They don't want to be rebuked again. They prefer to keep their questions to themselves.

Instead they move away from the topic. "Why do the scribes say that first Elijah must come?" (**v 11**). They could be thinking, *We know that Elijah will return before the great day of the Lord, when God is going to put everything to right. We just saw Elijah up there. So isn't the day of the Lord near? Why are we talking about death and resurrection still? Let's talk about the restoration of all things instead!* They're trying to change the subject—but Jesus will take them right back to it.

The disciples have a partial blindness. They only know half of the story. They have missed the suffering part of the picture again! Once again Jesus is going to help them connect the dots of Scripture.

He shows that the disciples' question about Elijah is not a separate subject from his own death and resurrection.

Jesus acknowledges that they are right about Elijah's coming (**v 12**). It is prophesied in Malachi 4:5-6. Then he asks, "How is it written of the Son of Man that he should suffer many things?" (Mark **9:12**). He is connecting the dot of the coming of Elijah with the dot of his own suffering.

The truth is that Elijah must suffer too. In fact (and this is the gotcha moment) he already has suffered (**v 13**). So Jesus is essentially saying, *Elijah was handed over and executed; why does it surprise you that I am going down that same road?*

There is no single text that says Elijah would suffer. Jesus is pointing to a general pattern in Scripture of the persecution and suffering of prophets. Later, in Mark 12, he will highlight this by portraying Israel as tenants of a vineyard who keep rejecting and even killing the messengers of the owner. At last, the Master sends his beloved Son (v 6). The Master says, "They will respect my son." But they kill him too.

In what sense has Elijah suffered? Jesus is connecting him with John the Baptist. Mark has already prepared the ground for this by showing how John the Baptist preached in the wilderness and prepared the way for Jesus (1:2-4)—which is what the disciples expected Elijah to come and do. Mark also describes John as wearing the distinctive dress of Elijah (Mark 1:6; 2 Kings 1:7-8). John the Baptist was not literally Elijah. They were two distinct people. But in God's plan they came together as one. John the Baptist came "in the spirit and power of Elijah" (Luke 1:17) to accomplish Malachi 4:5-6. This is one of the things that the disciples have failed to understand.

These stories of partial blindness can function like a spiritual check-up. They're like the little instrument that the doctor uses to hit your knee and test your reflexes. How do you reflexively respond to these stories? Do you question and doubt and change the subject as the disciples did? Or do these truths thrill your spiritual tastebuds?

"I Believe, Help My Unbelief"

In Mark **9:14** we move from the scene of glory to the troubled world below. The move is jarring. There is a painting in the Vatican Museums called *The Transfiguration*, painted by Raphael, which captures the scene with skill. R. Kent Hughes describes it very well in his commentary:

> "The uppermost part pictures the **transfigured** form of Jesus, with Moses on the left and Elijah on his right. On the next level down there are three disciples, Peter, James, and John, recently awakened and shielding their eyes from Jesus' blinding brilliance. Then, on the ground level is a poor demon-possessed boy, his mouth hideously gaping with wild ravings. At his side is his desperate father. Surrounding them are the rest of the disciples, some of whom are pointing upward to the glowing figure of Christ—who will be the boy's only answer. Raphael has brilliantly captured something of the overwhelming contrast between the glorious Mount of Transfiguration and the troubled world waiting below." (*Mark*, vol. 2, p 21)

The story starts with the usual cast of characters: the crowd, the scribes, and the disciples. Jesus and Peter, James, and John are reunited with the other disciples. We are not surprised that the scribes are arguing with the disciples again (**v 14**). Jesus comes on the scene to much fanfare and amazement (**v 15**). He immediately asks about the argument (**v 16**). Someone emerges from the crowd to tell the story. He is the father of a demon-possessed boy. He brings a charge against the disciples in **verse 18**: "So I asked your disciples to cast it out, and they were not able." Apparently, this is what everyone is arguing about.

This dad describes the horrible drama that he deals with every day (**v 17-18, 21-22**). These demons degrade this little boy until he grinds his teeth and foams at the mouth like a rabid animal. They seek to disable and distort the image of God by making the boy mute or stiff and lifeless. Then they try to destroy the image of God altogether by burning or drowning the boy (**v 22**).

Jesus asks them to bring the boy to him, and we see all this happen for ourselves in **verse 20**. "Immediately [the spirit] convulsed the boy, and he fell on the ground and rolled about, foaming at the mouth."

Watching the demons do this to a beloved son is a form of suffering for the father, too, and so this is a shared request for mercy. The father does not say, *Have compassion on him and help him*; he says, "have compassion on *us* and help *us*" (**v 22**, my emphasis). This father is strung out by one disappointment after another. His hopes have been dashed by the failure of the disciples. He is at the end of his rope.

So he adds to his request the phrase "if you can do anything" (**v 22**). He does not doubt Jesus' willingness to help—he doubts Jesus' ability to help. The man assumes the problem is probably with Jesus, not with himself. Jesus gently shows him it is the other way around.

"And Jesus said to him, 'If you can'! All things are possible for one who believes." (**v 23**)

Faith recognizes that there is nothing that can hold Jesus back—he is both willing and able. This man has the beginnings of trust in Jesus' compassion, which is why he is asking, but he also doubts Jesus' ability. This is the very real struggle for faith in Mark's Gospel.

> The struggle for faith is very real.

The father takes Jesus' word to heart. He suddenly sees the real source of the problem: he believes partially, not fully. What should he do about that? Try harder? Resolve to doubt less? No, he brings even his unbelief to Jesus. "Immediately the father of the child cried out and said, 'I believe; help my unbelief!'" (**v 24**)

It is hard to bring out the force of this word for "cried out." This phrase is used ten times in Mark, and it always refers to a strong emotional outburst. Don't think of a gentle rain or drizzle—think of a thunderclap. This word is something the demons do when they see Jesus (3:11; 5:5, 7; **9:26**), and what people in need do when they see

Jesus and cry out for mercy (Bartimaeus in 10:47-48), or shout "**Ho-sanna!**" (11:9), or shout loudly for his crucifixion (15:13, 14).

You should hear this word "crying out" as a desperate shout—something you do when one thing becomes everything. This desperate desire has seized him; it has become the only thing that matters in this moment.

Pride will keep someone from crying out like that. You don't want people to see you desperate or that needy. Sometimes if we face difficulties, the impulse is to try harder, do better, or persevere longer. It is a symptom of the same problem—proud unbelief.

Ironically, this confession of unbelief is actually an example of belief—it is a prayer of faith. The father has faith that Jesus can even help him with his lack of faith. Bringing our doubts to Jesus does not offend Jesus. He already sees what is in our hearts. He knows the problem. But have we reached the point where we will humble ourselves, confess our need, bring it to him, and beg him to do what only he can do?

The reader gets a front row seat to watch what Jesus can truly do in **9:25-27**. These three verses show us three things about Jesus' power. First, he has irresistible authority. We have seen this time and time again in Mark. No one and nothing can resist Jesus' power. When Jesus tells the demon to come out of the boy, it comes out.

Second, Jesus has irreversible authority. What he does cannot be undone: "Come out of him and never enter him again" (**v 25**). This is the glory of the Jesus of Revelation 3:7—"the true one … who opens and no one will shut, who shuts and no one opens."

Third, Jesus has resurrection authority. Mark does not want us to miss this point. The boy is "like a corpse" (Mark **9:26**). Some people say, "He is dead." But Jesus takes this boy by the hand. He "lifted him up" and "he arose" (**v 27**). In the preceding story, the disciples were confused about what it means to rise from the dead (**v 10**). Now they have a stunning demonstration of that very reality. This is a preview of how the Gospel of Mark will end and Jesus will once again show his resurrection power.

The boy's healing would have been a perfect way to end this story. It seems like that is the resolution—the climax of the resurrection picture. But this story ends once again with a comment on the problem with the disciples. They ask why they were unable to do what they had done so many times before. Jesus gives an answer that highlights their lack of prayer (**v 29**).

Nearly everyone who receives help in Mark first sees their need and then asks for help. The disciples often do not see their need, and thus they do not ask—as they showed when they did not ask Jesus to explain the resurrection (**v 10**). Jesus shows them that their perennial problem is their prayerlessness. They are afraid to ask Jesus for help. They are relying on their own strength.

The father of the demon-possessed boy modeled something the disciples are missing. He had partial faith and partial unbelief, and he asked for help with his unbelief. The disciples are in the same position, and they need the same solution: "I believe; help my unbelief!"

I have met many people who truly believe that they need to work through their difficulties on their own. If they have doubts, they try to think more or read more or study more until they are convinced. If they struggle with sin, they try to sort themselves out instead of going to Jesus. That, in effect, is the same thing that the disciples were doing.

What about you? Do you despise weakness and desperation or have you reached the surprising insight that it is actually a gift? The hymn writer Joseph Hart says it well in the song "Come Ye Sinners." What does it take to come to Jesus? "All the fitness he requires is to feel your need of him." The only thing we really need is to feel our need for him. Paul Miller summarizes this principle for prayer:

"We don't need self-discipline to pray continuously; we just need to be poor in spirit." (*A Praying Life,* p 54)

Questions for reflection

1. Does pride ever keep you from prayer?

2. For what reasons might this passage encourage you to pray more?

3. What will you ask Jesus for as a result of reading this passage?

8. WHO IS WELCOME?

The travel narrative now gains a sense of decisiveness. Jesus is passing through Galilee for the final time and does not want anyone to know because he is not stopping (**9:30**). Galilee is not his destination; Jerusalem is. His date with destiny is drawing near. He will die there and rise again on the third day—as he informs the disciples once again (**v 31**).

Blindness

The disciples have not learned the lesson that the father of the demon-possessed boy modeled for them. Despite Jesus' constant teaching on his death and resurrection, they fail to understand, and they are afraid to ask for help (**v 32**). The rest of the story is going to help us see that "afraid to ask" really means "too arrogant to ask."

The next verses put this mindset on display. A lively conversation is happening on the way. Jesus asks them, "What were you discussing on the way?" (**v 33**).

Mark makes it clear that they kept silent. They were not going to go there. They refused to bring that conversation into the light. Why? "For on the way they had argued with one another about who was the greatest" (**v 34**). They are consumed by debates about their own greatness, and stay silent because they don't want to look bad.

This series of events is strikingly jarring and disorienting. What would you do if you just heard your beloved master say that he was going to die? Imagine this scenario: I get home from church one Sunday and my wife tells me to sit down. She explains that she has an aggressive form of cancer that is very advanced. She only has a few weeks to live.

How do I respond? I will tell you how I should not respond! I should not suddenly interject, "Wow. Interesting news. Well, did you hear my sermon today? I think it was one of my best—maybe my greatest. At least in the top five."

It would be a totally insensitive and self-centered response. But that's effectively what the disciples are doing.

Their blindness flows from their delusions of grandeur. Mark explicitly says that this argument took place "on the way." He repeats the phrase (**v 33, 34**) so that we won't miss it. This phrase "on the way" is a reference to the journey they are taking to Jerusalem. They think it is a glory road leading to exaltation. But this is the Calvary road. This journey is leading to humiliation. Suffering must precede glory. Jesus has work to do in resetting the disciples' expectations.

Correction

Jesus starts with a lesson in humility. He does not rebuke them for wanting to be first or great. Their endeavour to be first is not wrong—just misguided. It is category confusion. They are thinking the things of the world, not the things of God, again (compare 8:33). They are using worldly categories for greatness. Jesus teaches them about his upside-down kingdom, where the way up is down and the way to real happiness is to seek the happiness of others. Being first of all in worldly terms means being last of all in the kingdom. Being greater than all in the kingdom means being the servant of all (**9:35**).

Jesus uses a child to reinforce this lesson (**v 36-37**). The meaning of this lesson centers not on the worth of the child but the worth of Jesus. He tells them that when they receive even a child "in my name," they are really receiving him. The child has no reason to be received on his or her own. The reason is owing to Jesus.

This is a test to see if the disciples will prize Jesus' name and put it above everything else. There is a single criterion for receiving others: Jesus. We do not define people in relation to ourselves—especially not by what they can do for us. The disciples seem to make everything about themselves, but Jesus is making it all about himself.

Then he raises the bar higher. What is at stake in receiving and serving the lowly? Receiving Jesus is at stake. Receiving God the Father is at stake. They cannot receive Jesus and reject others who name the name of Jesus. And they cannot reject others in Jesus' name and receive the Father who sent Jesus. Rejecting others in the name of Jesus is spiritual suicide, which rejects Jesus and his Father. It is Jesus' way of saying what John the apostle says later:

"If anyone says, 'I love God,' and hates his brother, he is a liar; for he who does not love his brother whom he has seen cannot love God whom he has not seen. And this commandment we have from him: whoever loves God must also love his brother."

(1 John 4:20-21)

True greatness is a big-heartedness that can't bear to stiff-arm any of the children of God. It cannot stand spiritual snobbery in the family of God. This is very different than the world's understanding of greatness.

Michael Jordan's Basketball Hall of Fame acceptance speech is infamous. He gave a 23-minute speech in which he named people who helped him become great because they were obstacles for him to overcome. Greatness for Jordan was elevating himself at the expense of others—they were like rungs on the ladder of greatness, which he had stepped on to climb up higher.

> True greatness sees how to empower, not overpower.

Jesus' definition of greatness is diametrically opposed to this. Greatness does not tear down others to elevate oneself. True greatness elevates others. True greatness sees how to empower someone, not overpower them. We become a servant; we do not make others our servants.

These words test our hearts today. Do we size people up to measure if we are better than them? And do we use people, or do we love people? A flourishing church is a place where the weak and poor and frail flourish. A flourishing church is a church not of big shots but of big hearts. We do not view people as those to evaluate and compete with but those to serve.

Jesus is the ultimate standard of greatness. He is the servant of all. He has welcomed all the weak and needy in Mark's Gospel. And the same is true today. Those who come to him he does not cast out. That would be to "un-Jesus" himself. He is more ready to receive you than you are ready to be received. Indeed, the Father's arms are open to you and the family of God is open to you only because the Son stretched out his arms *for* you on the cross.

David Robinson was inducted into the Basketball Hall of Fame at the same ceremony as Michael Jordan. His speech was radically different. He first thanked everyone who had touched his life. Then he closed with the passage from Luke 17:11–19 about the ten men with leprosy who were healed, with only one coming back to give thanks. Robinson presented himself simply as someone healed of his leprosy by Jesus. He had come to the microphone to give thanks to Jesus.

Robinson was right. Christians are those who suffered from leprosy who gather to give thanks to Christ for how he has healed us. We are not impressed with ourselves; we are thankful to him. It is what we celebrate every time we partake of the Lord's Supper. There, there is no VIP section or special seating for the somebodies of the world. It is the great leveler. Salvation is not a potluck where we all bring something to the table. We dine with the King only because the King purchased our seat.

Another Eye Exam

How do we view others? The eye test in the next passage (Mark **9:38-41**) is really a heart test—and the disciples fail once again.

The whole scene is ironic from start to finish. Jesus has barely finished teaching them that they need to receive people in his name (**v 36-37**). Perhaps those words are still hanging in the air when John tells him that someone has been casting out demons "in your name" (**v 38**). Did the disciples receive this man? No. They rejected him and tried to stop him. The scene is doubly ironic because the disciples have just failed in their attempt to cast out a demon (v 17-18) and this person was successful. "To see an 'outsider' apparently succeeding where they, the chosen agents of Jesus, have failed is doubly distressing" (R.T. France, *The Gospel of Mark*, p 376). So, rather than celebrate the defeat of dark spirits, they try to put a stop to it.

Many commentators point to the similarities between this story and Numbers 11:26-29. Some people began to speak as prophets who were not official prophets like Moses. Joshua was troubled that others were speaking for the Lord. He didn't want them sharing the limelight with Moses. This is the conversation between Joshua and Moses:

> "Joshua the son of Nun, the assistant of Moses from his youth, said, 'My lord Moses, stop them.' But Moses said to him, 'Are you jealous for my sake? Would that all the LORD's people were prophets, that the LORD would put his Spirit on them!'"
>
> (Numbers 11:28-29)

The disciples have narrow, prideful hearts that seem bent on cornering the market on ministry—but Jesus' heart is more expansive. It is as if Jesus is saying, *Would that all the Lord's people were exorcists who would cast out demons in my name!*

He rebukes John: "Do not stop him" (Mark **9:39**). Then he gives three reasons for the command. First, don't stop the one ministering in my name, "for no one who does a mighty work in my name will be able soon afterward to speak evil of me." Jesus has a standard—mighty works must be matched with honor for the mighty name of Jesus. People can only do miracles in his name if they are in a proper relationship to himself.

Here's the second reason for the command: "For the one who is not against us is for us" (**v 40**). Notice that Jesus redefines "us" beyond the scope of the disciples. In their preoccupation with themselves, they draw the circle of insiders around themselves only. Jesus draws the circle much wider: *if they are not against us, then they are for us.*

This is a war: the kingdom of God versus the kingdom of Satan. One must take sides, and there are only two sides. The true adversary is Satan. He and his demons are the ones "against us." The problem with the disciples is that their pride leads to cutthroat competition that would draw really small circles based on who is part of their group. The problem with this person is not what he is doing or the name he is using—he simply fails to be in their company.

We really need to let this text speak to where we are today. Tribalism and party strife have no place in the body of Christ. I love what J.C. Ryle says about **verse 40**:

> "Here is a golden rule indeed, and one that human nature sorely needs and has too often forgotten. Members of all branches of Christ's church are apt to think that no good can be done in the world unless it is done by their own party and denomination. They are so narrow-minded that they cannot conceive the possibility of working on any other pattern but that which they follow." (*The Gospel of Mark*, p 138)

Ryle goes on to say that we can blame some of the blackest pages of church history on this intolerance:

> "Christians have repeatedly persecuted Christians for no better reason than that which is here given by John. They have practically proclaimed to their brothers and sisters, 'You must either follow us or not work for Christ at all.'" (p 138)

But Jesus goes even further in his third reason not to stop the man.

The phrase "in my name / in your name" has occurred three times in rapid succession in **verses 37-39**. Now we come to the climax in **verse 41**, where the actual name is explicitly spelled out:

"You belong to Christ." Never mind casting out demons—even the smallest act has great significance when it is done for the greatest Name. A small act like giving a disciple a drink signifies something: we belong to Christ together.

Jesus' words are a full-frontal assault on our pride. Pride is quick to exclude people and draw the circle really small. Pride is also quick to judge the supposed size of the actions. We are quick to notice large, sensational works, and overlook small, everyday acts of kindness. Jesus will receive and reward what anyone does in his name—whether it is the sensational act of casting out a demon or the seemingly small act of pouring a cup of water.

How much more does this truth apply to the church in our day on the other side of the cross. Christ came and tore down the dividing wall between us by his blood. Imagine the offense of building it back up, issue by issue. When the church is filled with a **party spirit**, it is our names, not the name of Jesus, that are lifted high.

The influential evangelist of the **Great Awakening**, George Whitefield, exemplifies Paul's preoccupation with the name of Christ over his own name. Whitefield decided to hand over the reigns of leadership of the **Methodist** movement to John Wesley because the movement was in danger of being divided over allegiance to either Whitefield or Wesley. Whitefield's followers urged him to take back his position of leadership. They warned him that his name might be forgotten. He replied by saying, "My name? Let the name of Whitefield perish if only the name of Christ be glorified." The single passion of a faithful Christian is to make much of the name of Christ.

Questions for reflection

1. How is Jesus the perfect expression of true greatness?

2. Have there been moments in your life when you sounded like Michael Jordan in his Hall of Fame speech? Have there been moments in your life when you sounded like David Robinson in *his* Hall of Fame speech?

3. How can you grow to be a disciple who welcomes other disciples? What can you personally do in order to make your church a more welcoming, big-hearted, open-armed church?

PART TWO

Be at Peace with One Another

Mark **9:42-50** makes many people very uncomfortable today because it speaks very directly of the **doctrine** of hell. This doctrine did not embarrass Jesus. He taught about it more than all other biblical authors combined.

Please do not ignore the warning in this passage and think that it is only for those who do not follow Jesus. That would be going against everything Jesus is doing in this text, because he preached it to his disciples—followers of Christ!

And do not check out at this point because you think the danger of hell only applies to those who are caught in "big" sins. Jesus says we should take sin so seriously that if our hand or foot or eye causes us to sin, we should cut it off or tear it out. Both Matthew and Mark use these metaphors of fighting sin, but it is worth noting that these texts address different sins. In Matthew, Jesus focuses on lust (Matthew 5:28), but in Mark, he addresses sinning in a way that causes others to sin or stumble (Mark **9:42**). We must not exclude a fellow believer and cause them to stumble because eternal punishment is at stake. We must be at peace with one another, not at peace with sin.

The passage begins and ends with the same point. **Verse 42** says it negatively (Don't cause a fellow Christian to sin) and **verse 50** says it positively (Be at peace with one another). These are two sides of the same coin. Jesus is still responding to the fact that the disciples have just been rejecting a fellow believer. When he speaks about causing someone to stumble or sin (**v 42, 43, 45, 47**), he is referring to the creation of confusion in someone as to whether he or she is in the kingdom and truly belongs to Christ. The idea is that a little one (a seemingly insignificant follower of Christ) has a fragile faith and they could be so undone by the rejection of other Christians that they abandon the faith and abandon following Jesus.

This warning is very timely for the disciples because they are in danger of doing this very thing. They have been shrinking the circle of those who follow Christ and belong to Christ to themselves, and they are in danger of excluding everyone else. In fact, the disciples have not only reduced the circle to twelve but they are further subdividing the circle in cutthroat competition and arguing over who is the greatest. They want to shrink the circle to twelve and then rank those twelve from greatest to least.

Jesus' warning—to fight the sin of causing a fellow believer to stumble—involves the most serious exposition of eternal judgment found anywhere in Mark. Don't cause a believer to stumble or you will face the fires of hell.

Metaphor and Reality

The word that Jesus uses for "hell" is the Greek word *Gehenna*. Gehenna was a valley to the southwest of Jerusalem. It was a place where the garbage and rubbish would be burned up. The fire kept burning and smoldering there continuously. In Jesus' day, that place had become a metaphor for the place where those who reject God and his rule will end up after death. There are several points that Jesus makes concerning the meaning of this metaphor.

First, the suffering of hell is *unending*. Two times in these verses Jesus adds a further description about the nature of hell.

- "... to go to hell, to the unquenchable fire" (**v 44**)

- "... where their worm does not die and the fire is not quenched" (**v 47-48**)

We can understand the phrase "unquenchable fire": it means a fire that does not go out—it just keeps going. But why does he talk about worms? The valley of Gehenna had piles of garbage that were burned, but there were also dead bodies—of those who did not have families to bury them. The worms are maggots that lived in these corpses. In the original garbage heap, when the bodies were consumed, the maggots died too. But the difference with hell is that even the maggots do not die—there is no final decomposition to the point of total elimination.

The fire never dies down, and what is in the fire never dies from the fire. The people in hell don't die out, and the fires of hell don't die down. It is the worst possible place—a horror movie that never stops.

Second, the suffering of hell is *incomparable* to any earthly torment. At the heart of these verses, there are repeated comparisons between something on the one hand and hell on the other hand. The first thing is always a terrible torment, yet each one is portrayed as far better than hell.

Jesus wants to show that the horrors of hell are worse than anything one could face on earth. That is because temporary torment is better than eternal torment. Being chained and thrown into the sea, where you are helpless to save yourself (**v 42**), is like something from a horror movie. You would just sink until you run out of air and cannot struggle any longer. Jesus says hell is worse than that.

He also uses the imagery of gruesome physical dismemberment: tearing out an eye, cutting off a hand, or cutting off a foot (**v 43-47**). He says that being physically maimed or disabled *and alive* is far better than having a whole body only to have it all burn in hell.

Third, the suffering of hell is *real*, not metaphorical. Because Jesus uses metaphorical language to describe hell, many people wonder if it is actually a real place with real suffering. But the fact that Jesus uses a metaphor does not mean that hell is imaginary and not literal. In fact, Jesus' metaphor about bodies burning on the garbage heap demonstrates that hell involves both the spiritual and the physical. Jesus is saying that the final punishment of hell will include our bodies. Elsewhere he says, "Do not fear those who kill the body but cannot kill the soul. Rather fear him who can destroy both soul and body in hell" (Matthew 10:28). Clearly, for Jesus, hell was a real, physical place.

Yet Jesus does use metaphor to describe hell. A few moments' reflection will show that the imagery of the unquenchable fire is metaphorical. First, the other dominant metaphor for hell is being cast into "outer darkness" (Matthew 8:12). How could hell be a place of "outer darkness" if it were aflame all the time forever? Second, since souls are in hell right now, without bodies, how could the fire be literal, physical fire?

When we say that the unquenchable fire is a metaphor, we are not watering down the horrors of hell in any way. Metaphors are used when other words fail to capture the full weight of something—when the reality is so full that one or two ways of talking about it are not enough. Multiple images are needed. Saying that Scripture uses metaphors for hell does not compromise the reality of hell at all. The metaphors for hell declare that the reality is fuller and worse than one can put into plain words.

Take the metaphor of outer darkness. What does that symbolism communicate about hell? It is a vivid way to talk about losing the presence of God—and a direct contrast to the Bible's description of heaven, which does not need the sun because God himself is the sun (Revelation 21:23).

> The worst thing that could happen to us is to be kept away from God.

The worst thing that could happen to us is to be kept away from God. Humanity was created to walk with God—which speaks of his immediate, direct presence. The Bible affirms that his nearness is our good. God's presence is where all goodness, life, joy, and love come from. The sinful path of rebellion against God took us away from what ultimately gives us life.

The metaphors of fire and outer darkness both point to a total destruction which stems from being separated from God. In hell, a person does not cease to exist but is sustained in a state of being ruined—cut off from what gives us life and light and goodness and joy. This is a far greater suffering than any literal fire or darkness we could imagine.

Salted with Fire

The word "For" (Mark **9:49**) provides the logical link between **verses 42-48** and **verses 49-50**. It raises a question: how does the fire of **verse 49** relate to the fire of **verses 42-48**? The key to the logic is found in the meaning of the phrase "salted with fire" (**v 49**). Some scholars think that being "salted with fire" means Jesus will purify ("salt") his disciples through persecution ("fire"). This reading is possible, but the theme of persecution has to be borrowed from the next chapter (10:29-30, 38-39) and so it must be inserted into the context of **verse 49**. A more natural reading comes from the Old Testament sacrificial system. Offerings were not only burnt with fire but also seasoned and purified with salt (Exodus 30:35). Salt represented "the covenant with your God" (Leviticus 2:13)—the commitment that God had made to be faithful to his people, and the commitment the people had therefore made to live according to God's law. Nothing was to be offered without salt.

In the same way, the followers of Jesus are living burnt offerings purified with salt. The new-covenant community should be marked by the moral purity that comes from committing our lives to God. These living sacrifices have a distinctive flavor profile. Salty disciples resist the moral decay that characterizes this world. In the context of Mark 9, the saltiness or purity of believers will counteract the impurity of pride, which would sinfully exclude others instead of receiving and welcoming them.

Verse 50 helps reinforce this reading. What difference does the saltiness of disciples make? The good salt of purity that characterizes disciples should make them "at peace with one another" (**v 50**). Someone who has not been "salted with fire" is not offering his or her life to God and is not acting in a morally pure way. He or she will cause others to stumble as part of their prideful exclusion of others.

You might wonder how salt can "lose its saltiness." Strictly speaking, sodium chloride is a stable compound, which cannot lose its quality. But the "salt" used in Palestine, which was derived either from deposits around the Dead Sea or from salt pans in which water was evaporated, was not pure sodium chloride. The salt could leach out, leaving other minerals like gypsum. "Salt" in Jesus' day really could lose its saltiness (R.T. France, *The Gospel of Mark*, p 384-385). And if salt stops being salty, no one is going to season the seasoning. They will simply throw it out. Disciples who are not salty are not disciples.

So how does the fire of **verse 49** relate to the fire of **verses 42-48**? Those who have not been "salted with fire" (**v 49**) are impure and thus are in danger of the unquenchable fire (**v 42-48**). There is a holiness or saltiness without which no one will see the Lord (Hebrews 12:14).

Prideful tribalism is a serious sin because it may cause someone to stumble. Is it a serious enough sin to warrant damnation and hellfire? Yes—because only followers of Jesus enter into eternal life and escape eternal damnation. Jesus' point is that prideful tribalism is proof that you are not really a disciple: not really a believer at all.

I remember a haunting story from seminary about a missionary who ended up living a life of sexual immorality on the field. The church led him through the process of **church discipline**, but he steadfastly refused to repent. When I asked some of the pastors at the church about it, they said that as they looked back over his seminary days, they remembered that he had always been quick to argue with others and turn things into doctrinal debates. He had an impulse to debate and divide. Sadly, it seemed as if he had never been a real follower of Jesus. He had made peace with the sin of pride, and he had kept going in that direction.

Let us heed the words of Jesus carefully. A prideful heart, always ready to prove others wrong, could very well be an unconverted heart. We must fight the root of pride, and its flowering blossoms of divisive tribalism, and uproot it from our hearts daily.

We also must not lose the terrors of hell or we will lose the glory of the gospel. People tone down the wrath of God because they want to save the idea of the love of God, but they actually destroy both because they miss the gospel. The wrath of God is an essential dark backdrop against which we can see the bright, shining beams of the love of God in the gospel of Christ.

Have you ever eaten an insanely hot habanero pepper? My friends once dared me to do it—seeds and all. My mouth felt like a forest fire. They told me that milk was even better than water at extinguishing the burning. I don't think I have ever wanted a glass of milk more in my entire life. I don't think I ever loved milk so much as in that moment after drinking it. The gospel is a little like that milk: it is when we appreciate the heat of God's anger against sin that we fully feel the gratitude we should feel for his love in sending Jesus.

Questions for reflection

1. How can you take seriously the dangers of a proud, divisive spirit that excludes other believers?

2. Why is it important to be able to address objections to the existence of hell?

3. How does this passage change or challenge your perception of hell?

9. THE UPSIDE-DOWN KINGDOM

Mark **10:1** lets us know that Jesus is now in a different setting and a different teaching situation. He has now left Galilee and traveled south to Judea—the region around Jerusalem.

Mark puts together a pair of "blindness" stories in **verses 2-16**. He demonstrates that the Pharisees are totally blind (**v 2-12**), but the disciples are still partially blind (**v 13-16**).

Is It Lawful?

The Pharisees come and ask a question in order to test and trap Jesus. "Is it lawful for a man to divorce his wife?" (**v 2**) There is a hidden landmine behind this question: a heated debate within Jewish culture about how to interpret a phrase in Deuteronomy 24:1 on divorce.

> "When a man takes a wife and marries her, if then she finds no favor in his eyes because he has found some indecency in her, and he writes her a certificate of divorce and puts it in her hand and sends her out of his house…"

The rabbis of Jesus' day were debating what qualified as "indecency." One way to translate the Hebrew is "the nakedness of a thing." One school of thought, led by Rabbi Shammai, took that literally. They restricted the meaning of indecency to physical nakedness—that is, the husband discovers that his wife is committing adultery. Another school of thought, led by Rabbi Hillel, said that the "indecency" could be anything—even something as minimal as burning the husband's toast. Anything could be a reason for divorce.

Which side will Jesus choose? Either way, the Pharisees think they have him. He has to alienate one side or the other. But let's watch what Jesus does to avoid the trap.

They asked what was lawful, and so Jesus takes them back to the actual law (not the rabbis). What does Moses say (Mark **10:3**)? They answer correctly: "Moses allowed a man to write a certificate of divorce and to send her away" (**v 4**).

They seem to think that they have said enough. Case closed. Moses permitted it. He gave an official series of steps to take: (1) write a certificate of divorce, and (2) send her away.

But the problem with the Pharisees (as usual) is that they are staring at the law and seeing the external issue without stopping to consider the underlying heart issues. Jesus turns the tables on them. "Because of your hardness of heart he wrote you this commandment" (**v 5**). Jesus is saying, *The problem here is you. You are trying to test me, but you fail to see that the law judges your hearts.* The law had to make legal allowance for the people's sinful heart issues. In a perfect world, divorce would not happen, but God gave this commandment because he knew it would.

Now Jesus does something masterful. He shows them that their question is out of order. They should not center the debate around two rabbis. In fact, even looking at Deuteronomy is not going far enough. If they want to know God's heart and his intent for marriage, they need to go all the way back to the beginning in Genesis. *Do not look merely at what Moses allowed; go to what God designed* (**v 6-9**).

Divorce will never be understood unless you start by understanding marriage as something God made. He made humanity male and female. He designed marriage with the blessing of intimacy. The man leaves his family and makes a new one. Husband and wife are no longer two but one flesh. God did this. If God joined them, then man should not separate them.

Inside the house, the disciples—unlike the Pharisees—take the posture of genuine learners (**v 10**). So now Jesus answers in a more straightforward way.

> "Whoever divorces his wife and marries another commits adultery against her, and if she divorces her husband and marries another, she commits adultery." (**v 11–12**)

This is how seriously Jesus takes wrongful divorce and remarriage. He calls it adultery. Jesus presents divorce and remarriage here as an act of rebellion against God. It is the act of undoing a union that God made and then making a different union that God did not make. That is the main point: don't tear apart what God has joined, and don't join together what God has kept separate.

A "no-fault" divorce culture is at odds with the biblical view of marriage. Many biblical scholars do see two legitimate reasons for divorce and remarriage in the Bible (see Matthew 19:9; 1 Corinthians 7:15). We should emphasize those two exceptions, but we should not open the floodgates to divorce for any and every reason. Do not believe the lie that you will be happier by defying God's commands and going your own way. A life that directly challenges God's sovereign and loving design is the path of folly, not wisdom.

Love and Correction

As a professor, I once told my students that a particular question was going to be on the test. I gave them the question in advance and told them how I wanted it to be answered. I was shocked when a few of the students still got it wrong.

I am even more shocked by this next scene, where the disciples once again rebuke those bringing children to Jesus (Mark **10:13**). I am not sure how Jesus could have prepared the disciples better. He put a child in their midst back in 9:36-37. He not only gave them a hint—he gave them the test question and the answer. But the disciples fail the test.

Jesus is "indignant" (**10:14**). This is an overflow of love. When you love something and you find it attacked, righteous anger should flare up to protect it. Jesus clearly loves the disciples. He never says, *That's it. I can't take it anymore. I am done with you.* But he also loves the children. There is no way that he would wish to be denied the opportunity to take them in his arms and bless them (**v 16**).

This text should purify our picture of Jesus. Is your view of Jesus big enough to include him being indignant with you? Jesus does not say, *Oh, that's ok. Don't worry about it—no big deal.* He can be offended by you, and he can offend you. Conversely, perhaps you imagine Jesus as stern—so serious that he is unapproachable. But the truth is that he is not hesitant or reticent to receive us.

Jesus loves the children by receiving them, and he loves the disciples by correcting them: "Let the children come to me; do not hinder them, for to such belongs the kingdom of God" (**v 14-15**). This is remarkably similar to his response to the man who was casting out demons in his name. There he said, "Do not stop him" (9:39). Here he says, "Do not hinder them" (**10:14**).

We would misuse this text if we made it merely about physical children. This story is about who can enter the kingdom of God (**v 15**). The word "such" is the main clue (**v 14**). Not everyone can enter the kingdom. Indeed, the kingdom belongs to a certain kind of person. Only those who receive the kingdom like a child can enter it.

The Rich Young Man

The concept of entering the kingdom of God continues in the next story (**v 17-22**). A rich young man brings a question to Jesus: "Good Teacher, what must I do to inherit eternal life?" (**v 17**)

The disciples have been told to receive the kingdom like a little child. But the rich young man is the polar opposite of childlike. He has "great possessions" (**v 22**), and he seems to believe that his obedience is great (**v 20**). Even his question seems to focus attention on eternal life as something to "do" (**v 17**) rather than something to receive (**v 15**).

Jesus asks a counter question: "Why do you call me good? No one is good except God alone" (**v 18**). This is puzzling at first glance; it's not an answer to the man's question. What is Jesus doing?

The clue is that this whole section is about spiritual blindness. Mark highlights the blindness of the Pharisees (**v 1-9**), the disciples (**v 13-16**), the rich young man (**v 17-22**), and the disciples (**v 23-28**). Jesus' words in verse 18 are like an eye chart to test what the young man sees. Jesus doesn't say, *Don't call me good—only God is good.* He says, "Why do you call me good? No one is good except God alone" (**v 18**). Jesus is trying to help the young man to see that calling him "good" would be like calling him God. He is showing him that he is blind to what true goodness is.

> God's commands are not a ladder but a mirror.

This eye exam continues as Jesus gives the young man a snapshot of the good he would have to do in order to inherit eternal life (**v 19**). The young man replies that he has done all these things from his youth (**v 20**). He seems to assume that he himself is good. The problem with the young man's thinking is that the commandments are not a ladder we use to climb up to God by our obedience. They actually function as a mirror to show us that there is no one good except God alone.

Jesus pokes more holes in the young man's idea of goodness and self-righteousness when he adds a commandment not originally found in the Ten Commandments:

"Do not murder, Do not commit adultery, Do not steal, Do not bear false witness, *Do not defraud,* Honor your father and mother." (**v 19,** my emphasis)

This addition seems to call into question how this man became rich. Could it be that his wealth came from defrauding the poor?

Now Jesus issues a command to the young man to sell all that he has, give to the poor, follow Jesus, and gain true riches in heaven (**v 21**). This command reflects the wisdom of another world. The way to become truly rich is to give riches away. These words will help expose the young man's blindness. He has claimed that he has kept all the commandments, and so Jesus effectively says, *Ok, let's start with the first commandment: "You shall have no other gods before me."* What if the young man's money was all gone, and everything that comes with it—respect, admiration, mansions, servants, freedom to do whatever he wants? Will he give it up to follow Jesus? Or has money become his god?

Mark makes Jesus' motive here explicit. Jesus looks intently at the young man and loves him (**v 21**). The piercing words come from a loving heart. It was loving for Jesus to expose the blindness of the disciples, and it is loving to expose this young man's blindness.

Two vivid words capture the young man's response: "disheartened" and "sorrowful" (**v 22**). The first word only occurs once elsewhere, in Matthew 16:3, translated a different way: "It will be stormy today, for the sky is red and *threatening*" (my emphasis). What Jesus said did not merely sound disheartening, but alarming and threatening. It was alarming to think about life without money.

The second word also describes an intense emotional response. The same term is used in Mark 14:19, when Jesus tells the disciples that one of them will betray him. They are devastated and are grieved to the heart. Another use of this term is illuminating. Matthew 26:37 says that Jesus was "grieved" or "troubled" in the Garden of Gethsemane. But what grieved Jesus was not merely the physical suffering but the emotional anguish at the thought of separation from God. The rich young man has a similar experience here. He has to contemplate what it would be like to be separated from what he loves more than anything: his great possessions (Mark **10:22**).

This is the response of someone trapped in the snare of idolatry. He can't let go of his money. The alarm goes off in his heart, and he cannot let go of what he loves most. His possessions have taken possession of his heart.

What a contrast is found here between the little children and the rich young ruler. The children possess nothing but receive Jesus' blessing—the kingdom of God belongs to them. The rich young ruler seems to possess everything (both financial attainment and moral accomplishment), yet he walks away from the kingdom.

Questions for reflection

1. How does Jesus' view of marriage challenge your view of marriage—and your pursuit of it or your attitude and behavior within it?

2. How do the verses in this section correct or challenge your view of Jesus?

3. What is the most tempting aspect of money for you? Success? Status? Security? How does this passage help you gain a better view of money?

PART TWO

The Blindness of the Disciples

The rich young ruler walked away from eternal life because he was self-sufficient like an adult and not dependent like a child. This story raises an alarming question: how can an adult stop being an adult and become like a child? Answer: it is a miracle, and only God can do it. Jesus brings this lesson to the disciples in this opportune moment.

The disciples are amazed by the idea that the wealthy will have a difficult time entering the kingdom (**10:23-24**). They evidently held to the common belief of their time that wealth was a sign of God's blessing or favor. In other words, if anyone was in the kingdom, it would be the wealthy. Jesus is turning that assumption on its head.

Then he raises the stakes. It is not just difficult for the wealthy to enter the kingdom but impossible (**v 24-27**).

It is easier for a camel to go through the eye of a needle than for a rich person to enter the kingdom of God (**v 25**). You may have heard the idea that there was a gate somewhere called the "eye of the needle" that camels entered through. But such a gate doesn't exist, and that interpretation totally misses Jesus' point. We sometimes talk about how hard it is to put a square peg through a round hole. It is hard because they are different shapes, even though the size may be similar. That is nothing compared to a situation in which both size and shape are radically different: putting a huge camel through a hole meant for a thin thread.

And Jesus says getting a camel through the eye of the needle is actually easier than a rich man entering the kingdom. The disciples are now exceedingly astonished (**v 26**), and they should be. They understand exactly what Jesus is saying, and they ask the right question: "Then who can be saved?" No one can be saved in human terms by human effort. It is impossible.

This text demolishes the idea often called "decisional regeneration." This idea says that someone can just *decide* to go from being adult-like to childlike—in other words, can decide to be saved. But it isn't true. The rich young man could not make himself a dependent child. Nothing he could do could fit him through the entrance to the kingdom. He was wrong to think that his moral attainments would be enough.

Jesus is saying that salvation is the work of God and must be the work of God, not the work of man. "With man it is impossible, but not with God" (**v 27**). If it was the work of man or the decision of man, no one would be saved. It is a miracle. Miracles are no problem for God! He made the world out of nothing, and he needs to do a similar miracle again; no human will ever become like a little child without a new birth.

The rich man is totally blind, but the disciples now display once again that they are partially blind. Peter says, "See, we have left everything and followed you" (**v 28**). It is true that they have not made the mistake of the rich man. They have left everything to follow Jesus. But that does not mean they have figured out discipleship. They still have a glaring error in their understanding.

Peter puts himself and the disciples forward and says, "See" (**v 28**). In effect, he says, *Look at us! We are different than that young man who walked away from the kingdom. You asked him to give it all away to follow you, and he couldn't. But we could. We did. We have left everything and followed you.* This is the language of sacrifice and self-denial. The emphasis is set upon how much they have given up. I am sure that Peter thought that Jesus would commend them for this.

But Jesus' answer in **verses 29-31** does not sound like a commendation at all. This is no verbal pat on the back. It is a verbal kick in the pants. *Get off your self-exalting kick, Peter. You sound like you made a huge sacrifice to follow me! Do you think following me is about what you have left behind—what you have lost?* Yes, it is technically true that they have left things: house, brothers, sisters, mother, father, children, lands (**v 29**). But they are not suffering from a deficit. This is not loss but gain—a hundredfold gain (**v 30**). And not just someday in heaven but today in Christian community. "Now in this time," they will gain houses, brothers, sisters, mothers, children, lands (**v 30**). They have a new family now.

Jesus is talking about a two-part miracle. The first part is the miracle of the new birth, which leads to the second part, the miracle of a new family. People who are new creations in Christ form a new community in Christ. I have lived away from my immediate family for many years now, and I have seen people in the wider family of God become like fathers, mothers, brothers, sisters, and children. It took a long time for me to understand these verses, but now I see that they are true.

The disciples seem to be oblivious to the pre-eminent point of discipleship: Jesus is worth it. They have had to leave things behind, but they should do so gladly "for my sake and for the gospel" (**v 29**)— because it is gain to have Christ and his kingdom.

I grew up believing that Christianity was a religion of rules. God seemed like a cosmic kill-joy: *Don't do this; don't do that.* I heard the call of Christianity as the need for bad people to become good through self-denial.

> The gospel is good news, not good advice.

But conversion to Christ changed everything. The gospel is not about bad people becoming good but dead people becoming alive. The gospel is good news, not good advice. We do not boast in what we do or what we give up, but in what we gain through what Christ has done for us. When Jesus asks you to deny yourself something, it is always to get something better, longer lasting, and more satisfying. We put to death things that would kill our joy because they lead us away from Christ as our chief joy.

Jesus' words to the disciples are like smelling salts, which used to be used to revive patients who had fainted. He teaches about the danger of money in a way that makes you feel you should wear a hazmat suit when dealing with it.

The problem with money is really the heart. We do what we do because we want what we want because we love what we love. We have a hard time believing that the way to become truly rich is to give away our riches. We love money because we love the security it gives. We believe that we are vulnerable without it. We can't give it away because it is a god. The only way we can give it away is if Christ so captures the heart that money ceases to be a god and goes back to being just money.

But Jesus can set us free from the love of money. The Son of God had riches and wealth and status like no one has ever dreamed of having. But he gave it all away. "Though he was rich, yet for your sake he became poor, so that you by his poverty might become rich" (2 Corinthians 8:9). All of this eternal, ultimate wealth he gave to spiritual beggars who had nothing to commend them to God. The gospel gives better security than money can give because it gives us our almighty Father.

The Third Passion Prediction

Jesus has been leading the disciples on this journey to Jerusalem for three chapters of Mark's Gospel now. Peter confessed that Jesus is the Messiah up in the northern part of Israel in Caesarea Philippi. From that point on, Jesus has stated twice that this journey will end in Jerusalem, and has taught them in no uncertain terms what awaits him there: suffering and death (Mark 8:31; 9:31). Yet he is the one setting the pace and leading the way (**10:32**).

The disciples are amazed and afraid. They cannot fathom why Jesus is so driven to get to Jerusalem. They do not yet understand his mission. Jesus' next piece of teaching will clear up the confusion.

He now predicts his death and resurrection for the third time (**v 33-34**). This third prediction is the most detailed. He begins once again with the title "Son of Man" from Daniel 7:13. He says that both Jews and Gentiles will reject him. First the Jewish leaders will put him on trial and condemn him to death. Then they will deliver

Jesus to the Gentiles to carry out the verdict. The Gentiles will mock him, spit on him, flog him, and kill him (Mark **10:34**).

These details do not just point forward to Mark 15; they also point back to Isaiah 50 and 53, the songs of the suffering servant. Jesus says his back will be flogged or scourged and he will be spit upon. This is the picture of Isaiah 50:5-6:

"The Lord GOD has opened my ear,
    and I was not rebellious;
    I turned not backward.
I gave my back to those who strike,
    and my cheeks to those who pull out the beard;
I hid not my face
    from disgrace and spitting."

Isaiah 50:5-6 will be fulfilled in Mark 15, but Isaiah 50:7-8 is being fulfilled in Mark **10:32**.

"But the Lord GOD helps me;
    therefore I have not been disgraced;
therefore I have set my face like a flint,
    and I know that I shall not be put to shame.
    He who vindicates me is near."

Now we learn why Jesus was leading the way and why the disciples were amazed and afraid. Jesus had set his face like flint to go to Jerusalem. He had purpose in every step because the plan of the Father was the mission of the Son. And he went into it all knowing how it would end. "After three days he will rise" (**v 34**). Jesus would rise from the grave and, by doing so, bring many sons and daughters to glory. He would not fail. He would fulfill the Father's plan.

The disciples could not see that Daniel's son of man is also Isaiah's suffering servant. Jesus brings them together. The "Daniel 7" kingdom will be established through the "Isaiah 53" death and resurrection.

Questions for reflection

1. How would you describe the difference between the kingdom of God and the kingdom of self? How does our attitude to money demonstrate our allegiance to one or the other?

2. How can you walk in the truth that being a disciple is all about what we gain in Christ as our greatest joy?

3. What things have you had to give up for Christ? What have you gained? How grateful are you for the gifts you have in him?

PART THREE

Mark **10:35-41** has an air of drama. The disciples are finally going to bring a question. "Teacher, we want you to do for us whatever we ask of you" (**v 35**). Jesus has been talking about his death and resurrection for three chapters. For three chapters the disciples have been blind to what he was saying. And for three chapters they have been afraid to ask him to help them see it.

But now, James and John finally work up the courage to ask Jesus a question. Could this be the moment when they ask for help with their unbelief?

No. When you read **verses 36-41**, you want to put your head in your hands and sigh. They are not humbly asking to see—they are arrogantly asking to be seen. They just heard Jesus say that he was going to get mocked and spit upon and flogged and killed. But they don't seem to get it. They think he is a king who is about to conquer Jerusalem. They want positions of power for themselves in the new regime.

Jesus tells them that they don't know what they are asking. Do you feel the irony? Jesus is going to the cross. There will be someone on his right and someone on his left—but they will be crucified criminals.

So Jesus asks them if they are able to endure what he is about to suffer: to drink the cup he must drink, and to enter the waters of baptism (death) that he is about to wade into (**v 38**). They say yes (**v 39**). But they are saying yes to something they don't even understand. These disciples are a sad and tragic mix of ignorance and arrogance.

Jesus does not get angry. He simply tells them that they will taste and experience what is about to happen to him, but it is still more than they can comprehend. The Father is working out his plan, and the places next to Jesus are already prepared (**v 40**).

The disciples respond to this dysfunctional drama by adding more dysfunction to the mix. They are "indignant" at James and John (**v 41**).

This has to feel like **Groundhog Day** for Jesus. The whole scene is similar to the situation in 9:31-34. There, Jesus announced that he would die and rise, and the disciples didn't understand what he meant. Instead of asking about it, they argued about who would be the greatest. The only difference here is that now two of them have brought their desires out into the open. All the disciples want the same thing—power and influence—but only James and John have enough gumption to make the request.

How will Jesus respond? He gives this dysfunctional bunch some sorely needed counsel (**10:42-45**). This is an expansion of what Jesus has been saying to the disciples all along. Jesus in effect claims that they are blind because they are wearing the world's blinders.

Their whole argument about who will be the greatest is rife with worldly thinking. Worldly rulers have something in common: they are elevated above others. Rulers "lord it over" others—the great "exercise authority over" others (**v 42**). Their position is higher. That is how the disciples think: *how can I rise above all the rest and gain power and position over them?*

Jesus does not tell them, *Stop wanting to be great!* He does not rebuke the quest for greatness; he redefines the quest by redefining greatness. He teaches them about the upside-down kingdom once again. True greatness is

> Jesus does not rebuke the quest for greatness but redefines it.

not about how high you can climb as you step on and over as many people as possible. It is about how low you can go in serving as many people as possible.

The disciples do not see the greatness of servanthood because they cannot see the servant of Isaiah's prophecy right in front of them. Instead of looking at the world to see greatness, they should look at Jesus. "For even the Son of Man came not to be served but to serve, and to give his life as a ransom for many" (**v 45**).

The "Daniel 7" Son of Man is the Lord over all, but he did not come to lord it over all. He did not come to make servants but to be a servant. Most rulers get rich from the resources of those that they rule over. This King comes not to get but to give. He gives and gives until he has given all—his very life—as a ransom for many.

The word "ransom" in the culture of Jesus' day was a financial term. If you owed a debt, you could sell yourself into slavery and work to pay it off; or someone could pay a ransom to release you. Humans have a debt they cannot pay—the debt of sin—and when it comes due, there will literally be hell to pay. But Jesus took our place. He paid our debt. The highest person took the lowest place to serve, rescue, and ransom hell-bound humanity.

We serve because he first served us. In other words, this new way of life comes from a new-creation work. When Jesus speaks to the disciples about kingdom realities, he uses the present tense. The ESV translation makes this very hard to see: "But it shall not be so among you" (Mark **10:43**). The verb is actually in the present tense and should read, "But it is not so among you."

The contrast is not between what is and what will be. It is a contrast between the way things are in the world and the way things are in the kingdom. Jesus is speaking about who kingdom disciples *are*—who he enables them to be. "You are the light of the world" (Matthew 5:14). He doesn't say, *Be the light*. He says, "You *are* the light."

Without the coming of Christ, we are incapable of love in the purest sense because we all need love like we need air and water. We have an ulterior motive: we want to gain the love of others. The only person that could truly love, with no strings attached, is someone that does not have that need. God doesn't need us because God is a Trinity. He already enjoys within himself a relationship of perfect love between the Father, the Son, and the Holy Spirit. That is why the Bible says that God is love (1 John 4:8). **Redemption** came out of the overflow of that infinite, perfect love. This is how we know what love is: Jesus Christ laid down his life for us (1 John 3:16).

When our love needs are met in the gospel—when we become part of that loving relationship that the Trinity enjoys—we, too, can actually love. We love because he first loved us. We can give because we have received.

The Healing of a Blind Man

In the final section of Mark 10, Mark highlights a stark contrast with the disciples: Bartimaeus. This man is introduced to us as a "blind beggar" (Mark **10:46**). He is a disabled man and a dependent man. He can't make it on his own, and he knows it. He is childlike. He lives on the care of others. In fact, he has learned how to be strategic in his dependence. He wisely positions himself on the path where people will pass by.

But the blind man has eyes to see clearly who Jesus is: the Son of David (**v 47**).

The crowd does not encourage the blind man in his faith. They "rebuke" him (**v 48**). The rebuke does not come from a few but "many." Imagine sitting in the library talking and having everyone in the library come around you and with irritated scowls say, "SHHHH!" That gives you a small hint of how the crowds feel about Bartimaeus. They do not think he merits Jesus' attention. Jesus is a somebody, and Bartimaeus is a nobody. Bartimaeus should quit bothering him.

That is a common theme in Mark. The world values power and greatness that rules over others and commands respect and attention. But that is not the way the kingdom works, and it is not the way that the Savior responds.

Bartimaeus will not be silenced. "He cried out all the more" (**v 48**). Public shaming does not work on him because he is desperate. He cries out with a singular fervor because he has a single hope: *Only the Messiah can help me.* He does not come wondering if he is the greatest, like the disciples. He comes with empty hands as a beggar.

This cry for mercy stops Jesus dead in his tracks (**v 49**). This is the same thing that happened for the woman with the flow of blood. It seems that the cry for mercy is the sweetest sound to Jesus' ears.

Mark does not simply say that Bartimaeus "came to Jesus" (**v 50**). He emphasizes how he came. He sprang up with joy, and he threw off his cloak. The fact that Bartimaeus left his cloak is significant. He knew he would not need it anymore. He used his cloak to collect money, like a musician who lays out his guitar case for people to throw in their coins. By faith he now believes he is as good as healed, so he does not need it anymore. Mark is also showing us that Bartimaeus fits the pattern of a disciple. Disciples leave everything to follow Jesus. The rich man was not willing to leave his wealth, but Bartimaeus was happy to leave behind the little he had.

Jesus asks a question that stands out as perplexing. "What do you want me to do for you?" (**v 51**). Isn't the answer obvious? The reason Jesus asks this is that it is the same question he asked James and John (**v 36**). But the answers are totally different. The disciples asked to be seen (**v 37**), but Bartimaeus asks to see. This blind beggar is the one who answers rightly.

Jesus tells him that he can go because his faith has saved him (**v 52**). This is a common response after a healing, but Bartimaeus responds in a unique way. After being told to go his way, he does not go away but follows Jesus on the way. He has cast off his cloak, and now he refuses to leave Jesus. This is a picture of true discipleship. When your blindness is removed, then you can follow Jesus as a disciple—on the Calvary road to Jerusalem.

Bartimaeus models what true discipleship is in three ways. First, he sees Jesus rightly. Jesus is the Son of David, who can and will help. Second, he sees himself rightly. He is totally dependent and in need of help. Third, he responds rightly to Jesus. He leaves all that he has—his cloak—and joyfully follows Jesus on the way.

Mark highlights that Jesus is Isaiah's prophesied servant. He has come to open the eyes of the blind and lead them on the way. Isaiah 42 says the servant of the Lord will be compassionate and responsive to the weak. He will not break a bruised reed. He will not let a lightly burning wick go out (v 3). He will open the eyes of the blind (v 7). Isaiah 42:16 points even more clearly to the story of Bartimaeus:

"And I will lead the blind
   in a way that they do not know,
 in paths that they have not known
   I will guide them.
 I will turn the darkness before them into light,
   the rough places into level ground.
 These are the things I do,
   and I do not forsake them."

Without Christ, we are all blind. The Bible says that we are born spiritually blind to the gospel of the glory of Christ (2 Corinthians 4:4). You cannot make yourself see, but you can strategically sit on the path of grace, where you know Jesus will pass by in the preaching of the gospel. Then God enables us to see his glory in the face of Christ (2 Corinthians 4:6).

Without Christ, we are all spiritual beggars. We have empty hands. But Jesus does not come and give us some spare change; he gives us eternal life at the cost of his own life.

Mark demonstrates that awareness of weakness and crying out in dependence is a prerequisite for the display of divine strength. If you cry out to him for mercy, Jesus is the Savior who stops. Jesus had his own suffering and death in mind as he led the way to Jerusalem. If anyone ever had the right to be preoccupied, it was Jesus. But then he heard the cry for mercy. And he stopped (Mark **10:49**).

A cry for help is the sweetest sound to the Savior. He will stop. He will save. Do not let fear of what others in the crowd may think keep you away. Cry out all the more for mercy. See Jesus rightly, see yourself rightly, and respond rightly.

Questions for reflection

1. Think of some times when you cried out for mercy and Jesus stopped and showed up in mercy. What mercy do you need in your life right now? What is keeping you from crying out?

2. Why is Bartimaeus' response so significant in the Gospel of Mark?

3. What things from this chapter would you share with an unbelieving friend?

10. JESUS IN THE TEMPLE

The third section of the main body of Mark (11:1 – 15:9) narrates the last week of Jesus' earthly life. He and his disciples arrive in Jerusalem. The second half of this section will move to Jesus' suffering and death, but first Mark tells us about three trips to the temple (11:1 – 13:37). The theme here is Jesus' confrontation with the Jewish religious system.

Jesus has almost reached Jerusalem (**11:1**). He is going to enter into the temple. But the text will build to a quite unexpected surprise and shock. Mark starts the story by narrating the preparations for entry into Jerusalem.

Mark gives the reader the instructions of Jesus (**v 2-3**): the disciples are to go into the village and find a colt, which they must untie and bring to him. Jesus knows that there is a colt. He knows where it is, and he even knows its history: no one has ever sat on it. He also tells the disciples exactly what is going to happen and what to say when it happens. Sure enough, the next verses relate an exact fulfillment of Jesus' words (**v 4-6**).

Jesus knows about the colt and has authority to take it because he is the Lord. That is the ultimate answer: "The Lord has need of it" (**v 3**). He needs the colt because the Scripture needs to be fulfilled. The Messiah is to ride into Jerusalem on a colt (Zechariah 9:9). A king always had the right to commandeer a beast of burden in ancient times (James R. Edwards, *The Gospel of Mark*, p 336). An unbroken beast of burden such as this one was regarded as sacred (Numbers 19:2; Deuteronomy 21:3) and was therefore especially fitting.

Unsurprisingly, then, when Jesus enters Jerusalem, there is a royal reception. People throw their outer garments on the ground before him, along with branches from the fields (Mark **11:7-8**). This is a symbolic recognition of royalty (see 2 Kings 9:12-13).

The crowd also quotes from Psalm 118:25-26:

"Save us, we pray, O LORD!

O LORD, we pray, give us success!

Blessed is he who comes in the name of the LORD!

We bless you from the house of the LORD."

There are three notes of irony in Mark **11:9**. First, there is the meaning of the word, "Hosanna." It means "Oh, save us now!" Or, as Psalm 118:25 has it, "Save us, we pray, O LORD!"

The people were saying more than they knew.

The people were saying exactly the right thing, but they said more than they knew. They did not understand the salvation that the King was going to bring.

Second, one wonders if they really knew what they were saying when they exclaimed, "Blessed is he who comes in the name of the LORD." The phrase has some ambiguity in Psalm 118. It could be a reference to people who come to the temple to worship: "Blessed is the worshipper who comes in the Lord's name into the temple." But Jesus is coming in the name of the Lord in a far greater sense. We know from Mark **11:3** that he is the Lord; Yahweh has sent him.

Third, the quotation of this particular psalm is highly ironic, because it predicts not just the coming of the Lord but the rejection of the Lord. Jesus will later use Psalm 118:22-23 as an explanation for why he is rejected (Mark **12:10-11**).

The other phrase in the crowd's shouts is another clue that Jesus is royalty. "Blessed is the coming kingdom of our father David" (**11:10**). Now there can be no doubt about what the crowd is saying. This is the Messiah, the King in David's line, and he has come in the name of the Lord to re-establish the Lord's rule and reign, as God promised to David. The people are joining in that expectation and crying out for Jesus to save them.

But they misunderstand salvation. They believe that salvation means the Messiah will come and destroy the people oppressing them. They will be saved or liberated, and the oppressors will be destroyed. They expect Jesus to judge the nations and save them. They never would have expected that he would judge them and save the nations.

What is missing in this story is a repentant people who realize that the true problem is not the Romans but themselves. Each person in the crowd should cry out and say, *I need a Savior for my sins*. But they do not.

Jesus enters the temple in **verse 11**. Then he leaves again. Mark says, "And when he had looked around at everything, as it was already late, he went out to Bethany with the twelve."

Why is this first trip to the temple such an anti-climax? The next verses (**v 12-15**) hint at the reason.

The Fig-Tree Sandwich

Jesus came to the temple and looked around (**v 11**). The next verses also describe Jesus looking for something: figs. The following day, Jesus is hungry (**v 12**). But the fig tree he spots has only leaves and no fruit (**v 13**).

Then Jesus utters a curse: "May no one ever eat fruit from you again" (**v 14**).

This is not a case of childish anger. Jesus has not made a mistake. He knows it is not the season for figs. The point of this story is not that Jesus is looking for literal figs. He is acting out a parable based on Jeremiah 8:13. Jeremiah described the people as being like a fig tree with no figs; they had not grown or borne good fruit but had rejected what God gave them. They were therefore bound for judgment.

Soon Mark will tell us about the fulfillment of Jesus' curse: the fig tree withered away to its roots (Mark **11:20**). But first we read of Jesus' second trip to the temple. This is another sandwich structure.

The "bread" of the fig-tree story should make us read the story in the middle in a different way than we would if it were on its own. We often say that in this passage Jesus was cleansing the temple—driving out those who were misusing it and restoring it to the house of prayer that it should have been (**v 17**). But in the context of the fig tree, I would argue that Jesus was not cleansing or reforming the temple; he was cursing the temple and replacing it.

As Jesus enters the temple the second time, he drives out those who are selling and buying, and forbids people from carrying anything through the temple (**v 15-16**).

It is often said that Jesus was reforming exploitative business practices or eliminating **profane** activity in the sacred space of the temple. However, Jesus' motivation could not have been to attack unjust business practices, because he threw out not only the sellers (those who were profiting unjustly) but the buyers too (**v 15**).

In fact, this was not ordinary commercial activity at all—that would not have taken place in the temple. The "tables of the money-changers" (**v 15**) were set up to receive the annual half-shekel tax that was required of every Jewish male and that funded the daily sacrifices in the temple for the atonement of sin. The pigeons being sold were to be sacrifices to the Lord. This was not a mere reform of the temple but a rejection of the temple system. A Jewish scholar, Jacob Neusner, captures this:

> "Only someone who rejected the Torah's explicit teaching concerning the daily offering could have overturned the tables … Indeed, the money-changers' presence made possible the **cultic** participation of every Israelite, and it was not a blemish on the **cult** but its perfection."
>
> (quoted in David Garland, *The Gospel of Mark*, p 436)

David Garland makes the same point:

> "If money cannot be exchanged into the holy currency, then monetary support for the temple sacrifices and the priesthood must end. If sacrificial animals cannot be purchased, then

sacrifice must end. If no vessel can be carried through the temple, then all cultic activity must cease."

(*Zondervan Illustrated Bible Backgrounds Commentary*, p 271)

Jesus has not cleansed or restored the temple. He has caused all activity in the temple to cease.

In **verse 17** Jesus gives the reason for this. His condemnation consists of two Old Testament texts: Isaiah 56:7 and Jeremiah 7:11.

Isaiah 56 is one of the greatest texts in the Old Testament to demonstrate that God's plan of salvation includes the nations. It says that salvation will come to those typically thought to be excluded from God's people. **Eunuchs** were not allowed to enter the temple (Deuteronomy 23:1), but now they will be included (Isaiah 56:4-5). Foreigners, also previously separated from God's people, will even "minister to [God] … love the name of the LORD, and … be his servants" (v 6). This went against all the usual rules about the temple, to which access was strictly controlled. It sounds like Gentile foreigners would be able to be priests—which means they would be able to go even further into the temple than Jewish males!

When Jesus quotes this verse from Isaiah 56, he has all this in mind. One day the temple worship was going to change, and there would be "a house of prayer for all nations." With Jesus, that day has arrived.

Why does Jesus add that the temple has been made into a "den of robbers" (Jeremiah 7:11)? The people in Jeremiah's day were treating the temple like a safe den—a place to go to protect themselves from God's judgment after they had been wicked. They participated in the rituals of the temple, but they were not serious about pursuing God; they were serious about pursuing their sin. They were coming into the temple because they believed it would keep them safe and allow them to keep sinning. That is what Jeremiah meant in calling God's house a "den of robbers." Thieves would rob people in Jerusalem and then run to the caves of the mountains to hide. The Israelites were treating the temple like a cave to hide from getting caught. Jesus is saying that the people of his own day are doing this, too.

How do the people respond to this? Does repentance finally come? No. The chief priests and the scribes do not show any signs of repentance. They strengthen their resolve to kill Jesus (Mark **11:18**).

Jesus and his disciples leave the city again (**v 19**). Next day, Peter sees that the fig tree has withered to the roots (**v 20-21**). He remembers Jesus' words in **verse 14** and realizes that Jesus' curse has been effective.

Real Prayer

Jesus uses this opportune moment to unpack the nature of prayer. He is essentially asking the disciples why they are surprised to see this answer to his words. Don't they understand prayer and the power of God?

Jesus teaches the disciples what true prayer is. Real prayer comes from a heart full of faith (**v 22-24**) and forgiveness (**v 25**).

"Whoever says to this mountain, 'Be taken up and thrown into
the sea', and does not doubt in his heart, but believes that
what he says will come to pass, it will be done for him." (**v 23**)

It is important to note that Jesus does not say, *Whoever says to* a *mountain.* He says, "*this* mountain" (**v 23,** my emphasis). He is talking about the Temple Mount. He is standing on the Mount of Olives, and he can see the Temple Mount and the Dead Sea. He is talking about destroying the temple.

The imagery is intensified if we get the wider context of Mark in view. Where have we seen something cast into the sea before in Mark? Pigs possessed by a legion of demons ran into the sea and drowned (5:13); and anyone who causes a little one to stumble would be better thrown into the sea with a millstone hung around his neck (9:42). The mountain of **Zion** has become unclean like pigs and causes the nations to stumble. Jesus will cause it to be cast into the sea.

Jesus teaches on prayer here because the temple is to be a house of prayer. If it is replaced, then where can prayer happen? What happens to prayer when the house of prayer is gone? Some people thought that the temple made your prayers more effective. Later rabbis even said that "from the day on which the Temple was destroyed, the gates of prayer have closed … a wall of iron divides between Israel and their Father in heaven" (quoted in David Garland, *The Gospel of Mark*, p 442).

It is vital to see that one can have a relationship with God without the formalism and external ritual of the temple. Jesus is doing the same thing that he did in Mark 7. The Pharisees emphasized external cleansing (the ritual of washing hands and objects used in eating and drinking). Jesus taught that nothing from the outside makes one un-clean, but what comes from the inside: from the heart. Jesus says the same thing about prayer. Prayer is not a matter of external ritual or **liturgy** or location. Prayer must come from a heart full of faith. One must say (**11:23**) or ask (**v 24**) with faith (that is, with belief and no doubt in the heart).

Real prayer comes not only from a heart full of faith but also one full of forgiveness (**v 25**). Forgiveness is not easy. C.S. Lewis said, "Everyone thinks forgiveness is a lovely idea until he has something to forgive" (*Mere Christianity*, p 110). It is not easy, but failing to for-give reveals a tragic double standard in us. When others fail us, we tend to put the spotlight on their evil actions. When we fail others, we tend to put the spotlight on our good intentions.

But there is a grave warning here for those who will not forgive. If you are praying and find that you have something against someone and you don't forgive them, then your Father in heaven will not forgive your trespasses (**v 25**).

Jesus takes forgiveness so seriously because God's forgiveness of us and our forgiveness of others are inseparably linked. If we will not for-give, it calls into question whether or not we really believe the gospel.

Jesus told a parable in Matthew's Gospel warning about the danger of not forgiving (Matthew 18:21-35). A king forgave his servant a debt of 10,000 talents (v 24)—an unthinkable amount of money. The servant then went and "found" his fellow servant and choked him for far less. The king responded by throwing the unforgiving servant into prison until he could pay off his debt (v 34). This is a picture of eternal judgment: such a debt could never be repaid. Jesus said that that is what will happen to anyone who does not forgive from the heart (v 35).

In other words, an unforgiving heart is proof that the gospel has not changed the heart. Someone is in spiritual danger if they lose sight of the cross. Unforgiveness happens when someone else's sin becomes bigger than the cross. The debt others owe us seems bigger than the debt we owed God.

Questions for reflection

1. The people of Jesus' day were participating in the temple not to pursue God but to hide from judgment and excuse their sinful behavior. How can those who claim to be Christians do something similar with the blood of Jesus?

2. How might people today rely on rituals or other external things in their relationship with God? How can we make sure that prayer in particular is an act of devotion, not just a discipline to master?

3. What is the relationship between prayer, faith, and a forgiving heart?

PART TWO

Rival Authorities

Mark **11:27** introduces Jesus' third trip to the temple, where he will now be until the end of chapter 12. First, the religious leaders bring Jesus a question (**11:27-28**). Jesus asks them a question in response (**v 29-30**). They refuse to answer his question (**v 31-33**), and so he refuses to answer their question (**v 33**).

The Sanhedrin (or Jewish ruling council) comprised 71 members in three groups: the chief priests, the scribes, and the elders. Members of all these groups were present for this confrontation (**v 27**). The first group, the chief priests, were former high priests and priests with permanent duties in the temple. The second group, the teachers of the law, were the trained legal experts of the day. The third group, the elders, were typically **lay people** who came from the wealthy aristocratic class.

This is not an honest inquiry. The previous scene in the temple ended with Mark noting that these rulers are seeking a way to destroy Jesus (**v 18**). They have been plotting murder since Mark 3:6. But they have to bring him down before they can safely move to destroy him.

They choose a topic on which to tackle him: authority. This always seems to be the issue with the religious authorities. Who has authorized Jesus to do "these things" (a reference to his recent actions in the temple)? They think they themselves have heaven's authorization, and they have not authorized Jesus to do what he is doing. So who has?

This is a trap—a thinly veiled accusation. What is Jesus supposed to say? *By my own authority*? They will jump all over that. Will he say that God himself sent him—something that in their eyes is blasphemy? They are looking for him to say something that will get him in trouble.

Jesus asks a counter-question. He first promises, "Answer me, and I will tell you by what authority I do these things" (**11:29**). The note of authority stands out sharply. He is subtly reminding them of who is really on trial. Jesus is testing them.

They clearly rejected John the Baptist's authority, and so Jesus quizzes them about him. Did John's baptism come from heaven (that is, was he sent by God) or from man (that is, did he invent the idea himself) (**v 30**)?

John's baptism is significant here for two reasons. First, John baptized Jesus—and it was at that baptism that God the Father declared that Jesus is the Son (1:9-11). So this is a reminder to the reader of where Jesus gets his authority from. Second, John was sent from heaven with a baptism of repentance for the forgiveness of sins. It did not involve the temple or the sacrifices. It was free. The only requirement was a repentant heart (David Garland, *The Gospel of Mark*, p 443). By mentioning John, Jesus is once again challenging the Jewish religious system.

The Jewish leaders find themselves on the horns of a dilemma (**11:31-32**). If they say, "From heaven," Jesus is going to say, "Why then did you not believe him?" But if they say, "From man," then they will be expressing an unpopular opinion, which they do not want to do because they fear the people. So they say, "We do not know" (**v 33**).

In so doing, they simply prove that they are not interested in the truth. Their hypocrisy is exposed. Mark highlights the fact that fear of the people is a chief motivating factor for them (**v 32**). The previous story highlighted the same thing (**v 18**), and the next story will do the same (**12:12**).

> They want to save face, not their souls.

Therefore, Jesus refuses to answer their question—not because he does not know the answer but because he knows their hearts. Jesus already knows the duplicity and hypocrisy of these religious leaders. They cannot trap him, but he traps them and exposes them.

This story makes an even greater point. The religious leaders were asked about authority from heaven or from men, but in the end what they really fear is man, not heaven. All they seem to care about is saving face; they do not see the need to save their souls.

Their answer also tells more truth than they realize. The story reveals that they really don't know how to distinguish between what comes from God and what comes from man.

A Final Parable

As a further challenge to the religious leaders, Jesus now tells his final parable in Mark: the story of the tenants of a vineyard (**12:1-12**).

This is an old, old story drawn from Isaiah 5, where the vineyard represents God's people. The Isaiah text emphasizes how well God cared for his vineyard—yet there is a note of surprise in how bad the grapes are in spite of how good God's care was. Isaiah's point is that Israel cannot say to God, *It is your fault that we ended up this way, because you neglected us.* They have to say, *It is our fault that we ended up this way, because we rejected you.*

Jesus' parable is even more suspenseful and shocking. The Isaiah story emphasizes the constant care of God and the surprise of how bad the grapes are. The twist in this story is how bad the tenants are—not the vineyard itself but the people who care for the vineyard. Isaiah's story was a condemnation of the people as a whole, but Jesus' version is an attack on the religious leaders.

The parable lays out a pattern of interaction between the owner of the vineyard and the tenants. It is a pattern of patience. The owner sends servants to collect the fruit, but they are mistreated or even killed (Mark **12:2-5**). The reference to fruit is almost certainly the fruit of repentance that God sent his servants (the prophets) to collect.

The owner keeps sending servants, but the result remains the same. Then **verse 6** features the climax. He has no one greater to send than his beloved son. Will he send his son to such murderers? The surprising answer is yes. The pattern of patience extends even to the sending of his son.

Surely they will respect my son, says the owner (**v 6**). Remember that this story is effectively the answer to the religious leaders' earlier question: "Who gave you this authority?" (**11:28**). The tenants should respect the authority of the owner's son. The religious leaders should respect the authority of God's Son.

The fact that the tenants so brazenly dishonor the son shows how bad they (and the religious leaders) really are. Their dishonor of the son goes beyond what could have been expected. The lack of honor is seen in the fact that they not only murder him but also refuse to bury him—an act of outright scorn and dishonor. The point of the story is not that the father is naïve to expect that they would honor the son. The point is that the tenants are even more exceedingly wicked than anyone would expect.

The tenants are calculated in their wickedness. They want more than murder. They see an opportunity to steal the inheritance by killing the heir (**12:7**). This logic involves a calculated risk. Killing the son will not give them control of the vineyard. The owner is still alive and now they will now have to reckon with his response. Perhaps they have begun to confuse patience with weakness. They must regard the owner as an absentee who is soft and powerless to do anything about their rebellion.

But this calculated wickedness turns out to be a serious miscalculation. The owner is more powerful than they expect. He will act decisively and destroy completely (**v 9**).

But the owner is also merciful in that he gives the vineyard to others. This unexpected gift to "others" is a reference to the nations—non-Jews. Jesus has already judged the leaders of the temple for turning it into a den of robbers, instead of ensuring it is a house of prayer for all the nations (**11:17**). Now he is saying that God will replace the temple system and bring foreigners to become part of his people—even to lead his people. The vineyard will belong to the nations after the owner brings judgment on the original tenants.

Jesus' parable raises a question. Did God expect that the religious leaders would honor his Son? Is he sitting in heaven with a stunned look on his face because things are going worse than he expected? In **12:10-11** Jesus shows that this very process of rejection and **vindication** is what God had planned all along, by quoting from Psalm 118:22-23:

"The stone that the builders rejected
  has become the cornerstone.
 This is the LORD's doing;
  it is marvelous in our eyes."

Psalm 118 is a celebration of going up to Jerusalem to participate in worship in the temple. One of the glories of the temple was the story of the temple architecture. There was a stone that would not fit any part of the building. It was rejected. But in the end, that stone fit perfectly as the cornerstone: the stone that stands at the summit of a corner and holds the whole structure together (see N.T. Wright, *Mark for Everyone*, p 160).

In its original context Psalm 118 focuses on the enemies of Israel's anointed king. By rejecting him, they were sealing their own fate, because the king was the stone by which God would execute his plan to judge the world. Jesus applies this psalm in a stunning way. The builders who reject the anointed king are not foreigners but the religious leaders of Israel. They believe they are building God's building, but they have rejected the cornerstone of the whole building. They are acting like the pagan rulers, not the people of God.

Jesus' parable stressed the rejection and dishonor of the son. Now this prophecy shows that God planned that the rejection of the Son would be reversed and would result in vindication. In the prophecy, the builders are the religious leaders, and the stone that they reject is the Son. After being rejected and discarded, he will become the cornerstone. This will lead to a new temple, composed of spiritual stones, with Christ Jesus as the chief cornerstone—as Peter would later explain in his first letter to Gentile Christians:

"As you come to him, a living stone rejected by men but in
 the sight of God chosen and precious, you yourselves like

living stones are being built up as a spiritual house, to be a holy priesthood, to offer spiritual sacrifices acceptable to God through Jesus Christ." (1 Peter 2:4-5)

The structure of this section in Mark reinforces these points. Jesus comes to the temple in the name of the Lord as the Messiah, greeted by the words of Psalm 118. He searches for the fruit of repentance, but it is not there, and so the temple is cursed. When the rebellious leaders ask who gave him the authority to do these things, he tells them a parable about how the Son comes with the authority of the Father. He returns to the prophecy of Psalm 118 to show that he is the stone that gets rejected but is vindicated as the cornerstone.

The prophecy of rejection ends with its fulfillment. The religious leaders reject Jesus. Indeed, they even seek to arrest him (Mark **12:12**). Jesus comes into the temple looking for the fruit of repentance—a moment which has been predicted for generations. But the people have rejected the call to repent with stone-cold hearts. God prophesied a final, climactic rejection, and it has now come. What does the future hold now? A climactic reversal: vindication of the Son, destruction of the religious system, and inclusion of foreigners and outcasts among God's people.

Questions for reflection

1. Do you recognize Jesus' authority in your life? When we struggle with sin or feel confused about what we believe, how can we bring our questions to Jesus in a way that recognizes his authority?

2. How does the image of the building with Christ as the cornerstone impact your life today?

3. How do some of the dynamics of the parable of the vineyard and the tenants show up in our world today? How do you respond to them?

11. A BATTLE OF WITS

In an iconic scene in the movie *The Princess Bride*, a mysterious Man in Black challenges a Sicilian outlaw named Vizzini to a test of wits. He presents him with two goblets; each of them will drink from one cup, but Vizzini must first work out which one is poisoned. The Man in Black is confident that he will win this battle because the game is rigged: he has put poison in both goblets, and he himself is immune. Whichever cup Vizzini chooses, he will die.

In Mark 12, the religious leaders are challenging Jesus to a battle of wits. They think the game is rigged because they have laced the questions with so much poison that he can't escape a poisoned response. They pose three challenges in **verses 13-34**. Here is the first: Should they pay taxes to Caesar? If he says yes, then they will say, *He supports Roman rule*. If he says no, then they have him on the charge that he opposes Caesar.

In *The Princess Bride*, Vizzini, convinced that he has made the right choice, tells the Man in Black that he is a fool. "You fell victim to one of the classic blunders … Never go in against a Sicilian, when death is on the line!"

We might say a similar thing about the religious leaders of Jesus' day. They fell victim to the most classic blunder of all time: do not put God to the test. The finite should never test the infinite, **omniscient** God in a battle of wits.

The First Challenge

The Pharisees were a religious purity group. They wanted the people to keep God's law and stay pure so that they would not be kicked out of their land again. They wanted Herod and the Romans out of Israel. The Herodians, meanwhile, were a political power group. They supported Herod and the Romans. These two groups of people could not agree on anything—except that they needed to get rid of Jesus.

Together they set their trap for Jesus (**v 13**). They try to lure him into the trap with flattery: "We know that you are true" (**v 14**). In other words, Jesus does not care about people's opinions and is not swayed by appearances, but truly teaches the word of God.

Their flattery is like a boomerang that comes back and hits them in the head. Jesus really is all those things—and they are none of them. Jesus is true, and they are false. Jesus is not swayed by the opinions of others but teaches the true way of God; they are en-slaved to people's opinions and teach the way of man.

Object Lessons

Jesus sees right through their poisoned, hypocritical game. He sends them to get a denarius—a silver coin which bore the image of the Roman emperor (**v 15**).

Then Jesus turns the tables on them:

"'Whose likeness and inscription is this?' They said to him, 'Caesar's.' Jesus said to them, '**Render** to Caesar the things that are Caesar's, and to God the things that are God's.'" (**v 16-17**)

Jesus' words give us not one but two object lessons.

Caesar's likeness is on the coin. Therefore, the coin belongs to the sphere of authority that God has granted Caesar. It is real author-ity, but it is authority derived from above (see John 19:11). Caesar has authority over some things, but he does not have authority over everything. All people living under his rule have real and genuine obligations to the government. Jews have obligations to honor that authority—like paying taxes.

But Jesus' second object lesson sets even this first point within a larger perspective.

When Jesus adds, "Render ... to God the things that are God's" (Mark **12:17**), he is saying something absolutely fundamental and stunningly far-reaching. We owe some things to political rulers, but we owe *everything* to God. The Roman coin is an object lesson for Roman rule. What is the object lesson for God's rule? *You are*. And everyone else is too.

> Jesus is saying something fundamental and far-reaching.

We can look at a coin and say, "Whose likeness is on this coin?" But we can also look at any person and say, "Whose likeness is on this person?" The answer is "God's." We are all made in the likeness and image of our Creator. Therefore, what should we render to God? Everything we have! We are accountable to God for what we do with every breath he gives us.

These religious leaders should be giving God their repentance and worship and obedience. They should be loving him with all of their hearts—not plotting to kill him.

The people marvel at what Jesus has said (**v 17**). Marveling is amazement that falls short of faith. You marvel when you see something that transcends normal experience—it is like shock and awe. But it does not lead to any lasting change.

The Pharisees and the Herodians tried to win a battle of wits with God incarnate—and lost. We should be quick to confess that we are not immune to trying the same thing. We confess with our lips that Jesus is the all-wise God, but at the same time we sometimes question his wisdom. We can be quick to wonder if his way really is best. But beware of doubting the wisdom of God. We should cry out to him when things are hard and we don't understand, but we should also believe that he is wise beyond our imagination. We can render all things to him, knowing that we are safe with him.

And as we live out the truth of accountability to God, we must recognize that our obedience is not the way to be accepted by God. Yes, we must render to God the things that belong to God. But we will never be saved by rendering to God the things that belong to God. We are not saved by what *we render to God*, but by what *he reckons to us*: the righteousness of Jesus (2 Corinthians 5:21).

And that is not the end of the good news. God took out the stony hearts of rebellion and put within us the soft hearts of obedience and love and trust. We are now a people who genuinely desire to render to God all that belongs to him.

The Second Challenge

Mark **12:18-23** contains yet another attempt to stump Jesus. This time it comes from the Sadducees—a group who did not believe in the res-urrection of the dead. We should read their words as being said with a sneer: they are trying to show how ridiculous the resurrection is.

The question hinges on part of the Jewish law written by Moses. It refers to what is called the levirate marriage commandment (see Deuteronomy 25:5-10). If a husband dies without children, then the man's brother has an obligation to marry his brother's wife in order to provide children who will carry on the brother's name and keep the inheritance in the family. We see the summary of this law in Mark **12:19**:

"If a man's brother dies and leaves a wife, but leaves no child,
the man must take the widow and raise up offspring for his
brother."

They ask about a hypothetical scenario based on this law. A family has seven sons. One woman ends up marrying all seven sons. All of them die. No one produces a child. Now comes the question. Which of the brothers will be her husband in the next life?

They think they have just dropped a ticking theological bomb on Jesus' lap. The question is a power play in which they now stand ready to judge Jesus' response. They do not realize that they are really the ones standing before the judgment seat of Christ. He does not waste any time in turning the tables of judgment upon them.

The Response

Jesus frames his response by repeating the fact that they are wrong at the beginning (**v 24**) and the end (**v 27**). The reason they are wrong is their ignorance of the Scriptures and of the power of God (**v 24**). Jesus offers proof of that claim in reverse order.

He shows first that their view of marriage fails to reckon with the power of God (**v 25**). They are denying the power of God by assuming that resurrection life is on the same plane as earthly life. They cannot understand resurrection life as a higher order—a great transformation of life as we know it now. Their question betrays this misunderstanding.

Then Jesus charges the Sadducees with a failure to read the Scriptures. He says, "As for the dead being raised, have you not read in the book of Moses…" (**v 26**). This rebuke cuts deep to the heart of who they think they are. "Have you not read?" They pride themselves on knowing the writings of Moses (the first five books of the Bible, also known as the Pentateuch) front and back. They have read, studied, memorized, and meditated on this five-part book. They have devoted their lives to it.

Jesus is meeting them on their own terms. The Sadducees only recognize these five books of Scripture. So Jesus chooses a text from there—Exodus 3:6—even though there are certainly clearer and more explicit texts about the resurrection elsewhere in the Old Testament (e.g. Job 19:25-27).

Jesus' case for the resurrection hinges on the tiniest but greatest detail: the tense of the verb "to be." God did not say, *I was the God of*

Abraham, Isaac, and Jacob. He said, *I am the God of Abraham, Isaac, and Jacob*. Therefore, Jesus says, "He is not God of the dead, but of the living" (Mark **12:27**). Abraham, Isaac, and Jacob are still alive. Those who enjoy a relationship with God actually enjoy an everlasting, never-ending relationship with God—a relationship which will survive beyond the grave. So the Sadducees are wrong to deny the resurrection.

Why won't anyone be married in the new creation as some are here on earth? Because God did not create earthly marriage to exist eternally for its own sake. It is a temporary, earthly pointer to something eternal and heavenly. Marriage between a man and a woman points to the eternal, heavenly marriage between Jesus and his bride, the church—and the symbol can cease when the real thing arrives. God sent his Son into the world to win his bride and defeat death. Because of Jesus, the relationship between God and his people is unbreakable and unstoppable.

The Third Challenge

Reading the religious leaders' final challenge (**v 28-34**) is a little bit like watching a tennis match. There is a back-and-forth dynamic as one of the scribes asks a question (**v 28**), Jesus answers (**v 29-31**), the scribe responds (**v 32-33**), Jesus responds (**v 34**), and then we see the conclusion of the match (**v 34**).

The scribe asks an amazing question: "Which commandment is the most important of all?" (**v 28**).

The first part of Jesus' answer takes us to the oneness of God (see Deuteronomy 6:4). God is one: he is exclusively and uniquely God (Mark **12:29**). No one else is worthy of everything. He is above all and must be loved more than all. He alone is worthy of every fiber of our devotion and affection and commitment. So, the greatest command is to love God more than we love anything else (**v 30**).

Jesus also gives a second, complementary command. We should love our neighbor as ourselves (see Leviticus 19:18). This is a breathtaking command. It is like Jesus is telling us to take off our flesh and put it on someone else. We look at them and love them with all the interest we have in ourselves. We give them all the care we would give ourselves. This command is a profound call to crucify selfishness and pour out self-sacrificing love on others.

The scribe asked for one command, but Jesus has given two. Jesus is saying that these two commandments are distinguishable, yet inseparable. Indeed, the New Testament tells us that we cannot say we love God and yet hate our brother (1 John 4:19-21). If you claim you can separate the two commands, the Bible does not just call you inconsistent. It calls you a liar.

The scribe recognizes the wisdom of Jesus (Mark **12:32-33**). *There is a hierarchy in God's commands,* he says. Loving God and neighbor is "much more than all whole burnt offerings and sacrifices" (**v 33**). This is self-evidently true: one could go through the motions in the sacrificial system without having love for God. But love for God should empower obedience to the other commands of God—like the command to participate in the sacrificial system.

Remember the context: Jesus has been speaking against what has been happening in the temple. The scribe has understood that loving God and neighbor mean more than participating in temple activities. We can see how Jesus' words relate to his cursing of the temple and turning over the tables that enabled Jews to participate in the sacrificial system. He is saying that it is all a sham. People have been doing all these activities without love for God or love for others. They have missed the main thing.

What is the outcome of the tennis match? No one dares to challenge Jesus anymore (**v 34**). They give up all hope of being able to trap him in his words or discredit him as a teacher of God's word. He is not going to be stumped or shamed or tricked.

We are in the presence of greatness. Jesus is God—and he takes all of the commands ever spoken in Scripture and says, *This is the essence of all I have been saying.* Jesus deserves all the worship and honor and love that belong to God. He proves it with his wise responses to these three questions.

Questions for reflection

1. In what ways do we sometimes try to engage God in a battle of wits?

2. How should Jesus' words about the resurrection affect the way we live now?

3. What would it look like to take the next steps of obedience in loving God with everything we have and loving others as ourselves? What do you need to give to God? Where do you need to step up in love for others?

PART TWO

The episode with the scribe is one of the few times that Jesus answers a question and then someone openly acknowledges that he is right. How will Jesus respond? Notice that he does not say, *You are in the kingdom*, but "You are not far from the kingdom of God" (**v 34**). This comment raises the question: What is the scribe missing? What does he need to see in order to enter the kingdom?

The scribe still does not understand the identity of Jesus. He says, "You are right, Teacher" (**v 32**). But it is not enough to call Jesus "right"; one must call him "Lord." Jesus makes this point in the next story.

The Question for the Religious Leaders

Jesus now makes a challenge of his own (**v 35-37**). He calls into question the scribes' understanding of the Messiah. Do they really know who they are looking for? They have taken the position that the Messiah is David's son. Jesus calls this position into question by quoting from Psalm 110:1. He does not start with what is being said in this psalm, but with who is saying it. The superscription of Psalm 110 matters: "A Psalm of David." David is the one who wrote it.

It's important to note that David is not speaking on his own. He is speaking "in the Holy Spirit" (Mark **12:36**). This is a doctrine called "concursus." We say that Scripture has a human author and a divine author. They work together concurrently or simultaneously. The human author is carried along by the Holy Spirit (2 Peter 1:21). The Spirit ensures that what the human author says is exactly what God wants him to say.

Why does it matter that David is speaking? To find out we have to see what he says. "The Lord said to my Lord" (Mark **12:36**). The answer to the puzzle of interpretation hinges on the work of identification. The first Lord must be a reference to Yahweh. And if Yahweh is "the Lord," then who on earth is the one David calls "my Lord"? Some would suggest that the divine Lord is speaking to Israel's king, because it is a "coronation psalm." But Jesus shows that the super-scription rules out that interpretation. At the time the psalm was written, David was the king. Who would a king call "my Lord"? This must be a reference to the Messiah.

And what does God say to David's Lord? "Sit at my right hand until I put your enemies under your feet." In the New Testament, this text is the most-referenced Old Testament text to demonstrate the exaltation and enthronement of Jesus after his resurrection (Acts 2:33-35; Romans 8:34; 1 Corinthians 15:25; Hebrews 1:3, 13).

Then Jesus asks the "gotcha" question: "David himself calls him Lord. So how is he his son?" (Mark **12:37**). How can the Messiah be David's son if he is David's Lord?

His question does not deny that the Messiah is the royal son of David. The Old Testament made it very clear that the Messiah was to be born in David's royal line (2 Samuel 7). Jesus has already been confessed as "the Son of David" by Bartimaeus (Mark 10:47-48). So, here in Mark 12, Jesus is not questioning the accuracy of the scribes' understanding on this point but the adequacy of it. In other words, the question is not whether the Messiah *is* the son of David but whether he is *only* the son of David.

These professional interpreters of the Bible don't know how to read the Bible! Not just on some minor matter but on the matter of their core and blessed hope: the Messiah. So it should come as no surprise that the scribes can't identify the Messiah when he is standing right in front of them.

Jesus takes the brush of Scripture—which describes the Messiah as both David's son and David's Lord—and paints this portrait of the Messiah that the scribes cannot refute. And the crowds love it (**12:37**)—but this glad hearing is not faith. Neither the scribes nor the crowd are saved. "Gladly hearing" does not get them into the kingdom any more than acknowledging Jesus' wisdom got the scribe in the previous story into the kingdom. It is not enough to say that Jesus is right—one must confess that he is Lord.

We must come to grips with this reality. You can read the Bible or listen to preaching about the identity of Jesus and hear the truth gladly without ever surrendering to it fully. This world in which we live will test whether or not we really believe these truths by testing our commitment to them. So many people are raised in church and just accept this as a point of doctrine instead of a point of identity. But we cannot play fast and loose with this truth. It deserves all or nothing. Augustine is right when he says, "Christ is not valued at all, unless he is valued above all."

Beware of the Scribes

Chapter 12 closes with two contrasting pictures: the scribes, who are a symbol of fake or counterfeit devotion to God (**v 38-40**), and the poor widow, who is a symbol of true devotion to God (**v 41-44**).

Jesus tells a cautionary tale about what the scribes do. They walk around in long robes. They seek greetings in the marketplaces. They sit in the best seats in the synagogue. They take the places of honor at feasts. They devour widows' houses. They make long prayers.

Why do they do these things? Because they are corrupt and counterfeit spiritual leaders. Jesus shows that their devotion is self-promotion. Their prayers are long like their clothes and for the same reason: to draw attention to themselves. The length of their prayers does not demonstrate the depth of their devotion to God but the lengths they will go to in order to be noticed as religious. Jesus calls it a "pretense" (**v 40**). It is all a sham. What they really want is not the approval of God but the approval of man. They ravenously crave greetings, recognition, and places of honor. They enjoy being religious celebrities.

It is bad enough that the scribes are spiritual peacocks that flaunt their devotion for the sake of self-promotion. But they are more than peacocks; they are predators, who prey upon the vulnerable. Jesus says that they devour widows' houses (**v 40**). This probably means that they abused the generosity and hospitality of poor and vulnerable widows.

They took advantage of their kindness and preyed upon it—eating them out of house and home.

The historical background provides a fuller picture of these predatory practices:

> "The scribes lived primarily on subsidies, since it was forbidden that they should be paid for exercising their profession … The extension of hospitality to them was strongly encouraged as an act of piety; it was considered particularly meritorious to relieve a scribe of concern for his livelihood. Many well-to-do persons placed their financial resources at the disposal of scribes, and it was inevitable that there should be abuses."
>
> (William Lane, *The Gospel of Mark*, p 441)

Jesus does not pull any punches. "They will receive the greater condemnation" (**v 40**). The grave warning here is that people are easily fooled by the scribes' pretenses, but God is nobody's fool. God sees right through their religious and self-righteous showmanship. God is also the defender of widows, and he will come after anyone who dares to prey upon them (Exodus 22:22; Deuteronomy 10:18; 24:17; 27:19; Psalm 68:5; 146:9; Isaiah 1:23; 10:1-4; Jeremiah 7:6; 22:3; 49:11; Ezekiel 22:7). It should come as no surprise to see a widow take center stage in the next story.

Rich in Faith

Here Jesus paints a picture of true devotion (Mark **12:41-44**). He has already shown the bankruptcy of ministry in the temple. God designed the temple to be a place in which to seek the Lord—a house of prayer (11:17). The Jewish leaders had corrupted it and made it "a den of robbers." The ministry of the temple was spiritually bankrupt, but physically profitable for the ministers.

Now Jesus sits down opposite the temple treasury, where people are putting money in the offering box. The treasury appears to have been located in the Court of Women, one of the outer courts of the temple, and consisted of 13 trumpet-shaped receptacles for both the temple tax and money given voluntarily for various purposes (see James A. Brooks, *Mark*, p 203). Jesus and his disciples watch impressive displays by rich people putting in large amounts of money (**12:41**). But then comes a stark contrast in **verse 42**: a poor widow comes and puts in two copper coins, which add up to a penny. (Mark is explaining the value of the coin for his Roman readers who are not familiar with it.)

Jesus wants us to know that appearances can be deceiving. Just as people should not be duped by the outward religious displays of the scribes, they should also not be dazzled by the larger amounts that some give and despise the smaller amount that the poor widow gives.

Jesus is like a spiritual optometrist: he helps his disciples see things as God sees them. Jesus calls the disciples to himself and turns their perceptions upside down. He says that the poor widow put more in the offering box than anyone else (**v 43**). If one looks only on the outside, this claim would not be true. She did not put more money in than others. But Jesus then gives the rationale to support his claim (**v 44**). He takes their eyes off the amount given and helps them look at the amount left over. The rich are still rich after their apparently generous donations. But the poor woman went from poor to poorer. She went from a little to nothing. She put all the others to shame by giving "all she had to live on" and leaving herself to rely completely on

She was not rich in finances, but in faith.

the Lord. It was a truly extravagant gift. It showed that the Lord was her hope and trust and security and treasure, not financial security. She was not rich in finances, but rich in faith.

The contrast is not merely between the greed of the scribes and the generosity of the widow but between the showiness of the scribes and the hiddenness of the widow. Their devotion is a shiny counterfeit. Her devotion has a hidden genuineness to it. She gives as an expression of praise, not as a strategy to get praise.

I remember that my daughter once taught me this lesson in a surprising way. She was going to put money in the offering plate. She decided to put in all of the money from her little purse. I told her, "Sweetheart, you do not have to put all of it in the offering plate. You can keep some back for yourself." I will never forget her response: "I don't need money. I have a daddy!"

I found myself greatly rebuked. I want to be rich in faith in the same way. The fact that we have a Father should change the way we think about our need for money.

Questions for reflection

1. Why does Jesus' identity matter so much? What difference does it make to your life?

2. What would it look like in your life to behave like the rich scribes? What would it look like to behave like the poor widow?

3. How could you put Jesus above all other things this week?

12. SIGNS OF THE END

For every reference to the first coming of Jesus in the Bible, there are eight references to his second coming. Why? Because it is essential for living the life of faith. No matter how hard it is now, we press on through trials because it's worth it. Jesus will come again and gather us to himself. We may be uncertain about what is going on around us. But we can be at peace. Certainty about what is ultimate can vanquish confusion about what is immediate. And then we can press on in obedience and faith.

There is a concept in childhood development called object permanence. Children can be easily alarmed and afraid when something is not right in front of them—the object that is out of sight seems to have gone completely. That is why children are often afraid of the dark. Their real fear is not fear of the dark but fear of being alone, which is accentuated by the dark. They can know that Mom and Dad are in the next room, but they can't see them—so they do not seem real or permanent.

But as Christians we know that the things that are most permanent and most real are eternal things. We set our eyes on things that are eternal, things that are unseen. Why are we afraid? Jesus said he is with us always. You may not see him, but he is near—and much closer than the next room. And one day we will see him face to face.

Therefore, there must be a connection between hope and patient endurance. "Now hope that is seen is not hope. For who hopes for what he sees? But if we hope for what we do not see, we wait for it with patience" (Romans 8:24-25). Too many people want to be certain about the immediate instead of bringing the ultimate into the immediate. Christians have an urgent need to bring "forever" to bear on what is right now.

The here-and-now is immediate but not ultimate. When you set your hope on the immediate, you set yourself up for failure and disappointment. You experience either a false sense of security or a false sense of despair because you are not resting your hope on the ultimate, just the immediate.

This is why, in the passage we are about to read, Jesus spends so long telling his disciples about what is to come. He wants them to endure to the end and be saved (Mark **13:13**). Knowing that Jesus will one day return is what will also give us the courage and confidence to do that.

The Future of the Temple

Mark 13 can be very confusing, and so we are going to take two laps around it. The first lap will focus on **verses 3-27**, where Jesus predicts certain future events. The second lap will go back and walk more quickly through all the movements of this text, showing how it works as a bridge to the following chapters.

As Jesus' third trip to the temple comes to an end, one of the disciples remarks on the temple's "wonderful stones" and "wonderful buildings" (**v 1**). But Jesus responds by prophesying that not one of these "wonderful stones" will be left on top of another (**v 2**). The temple will be totally destroyed. Next the disciples ask him privately the question begging to be asked. When? To be precise, they ask a twofold question: (1) when will these things be, and (2) what will be the sign (**v 3-4**)?

Jesus gives a three-part answer.

Persecution and Perseverance

Jesus first tells the disciples that their desire for a sign may make them vulnerable to being led astray (**v 5**). He encourages them not to place their trust in their ability to spot the signs and nail down the details of the precise timing of the end.

There will be wars, earthquakes, and famines (**v 7-8**)—and people will claim that this is the end of the world. They will even claim that they themselves are Jesus returning (**v 6**). But these things are not the end (**v 7**). In fact, Jesus says they are the beginning of labor pains (**v 8**)—the painful contractions preceding a birth. This is a profoundly hopeful metaphor. The disciples need not be alarmed when alarming things are happening around them. Why? They are not dying pains but birthing pains.

This is a profoundly hopeful metaphor.

Nothing is worse than pointless pain. But pain that is connected to a point or a purpose is so different. Childbirth involves incredible agony, but the joy of holding that newborn baby makes the pain worth it. The strife and pain that Jesus is speaking of are woes that will give birth to a whole new world—a world that is better than anything we could imagine. Yes, it will be worth it.

This metaphor leads to the call for us to be on our guard (**v 9**). Knowing the ultimate outcome will help us prepare to suffer and persevere.

Jesus does not go into detail about the particular signs; he focuses instead on the scope and severity of the persecution that is coming. It will take place in many different settings—among Jewish authorities (councils and synagogues, **v 9**) and Gentile authorities (governors and kings), but also in family settings (**v 12**). The hatred and animosity extends all the way to the most severe sentence (death, **v 12**) and to the farthest extent ("you will be hated by all for my name's sake," **v 13**).

But in the midst of the staggering scope and severity of this persecution, Jesus emphasizes three things: (1) a purpose, (2) a promise, and (3) a call for perseverance.

First, the purpose of this persecution is to provide a context for bearing witness to Christ (**v 9**). The disciples must move forward for the sake of proclamation, not move away for the sake of protection.

This proclamation will happen on a worldwide scale because "the gospel must first be proclaimed to all nations" (**v 10**). Disciples will be hated in all nations; the gospel will go to all nations. That is the power of the gospel—we all start as haters, but many become worshipers.

Second, the promise in the midst of the persecution is that Christ will provide the words for his disciples' witness through the power and presence of the Holy Spirit. They will need to speak, but the Holy Spirit will give them the words (**v 11**).

Third, Jesus stresses the call for perseverance: "But the one who endures to the end will be saved" (**v 13**). Once again, note the connection between perseverance and hope. The birth pains will give way to the birth of a new world.

The Abomination and the Tribulation

There are three main ways to read **verses 14-23**:

1. The historical view: Jesus is solely referring to AD 70, when the temple in Jerusalem was destroyed.

2. The **eschatological** view: Jesus is solely referring to the end of the age and the second coming.

3. The combination view: Jesus is referring to both these timeframes.

The phrase "abomination of desolation" originates from the book of Daniel (9:27, 11:31, 12:11). An abomination here is a sacrilege—a serious violation of God's law or a desecration of something holy. Most students of the Bible read Daniel's prophecy as a prediction of the desecration of the temple by a ruler named Antiochus Epiphanes (167 BC). The Jewish historian Josephus documented the sacrilege committed by Antiochus; he built a pagan altar on God's altar and sacrificed a pig on it (*Antiquities of the Jews*, 12.5.4). This was an "abomination … standing where he ought not to be" (Mark **13:14**). Using this phrase would have had a profound and startling effect on any Jew. It would make them think of Antiochus' sacrilege and make them wonder, *Could such sacrilege happen again?*

How should we read these verses? Let's see the case for each of the first two interpretations, detail by detail.

The Abomination

Jesus describes a desolating sacrilege involving something "standing where he ought not to be" (**v 14**). In the original Greek, Mark uses a masculine form of the word for "standing." One would expect a neuter form of the word (i.e. standing where *it* ought not to be) because that would grammatically agree with the neuter word "abomination." The masculine form suggests that Jesus envisions a person and not just an event or thing.

The historical view says that the desolating sacrilege refers in some way to the destruction of Jerusalem by the Romans in AD 70. It could be the moment when the Roman general Titus entered into the temple sanctuary, or when the Roman soldiers set their standards up in the temple and offered sacrifices while acclaiming Titus as emperor. Another strong possibility would be the actions of the **Jewish Zealots** and others who, in AD 67-68, made themselves priests and were thus standing where they should not be.

The eschatological view, meanwhile, says that Jesus is talking about an antichrist figure, probably the same person as Paul's "man of lawlessness," who will come shortly before the return of Jesus (2 Thessalonians 2:1-10; see also "antichrist" in 1 John 2:18 and the "beast" in Revelation 11:7, 13:1-18). Paul says the "man of lawlessness" will be where he ought not to be: "he takes his seat in the temple of God" and claims what he should not claim, "proclaiming himself to be God" (2 Thessalonians 2:4).

"Let the Reader Understand"

The historical view reads this phrase (Mark **13:14**) as an aside by Mark to his readers—alerting them to the fact that this will take place soon, and so, when they see it, they should be ready to take immediate action. That would date Mark's Gospel to the late 60s AD, just before the Jewish War began.

The eschatological view reads this phrase as a word from Jesus, not an editorial insertion from Mark. (The original language did not use speech marks.) In other words, these words would address all readers of the Bible, not just Mark's original readers in their particular time. In this way, the "reader" would also be the reader of the book of Daniel; so this phrase would be an exhortation to reflect further on the prophecies in Daniel about the end times.

The Tribulation

The historical view interprets Jesus' words as a warning to flee the city of Jerusalem as the Romans advanced (Mark **13:14-18**). The suffering would be so bad that people should not go back into their house to pack. There would be no time! (Flat rooftops in Palestine were used as living space and were accessible by an outside ladder or staircase— which is why people might be "on the housetop," **v 15**). Nor should they go back to get a cloak if they were in the fields (**v 16**).

Jesus then turns to the horrors of the siege and the terrors that those inside the city would face (**v 17-19**). He mentions the suffering of pregnant women and new mothers particularly. Jesus counsels his hearers to "pray that it may not happen in winter" (**v 18**), when food would be scarce and the suffering would be even worse.

The Jewish historian Josephus describes the horrors of the Roman siege of Jerusalem in great, graphic detail (*The Jewish War*, books 5-6). He comments that outside the city, the Romans crucified so many Jews that they ran out of wood for crosses. Inside the city there was also extreme suffering: disease, murder, starvation, and even cannibalism. Josephus makes the startling claim that 1,100,000 people died during the siege (*The Jewish War*, 6.9.3). Many scholars believe that these numbers are exaggerated, but they do give some indication of the terrors of this event.

The eschatological view, however, would read this "tribulation" as a future time of unprecedented suffering. All tragedies and travesties, including the siege of Jerusalem, pale in comparison with this future tribulation: "Such tribulation as has not been from the beginning of the creation that God created until now, and never will be" (**v 19**).

The Elect

Jesus adds that God has "cut short the days" of the tribulation for the sake of "the elect, whom he chose" (**v 20**). In the historical view, the "elect" or "chosen people" is the small number of Jewish Christians that were still in Jerusalem during the siege. The idea that God "cut short the days" is a reference to the siege lasting five months, which, though horrible, was a relatively short timeframe for a siege.

In the eschatological view, the elect would be all Christians living during this future tribulation. Remember that Jesus has already commented on the worldwide spread of the gospel (**v 10**). The elect are all those around the world whom God has chosen (see Ephesians 1:4).

False Signs and Wonders

When this time of tribulation comes, there will be those who claim that Jesus has returned, and even claim to be Christ themselves (Mark **13:21-22**). The Jewish historian Josephus uses similar language to describe what happened in the 1st century: many messianic imposters arose who tricked the masses through "wonders and signs" (*Antiquities of the Jews*, 20.8.6). The book of Acts mentions some of these pretenders by name (Theudas and Judas the Galilean—see Acts 5:36-37). So the historical view would once again say that Jesus was predicting things that happened in his own time and just afterward.

But on the eschatological view, these deceivers and false signs and wonders will come shortly before the day of the Lord. His language fits very well with what Paul says about the man of lawlessness (2 Thessalonians 2:9).

"Be on guard," Jesus says again; "I have told you all things beforehand" (Mark **13:23**). But what does he really mean? Which reading is right? Before we talk about the third way of reading this text, let's finish the interpretive challenge by looking at verses 24–27.

Questions for reflection

1. What implications would each of the views outlined so far have for us today?

2. What do you find encouraging in what Jesus says here? Is there anything you find worrying?

3. Based on the eschatological reading of these verses, what do you think it looks like to "be on guard" with regard to the second coming?

PART TWO

The Second Coming

When we reach **verses 24-27**, the historical view becomes difficult to justify. It would stretch these verses beyond the breaking point—like a rubber band stretched too far. Jesus says that the sun and moon will go dark and the stars will fall (**v 24-25**). The Son of Man will come in clouds with great power and glory (**v 26**). It is hard to see how this could refer to Rome's destruction of the temple!

Some do think that this "coming" of the Son of Man is metaphorical. Jesus' words will come true so that what he has said is vindicated. On that reading, this text talks about a change of rule: the Jewish temple or **sanctuary** is done, and now the Son of Man is ruling in the heavenly temple or sanctuary. People "see" him enthroned only conceptually or metaphorically.

But it makes much more sense to say that these verses refer to the second coming. There is a convincing parallel in Acts 1:6-11. There, an angel says to the disciples that they will see Jesus come back in the same way he left: visibly, bodily, and on the clouds. This interpretation also means we can read the words "coming" and "see" in a much more natural, literal way.

Furthermore, Jesus says that he will send his angels out to gather his elect "from the four winds, from the ends of the earth to the ends of heaven" (Mark **13:27**). This is global in scope. It seems to be connected with the gospel going to all the nations and then the elect of all nations being gathered at the end of the age.

Those who relate these verses to the destruction of Jerusalem rather than to the end of the age must identify the gathering of the elect (**v 27**) with the missionary expansion of the gospel in the 1st century. The "angels" (which is a Greek word meaning "messenger") would then be either human messengers of the gospel or angels viewed as supporting missionaries in the task of world evangelism. But if this is right, why would Mark use the word "gather"?

The language of gathering God's people comes from Old Testament texts that describe the final gathering of God's people: "ends of the earth" comes from Isaiah 45:22 (and elsewhere in Isaiah), and "ends of the heavens" from Zechariah 2:6.

In fact, this passage is saturated with the language of the prophets and what will happen at the end of the age. The phrases "the sun will be darkened, and the moon will not give its light, and the stars will be falling from heaven, and the powers in the heavens will be shaken" all echo Old Testament texts, especially Isaiah 13:10 ("the sun will be dark at its rising, and the moon will not shed its light") and 34:4 ("all the host of heaven shall rot away … like leaves falling from the fig tree").

The Combination View

It is hard to justify reading all the verses as a reference to AD 70. It is not natural to read the "elect" in one part of Mark 13 as only a few Jewish Christians in Jerusalem and the other references to the gathering of the elect as Christians throughout the world. Even though the siege of Jerusalem in the Jewish War was a horrific event, was it really the worst of its kind in history (Mark **13:19**)? And what does one do with all the parallels between Mark 13 and the man of lawlessness in 2 Thessalonians 2?

But it is equally hard to read all the verses as a reference to the last of the last times. This view does not seem to do justice to the connection between Jesus' prediction about the destruction of the temple and his answer to the disciples about when that would take place. Surely there has to be some reference to AD 70? Mark **13:14-15** seems to be very focused on a particular location, as people flee their houses in Judea; it makes most sense to connect that with the destruction of Jerusalem. The most natural way to take "let the reader understand" is to read it as Mark inserting something to get his first readers' attention—alerting them to what was about to happen. Finally, what does one do with all the similarities between Jesus' words in Mark 13 and Josephus' summary of the Jewish War?

This is why the most common position is to read this passage as a mix of both historical events and eschatological imagery. The main idea of this view is that history consists of repeating cycles and patterns. Judgments in history foreshadow and prefigure a climactic final upheaval and judgment. The destruction of the temple in AD 70 is therefore inextricably linked to the final judgment at the second coming and the destruction of the world as we know it. Some of what Jesus says refers to one event; some refers to the other; some refers to both.

The combination view does justice to the close relationship between Jesus' prediction of the temple's destruction (**v 2**) and the warning to flee Jerusalem (**v 14-15**). It explains the climactic finality that **verses 26-27** seem to communicate with the coming of the Son of Man and the gathering of the elect by the angels. It also makes sense of why Josephus' summary and Paul's words can be so similar.

All this is an important reminder about how to read any biblical text that is prophetic in nature. Sometimes biblical prophecy can be surprising in its fulfillment. The Old Testament contains many prophecies about the coming of the Lord. Jewish readers interpret these as referring to a single moment in time, but we know that what seems to be presented by the prophets as one package actually happens in two comings of Christ, not just one. This two-dimensional way of reading the prophets (one package with more than one event) has been compared to seeing mountains that in the distance look like they are side by side; as you get closer, you realize that they are actually miles apart. The prophecies about the coming of the Lord in the Old Testament may make it look like the fulfillments will all happen together, but we realize now that there are two fulfillments that are actually more than 2,000 years apart. The same goes for this passage in Mark.

In fact, I would argue that this passage doesn't only combine AD 70 and future end-time events, but also prefigures what will climactically and powerfully and surprisingly take place in Mark 14 – 16: the crucifixion and resurrection of Christ. These events are all intimately associated as part of the great drama of what God is doing in the world and the way that he is ruling the past, the present, and the future. This is what our second lap around Mark 13 will show.

Four Movements

Mark 13 has four movements: (1) total destruction (**v 1-2**), (2) the timing of the end (**v 3-27**), (3) the lesson of the fig tree (**v 28-31**), and (4) the warning to stay awake (**v 32-37**).

Total Destruction

In the first movement, the disciples seem to be blind to Jesus' confrontational curse on the temple. They are still dazzled by the external aspects of the temple (**v 1**). But Jesus has been addressing the internal corruption of the temple and its leaders. He brings crystal clear sight back to the situation. The buildings may look great now, but the time is coming when they will be utterly demolished. Not one stone will be left upon another. All will be thrown down (**v 2**).

The Timing of the End

The disciples ask when these things will be, and what will be the sign. Jesus' reply shows that the disciples' desire for a sign will open them up to the possibility of being led astray. There will be many cosmic disturbances in this world, but the end is not yet (**v 7**). There will be three stages: (1) signs or birth pains, (2) an abomination, and (3) the coming of the Lord. The abomination that causes desolation is a desolating sacrilege. Once this desolating sacrilege comes, people will flee. And then the Lord will come.

But Jesus does not end his discourse here with an end-times chart or further detail about the end. Rather, he returns to the fig tree.

The Lesson of the Fig Tree

Jesus says that certain signs on a fig tree show that summer is near (**v 28**). In the same way, when the signs which Jesus has outlined so far in chapter 13 happen, you will know that he is near (**v 29**). The Lord is at the gates! Jesus says that this generation won't pass away until these things take place (**v 30**). His words are more certain than the continued existence of heaven and earth (**v 31**).

This is where it starts to become clear that a third timeframe is needed in order to correctly interpret this passage. If Jesus is talking about the second coming, the question arises: was Jesus wrong? People of "this generation" did not see the second coming. So did Jesus' words pass away, even though he said that they would not?

Remember that Jesus did something similar back in chapters 8 and 9. He talked about the Son of Man coming (8:38). He said that some standing there would see the coming of the kingdom of God in power (9:1). Then some of them (Peter, James, and John) saw him transfigured in power and glory (Mark 9:2-3). This was what Jesus had been predicting.

This gives us a clue as to what is happening here. Jesus is now talking not about the second coming but about the events which are just about to take place. The next movement in Mark 13 makes this clearer.

The Final Warning: Stay Awake

Jesus tells the disciples that they don't know the specific time. Only the Father knows (**13:32**). Therefore, they must be on their guard, be vigilant, and stay awake, because they don't know when the time will come (**v 33**). It is like the master of a house going on a journey. The servants do not know when he will return. He leaves the servants in charge with work to do, and he commands the doorkeeper to stay awake (**v 34**).

Now comes the main command of this whole chapter. Everything has been building to this instruction: "Therefore stay awake" (**v 35**). Why?

Because the disciples don't know when the Master will come. They should be ready at any time of day: evening, midnight, when the rooster crows, or in the morning. They could miss him at all these times—he will come suddenly—and he must not find them asleep (**v 36**). So Jesus repeats the command again emphatically: stay awake (**v 37**).

Few people read this text with the right lens. They are so used to reading the whole chapter like a stand-alone, isolated prediction of the second coming. Let me be clear: Mark 13 *is* talking about the second coming, but not *only* the second coming. If the destruction of the temple and the second coming are our only lenses for reading Mark 13, then we miss the intentional connection Mark makes between chapters 11 – 13 and chapters 14 – 16. And we miss the way that chapter 13 brings the former section to a climax, which sets the stage (and the timeframe) for the next section.

Chapter 13 as the Bridge to Mark 14 - 15

Look at Mark **13:35** and you will see the times when the disciples must be awake and not be asleep in case they miss the coming of the Lord: evening, midnight, when the rooster crows, and in the morning.

Jesus has been talking about the destruction of the temple. We know from other texts (Mark 14:58; 15:29; John 2:19) that Jesus also spoke of his own body as the temple, saying that it would be destroyed and rebuilt in three days. This is key for our interpretation of the remaining chapters of Mark.

Mark 14:17 gives us evening as an explicit time frame. We are coming to the betrayal and arrest of Jesus. I think we are supposed to read this as an abomination, the sacrilege of **13:14**. The temple of Jesus' body is about to be woefully mistreated. This will bring tribulation and woe on those who have caused it:

> "For the Son of Man goes as it is written of him, but woe to that man by whom the Son of Man is betrayed! It would have been better for that man if he had not been born." (14:21)

Mark 14:32-42, the scene in the Garden of Gethsemane, contains the most explicit connections with chapter 13. Jesus repeatedly tells his disciples to stay awake and to keep watch (14:34, 37, 38, 41), and repeatedly finds them sleeping (v 37, 40). The language is exactly the same as in Mark **13:34-37**. Finally, when Jesus is arrested, all the disciples flee (14:50)—which is exactly what Jesus said people would do when the desolating sacrilege occurred (**13:14**).

In Gethsemane, the disciples have shown that they are asleep—they are not alert to the realities taking place around them. They have not been ready for Jesus' coming. The chief priests and scribes, too, have not understood his coming. As they condemn him for blasphemy, Jesus tells them that they will see him coming with the clouds of heaven (14:62). At the same time, Peter is also in a trial of sorts, before the servant girl of the high priest. Peter takes an oath and calls down a curse on himself in denying that he knows Jesus. The rooster crows (14:72). Peter breaks down and weeps. It is as though he has been asleep and his master has taken him by surprise.

Then it is morning (15:1). Jesus is delivered over to be crucified. Everyone still seems to be asleep, not recognizing the coming of the Lord. In 15:33, darkness comes over the whole land—just as Jesus predicted in **13:24**. As Jesus dies, the curtain in the Jerusalem temple is torn in two (15:38). The end of the temple is here.

> The last days are here. The future has broken into the present.

The way that Mark presents the cross and resurrection of Jesus is so significant. What we must realize is that we are not waiting for the end times; we are in the end times. They began with the first coming of Christ. Christ has come. He died and rose. He sent his Spirit. The last days are here. The presence of the future has broken into this present world.

Are we awake to the presence of the future? We should heed Paul's call:

"Awake, O sleeper,
and arise from the dead,
and Christ will shine on you." (Ephesians 5:14)

Questions for reflection

1. How have you responded to the cross and the resurrection of Christ? How do you show that you are awake to these realities?

2. In what ways do you sometimes find yourself drowsy or sleepy with regard to the reality of Christ's second coming?

3. How can you grow in pursuing the things that are above rather than earthly things?

13. TOWARD THE CROSS

Mark 14:1 – 15:37 narrates the ever-increasing abandonment of Jesus as he goes to the cross. He will be rejected, betrayed, and abandoned until the point that he is completely alone—forsaken even by the Father (15:34). Chapter 14 shows him being rejected by the Jews first of all.

The Plot against Jesus

It is two days before the Passover (**14:1**). The Passover was the beginning of the week-long Feast of Unleavened Bread (Exodus 12:15-20; Deuteronomy 16:1-8). This was a remembrance and commemoration of the hurried departure of the Israelites from Egypt when they could not wait for the dough to rise and had to eat unleavened bread.

The camera zooms in on the religious leaders. They are spending their time seeking how to arrest and kill Jesus—by stealth and in secrecy (Mark **14:1**). They do their work in the shadows because they are enslaved to the fear of man (**v 2**).

Skip down to **verses 10-11** and we see that the religious leaders have now found the answer to their search. One of Jesus' own disciples has sought them out, ready to betray Jesus (**v 10**). The religious leaders cannot contain their joy (**v 11**). They finally have what they want: a way to kill Jesus and protect themselves from the outrage of the people. Judas, in return, has something that he values: money (**v 11**).

But when we come to the middle of this sandwich, we will see something completely different being valued.

The Worship of Jesus

Mark does something he does not normally do—he tells us exactly where Jesus is. The house is in Bethany, a village two miles outside Jerusalem (**v 3**). Mark even tells us whose house it is: the house of Simon the leper (**v 3**). The note that Simon had leprosy suggests that he was an outsider in society. But presumably he is a *former* leper. If he still had leprosy, it would have precluded him from any social occasion. It seems likely that Jesus has healed him.

Most scholars believe that Mark's narrative here is the same story as the one in John 12:1-8, but in a somewhat different form. "If so, Mark's unnamed woman is Mary, sister of Martha and Lazarus, and Simon could be the father of the three." (James R. Edwards, *The Gospel of Mark*, p 413). Why is Mary not named? It is probably another installment in Mark's outsider theme. She is not enough of an insider to be given a name.

The repeated refrain of insider versus outsider sets up a surprise. No one would expect to see a display of discipleship here, outside Jerusalem, in the house of a leper, from this unnamed woman.

This element of surprise is enhanced further by the fact that the woman broke all social conventions and etiquette in coming directly to Jesus. Male fellowship among the Jews was not supposed to be broken by the "intrusion" of women unless they were bringing and serving food. But Jesus had captured her heart, and so she would not be held captive to such cultural constraints. Mark makes it clear that she did not bring Jesus food but her heart.

> Jesus had captured her heart.

Mark emphasizes how much she values Jesus by identifying the high value of the perfume she brings: "an alabaster flask of ointment of pure **nard**, very costly" (Mark **14:3**). I remember one of my friends in high school who used expensive cologne. It was pretty common for girls in my class to use perfume, but none of the guys did. I asked my friend what kind of cologne he used and made a mental note to look for it the next time I went shopping. When I finally found some (in a glass case), I saw the sticker price and I was shocked: $60! I remember thinking that $60 was more than I had in my entire bank account at the time.

But that was nothing compared to nard. The focus on the value of the nard is very pronounced in the narrative. In fact, the people present (presumably the disciples) immediately estimate its value: a year's worth of wages. "This ointment could have been sold for more than three hundred denarii" (**v 5**). A denarius was a day's wage for a laborer. In modern equivalence, 300 denarii would be worth roughly $25,000.

Women were by and large excluded from careers that afforded the possibility of earning such wages or procuring objects of such value. The nard was very probably a family heirloom, in which case it would have possessed a sentimental value in addition to its monetary value. Mark reports that the woman did not pour out the unguent but smashed the jar itself, which meant the vessel could never be used again—thus symbolizing the totality of the gift (James R. Edwards, *The Gospel of Mark*, p 413-414).

The response of the disciples is one of the saddest points of the whole story. They are indignant with the woman. They call this act of worship a waste (**v 4**). Why waste this perfume on Jesus? They scold her because they think it would be better to have sold it and given the money to the poor (**v 5**).

Mark presents a glaring contrast in this story between the way the woman values Jesus and the way the disciples value money. That same value difference is what frames the larger contrast between the story of the anointing of Jesus and the betrayal by Judas. In fact, the parallel story in John 12 shows that Judas was the disciple who became indignant about the nard. John adds an explanation: "He said this, not because he cared about the poor, but because he was a thief, and having charge of the moneybag he used to help himself to what was put into it" (John 12:6).

Mark, too, is making a connection between the anointing of Jesus and the treachery of Judas. Mark **14:10** introduces the story of Judas's betrayal with the word "then" or "and then." There's an explicit link between the two stories. In other words, Judas's love for money motivated him to betray Jesus. He would have loved to get his hands on some of that money, but it was "wasted" on Jesus, so he ended up selling Jesus for some silver coins.

Jesus does not pull any punches with his disciples. He rebukes them strongly and comes to the woman's defense. She should not be corrected; they should. They are blind to the true motives and value of this moment. Jesus calls it a "beautiful thing" (**v 6**). The disciples do not see the beauty of the woman's act because they fail to see the value of Jesus.

Jesus does not deny that the poor are important. He affirms that there will always be an opportunity to do something for them (**v 7**). But this woman has seized her only opportunity to declare how much she values Jesus. Meanwhile, the religious leaders are looking for an opportunity to kill Jesus (**v 1**), and Judas is looking for an opportunity to betray him for money (**v 11**).

Jesus says that the woman has anointed him for his burial (**v 8**). The disciples still do not understand his coming death, burial, and resurrection. They do not understand that just as this woman broke and poured out her most valuable treasure, so also the Father has sent his greatest treasure in the gift of his Son—whose body will be broken and whose blood will be poured out for the forgiveness of many.

Jesus did more than defend this woman. He gave her something greater. Her story is now tied to the telling of the gospel story throughout the world (**v 9**). What she has done will be told in memory of her. This text is being fulfilled right now as you read her story, wherever you are in this world. Her legacy is her love for Jesus. Don't you want that to be the one thing that stands out about your legacy as well?

Preparations for the Lord's Supper

The rejection theme will continue later in Mark 14, as Jesus predicts Judas' betrayal. But first, Mark wants us to know beyond a shadow of a doubt that Jesus is in control over all the plots and plans against him. In **verses 12-16** he inserts a story about how they got the room in which they celebrated the Passover.

This passage has similarities with the story of Jesus' entry into Jerusalem in Mark 11:1-11. Jesus sends two of his disciples (11:1; **14:13**) and tells them to go into the village (11:2) or city (**14:13**), to prepare for an event. Both passages have seemingly random, chance encounters ("You will find a colt tied," 11:2; "a man carrying a jar of water will meet you," **14:13**). In both passages, the disciples are told the exact words to say ("The Lord has need of it," 11:3; "The Teacher says, Where is my guest room?" **14:14**). Finally, in both stories, things happen exactly as Jesus said they would.

The effect of both stories in the narrative is to show us that Jesus is in complete control. In Mark 14, there are plots swirling around Jesus to kill him. His disciples are going to betray him, deny him, and abandon him. But he never responds with fear or desperation. He does not lash out or anxiously try to maneuver or manipulate the situation. He does not hide in fear or retreat from the dangerous plots around him. He walks through these events with a sovereign freedom and a striking note of authority. It is his colt, his temple, his guest room. No one outsmarts him, overpowers him, outmaneuvers him, catches him off guard, or takes his life from him. He will lay it down of his own accord (John 10:18)—and he will raise it up as well. *Don't you dare draw the conclusion that Jesus is out of his depth here,* Mark is telling us. *He remains in complete control!*

Jesus is still in control over all that happens on earth. His sovereign freedom is the best news in the world. Here I am, a small and limited creature, walking through this vast world of time. How will I make it? This text heralds the rock-solid truth that God rules and reigns over this world in meticulous detail. He is not just generally in control over some things or many things or most things, but meticulously in control of all things. "He is before all things, and in him all things hold together" (Colossians 1:17)—including our lives.

Questions for reflection

1. What similarities and differences do you see between the unnamed woman in Mark 14 and the unnamed woman in Mark 12? What does Jesus' response to both women teach us?

2. What do you do with your money? What does that say about your worship?

3. What threatens to get in the way of making Christ your highest treasure?

PART TWO

The next passage continues the theme of the betrayal, rejection, and denial of Jesus. Mark offers a rejection sandwich once more in Mark **14:17-31**. It begins with a prophecy of Judas' betrayal (**v 17-21**) and ends with a prophecy of Peter's denial (**v 26-31**). In the middle of the sandwich, Mark shows the divine purpose behind the drama of betrayal and denial.

Jesus Predicts Judas's Betrayal

Passover was a celebration commemorating how the Jews were delivered from the Egyptians. In the first Passover, the Jews put the blood of a lamb on the door frames so that the Lord would "pass over" their home and not permit **the destroyer** to kill their firstborn (Exodus 12:23). In the annual commemoration, the oldest man in the family would retell the story with emphasis on remembering the past deliverance and looking forward to the future deliverance that the Messiah would bring.

The celebration consisted of four parts, each one concluding with the drinking of a cup of wine. The actual meal was eaten in the third part of the evening. It is at this point that Jesus declares that someone in the room will betray him (Mark **14:18**).

Mark is being selective in his account. He focuses only on Jesus' betrayal and his coming death as a sacrifice in fulfillment of the Passover sacrifice. He does not record the entire Passover ceremony or mention the presence of other people besides the twelve—although it seems likely that others would have been there too (see James R. Edwards, *The Gospel of Mark*, p 422). Who among these will betray Jesus? They start asking, "Is it I?" (**v 21**). But Jesus narrows it down to "one of the twelve" (**v 20**). The suspects are those who have had their hands in Jesus' own bowl.

The betrayal does not take Jesus by surprise. He predicts it, and he says it was prophesied. All things will happen according to what

Scripture says (**v 21**). But he also condemns the person who is to carry out the betrayal. This betrayal is a great evil, and God will render judgment, but it is all part of God's all-wise, predestined plan. God is sovereign, but humans are still responsible for what we do.

Jesus Predicts Peter's Denial

The second piece of bread in this rejection sandwich is **verses 26-31**.

Mark says they sang a hymn (**v 26**). This is probably a reference to the singing of Psalms 116 – 118, which usually happened around midnight with the drinking of the fourth cup of wine. We have reached another time period that Mark 13 told us to watch for with respect to the coming of the Son of Man: midnight.

Jesus predicts the desertion of the disciples. They will all scatter (**14:27**). Once again, this will be a fulfillment of Scripture: Jesus quotes Zechariah 13:7. It is a stunning prophecy. Notice the first person singular: "I" will strike. God will strike Jesus the shepherd. Evil will be used by God to fulfill his saving purpose. It is just like Isaiah 53:10—"Yet it was the will of the LORD to crush him; he has put him to grief."

But there is a note of hope. *I will be struck. You will scatter. But I will be raised from the dead. Then I will go before you to Galilee* (Mark **14:28**). In other words, he will gather them again.

These words of prophecy trigger a response of spiritual bravado. Peter previously rebuked Jesus for saying he was going to die (Mark 8:32). Now he promises that even if everyone falls away, he will not (**14:29**). But Jesus tells Peter where the story will go. "Before the rooster crows twice, you will deny me three times" (**v 30**).

Peter responds emphatically: he would rather die than deny Jesus. "And they all said the same" (**v 31**). They all respond with bravado. They think that nothing could ever destroy their commitment and resolve.

The Last Supper

In the middle of it all, Jesus once again tells them about the coming cross and the coming kingdom—explaining the divine design for his death in pictorial form. He puts his death and resurrection into the symbols offered by the meal. The broken bread represents his body (**v 22**). The wine that is poured out really represents the shedding of his blood (**v 24**).

The climax of the whole meal comes with Jesus' words indicating that his work is really a covenant—a bond in blood that will unite God and his people. The blood here is significant. Throughout the Old Testament sacrificial system, the life of a creature was symbolized by its blood. Therefore, Jesus' blood is a reference to his very life. Jesus' life was the payment that would establish a new covenantal arrangement between God and his people.

The phrase "blood of the covenant" cannot be understood without reference to the old covenant. That covenant was established when Moses threw the blood of sacrificial animals over the people as they promised to keep God's commandments (Exodus 24:3-8). The blood symbolized the sealing of the covenant. But later prophets announced that a day would come when God would make a new covenant with his people (Jeremiah 31:31-34). Jesus says that that day has now come. This new covenant is about to be purchased and sealed with the lifeblood of the Lamb of God, slain for sinners. In fact, this blood will not simply be thrown over the people; they will drink it, taking it deep inside of themselves.

There are two points that merit further consideration. The first is how hard it is to spot counterfeit Christianity. Isn't it amazing that none of the disciples have figured out that something is off about Judas? When Jesus says, "One of you will betray me," no one says, *It must be Judas.* Judas has fooled all of them. He can talk the talk, and he looks like he belongs there. But it is all a sham.

The second is how patient Jesus is. The disciples have been spiritually blind and slow to understand when Jesus has told them about his coming death and resurrection. He tries again here with perfect patience. He says, *Let me give you a picture of what I am trying to say.* Jesus' predictions of the betrayals highlight this as well. He is eating with Judas. He is also eating with those who will deny him and leave him. Yet he continues to speak words of truth and love to them.

> The Lord's Supper is a meal for sinners, not achievers.

The **Lord's Supper** is a meal for sinners, not achievers. The use of the word "all" is somewhat haunting throughout this section. They "all" drank of the cup (Mark **14:23**). Even though they "all" swore that they would not fall away, they would "all" fall away (**v 27**) and they would "all" flee (**v 50**) from Jesus. This is obviously not a meal only for those who merit it. The prerequisite is need. People who eat and drink have to recognize their need for food and drink. Taking this meal means recognizing your need for Jesus' body and blood to save you.

On the cross, Jesus completed the work that would bring the people of God to God forever. To all the people like Peter, who say, "I got this," Jesus says, *No, look again. Don't trust in what you do. Trust in what I do. I have you. I paid for you. I will never let you go.*

The Agony in Gethsemane

The Gospel of Mark loves to put events together in threes. There are three boat scenes, where the disciples fail to understand who Jesus is (4:35-41, 6:45-52, 8:14-21). There are three **passion** predictions, and each time the disciples again fail to understand (8:31 – 10:45). There are three trips to the temple, and in each one the people fail to grasp that the Messiah has come to his temple. In this next section, Jesus prays three times in the garden, while urging the disciples three times to stay awake (**14:32-42**).

Gethsemane is on the lower slopes of the Mount of Olives—about half a mile from the city. Luke tells us that Jesus came here often to pray (Luke 22:39), and that is why Judas knew where to find him.

Jesus begins with a group of disciples. Instructing them to "sit here while I pray" (Mark **14:32**), he moves away with just Peter, James, and John. He becomes "greatly distressed and troubled" (**v 33**)—Mark piles up words for deep emotional turmoil.

Jesus tells the three disciples that his whole soul is overcome with sorrow and grief—not only to the point of exhaustion but to the point of death (**v 34**). So he commands Peter, James, and John to stay and pray and watch—and moves on alone.

Jesus does not just fold his hands and get on his knees. Mark tells us that he "fell on the ground" (**v 35**). Imagine a workout that is so intense that you virtually collapse on the ground. This is much more intense than that! Incalculable darkness has descended on Jesus and the strain is taking a toll on his very body. The weight of sorrow has made him collapse to the ground.

Then we hear the prayer of a heart, soul, and will in agony. Jesus is truly God, but he is also truly human. Here we see Jesus' human will wrestling with the divine will of the Father. He "prayed that, if it were possible, the hour might pass from him" (**v 35**). The "hour" is the moment God has ordained for his sacrifice as the Lamb of God. He is asking if the hour could pass—if there is some possible way to take a detour. In **verse 36** Mark zooms in for more detail on this prayer. It is filled with notes of reverence toward and intimacy with the Father. "Abba" is the Aramaic word for "father." The Son knows the Father as intimately and perfectly as possible. He knows that the Father can do all things—so he brings the request: "Remove this cup from me."

This is a holy moment. The Son knows the Father and his strength and power. Is there any other way than this cup? Isaac was spared even while Abraham held the knife over him because the Lord provided an alternative sacrifice (Genesis 22). But this time, heaven is silent. There is no other way and no other sacrifice.

In this sheer agony, can the will of the Son stay aligned with the will of the Father? Jesus has taught the disciples to pray, "Your kingdom come, your will be done, on earth as it is in heaven" (Matthew 6:10). He now prays the deepest and truest expression of that prayer ever uttered. He has come from heaven to earth to do the Father's will on earth as it is done in heaven, and so he prays in complete submission: "Yet not what I will, but what you will" (Mark **14:36**).

Jesus is totally awake to the plan of the Father. The disciples are the opposite. They are asleep (**v 37**). They certainly are not aligning their hearts and minds to the purpose of the Father! Jesus rebukes them: they must watch and pray in order not to enter into temptation (**v 38**). He warns them that the spirit is willing but the flesh is weak. He is saying, *Do not be content with good intentions. Good intentions in your spirit will be no match for the weakness of your flesh without the sustaining power of prayer.*

But we know the disciples' track record when it comes to understanding and obeying what Jesus says to them. Unsurprisingly, this awful scene is now replayed twice more.

Awake and Asleep Again

"Again he went away and prayed, saying the same words" (**v 39**). It is instructive to see that Jesus needed to pray multiple times. We do, too. We naturally shrink back from the prospect of suffering. Therefore, persistent prayer is the only way to stay aligned with the Father's will. We don't necessarily need to always pray new things. Sometimes we need to keep praying the same things in order to get God's will to be securely fastened within us.

Again, Jesus comes back and finds the disciples sleeping (**v 40**). They are without excuse, and they don't even have any words of response. Mark portrays the disciples as being almost in a total stupor—physically and spiritually. They are not awake, in any sense of the word.

A third time, Jesus comes to the disciples after praying alone. Are they *still* asleep (**v 41**)? Could they not watch and pray? Yet this time he does not rebuke them. The time to watch and pray is past; "the hour has come" (**v 41**). The Son is now betrayed into the hands of sinners. Jesus moves forward toward the cross like an arrow aligned with the aim of his Father.

Questions for reflection

1. What moment in Mark 14 do you find most moving so far?

2. Why do you think Jesus was so deeply troubled as he approached death?

3. Is your relationship with God in prayer gathering dust or growing in intimacy? What are some ways you can grow in prayer?

PART THREE

The Cup of Wrath

In the Old Testament, the "cup" of wrath or judgment is a symbol of the suffering and punishment that God's enemies experience (see Isaiah 51:17). God now held out the cup of wrath for his Son to drink. Would God really plan this for his only Son? Yes. "Yet it was the will of the LORD to crush him; he has put him to grief" (53:10). Jesus drank the cup in order to make "an offering for guilt" (v 10). Jesus is the sacrificial Lamb, and the Lord "has laid on him the iniquity of us all" (v 6).

Contemplate this cup for a moment. What would it taste like to drink to the dregs the cup of God's fiery wrath for every sin (in thought, attitude, or action) that we have ever committed? How much worse would it be to drink the cup of wrath for the sins of many other people? It is staggering. No wonder Jesus was in such anguish.

Mark is helping us to see that, in one sense, Jesus was already being crucified. Jesus' hands and feet were crucified on the cross, but his heart and will were crucified here. Gethsemane can be called the real earthly battle before Calvary.

It reminds me of something J.R.R. Tolkien said in *The Hobbit* about the decision of the main character, Bilbo, to walk down a tunnel into a dragon's lair:

"Going on from there was the bravest thing he ever did. The tremendous things that happened afterward were as nothing compared to it. He fought the real battle in the tunnel alone, before he ever saw the vast danger that lay in wait." (p 193)

This moment in Gethsemane was the definitive earthly step for Jesus. But unlike Bilbo, he knew the vast suffering that awaited him. And he still chose to go. Jesus' whole life was a life of obedience, but this moment tested his heart and mind more than any other earthly moment.

You may have noticed that I keep using the adjective "earthly." I make that distinction because there was an even more decisive step in heaven: the moment he stepped down from heaven to earth. He laid aside his glory and emptied himself in the incarnation by adding true humanity to his deity (Philippians 2:7). He took on the form of a servant so that he could be the servant prophesied in Isaiah. That first step down from heaven to earth started a journey of descent. Now he is ready to go to the lowest rung—to the excruciating depths of suffering in facing the wrath of God on the cross. Jesus prayed to stay totally awake to and aligned with the Father's plan and purpose. Let us pray that our hearts will be awakened with fresh awe as we see what the Son has done for us and for our salvation.

Forsaken by the Jews

The first half of chapter 14 focused on Jesus' predictions of Judas' betrayal and Peter's denial, and the second half focuses on the fulfillment of those predictions. Jesus and his claims are on trial in these verses as Mark narrates the betrayal of Judas (Mark **14:43-52**), the trial of Jesus (**v 53-65**), and the denial of Peter (**v 66-72**).

The Betrayal of Judas

Judas comes, together with a whole crowd, to arrest Jesus. Judas kisses him—the sign of betrayal (**v 44-45**). They seize Jesus (**v 46**). Then one of the disciples takes out his sword and cuts off the ear of the servant of the high priest (**v 47**). We learn in John 18:10 that it was Peter. This impulsive behavior certainly fits with the profile of Peter in Mark's Gospel. In John's Gospel, Jesus tells Peter that he is wrong for taking up the sword (John 18:11). In Mark's Gospel, Jesus tells the crowd with swords and clubs that they don't understand the things of God either (Mark **14:48-49**). They are treating him like a robber on the run who has finally been outmaneuvered. But Jesus has not been hiding but teaching in the temple. They knew where to find him. Why didn't they seize him during those times? Jesus answers his own question: they are only seizing him now because now his hour has come. It is time for Scripture to be fulfilled (**v 49**).

All the disciples scatter (**v 50**), just as Jesus prophesied (v 27). The camera then suddenly zooms in on one unnamed follower in particular. Mark tells us that he is a young man and he is only wearing a linen cloth (**v 51**). The soldiers seize him, but they only get hold of the linen cloth, and so he runs away naked (**v 52**).

Why does Mark zoom in here? Commentators go all over the place in explaining this part of the story. Some even think that this is a reference to Mark himself—but that is sheer speculation. My hunch is that this story is another bridge between chapters 13 and 14. Mark wants us to know that the man left his clothes. It is a reference back to Jesus' prediction that people would be in such a hurry to flee that they would not go back to grab their cloak (13:16).

Now we come to the centerpiece of this passage: the trial of Jesus (**14:53-65**).

The Trial of Jesus

Notice the way that Mark sets the scene. Jesus and Peter are not far apart. Jesus goes into the house of the high priest, while Peter stops in the courtyard (**v 53-54**). Peter will come back into play soon—but first of all we come to the judicial proceedings against Jesus.

This "trial" is meant to serve justice, but it is actually a mockery of justice. Many scholars have written about how it contravened the rules for such trials (see David E. Garland, "Mark," in the *Zondervan Bible Background Commentary*, vol. 1, p 291).

Mark takes pains to inform us that Jesus faced trial alone, against many opponents. "The whole council were seeking testimony against Jesus" (**v 55**); "many bore false witness against him" (**v 56**); "they all condemned him as deserving death" (**v 64**). Mark does not record the voice of anyone who defended Jesus. He stood trial all alone, and everyone spoke against him.

As they make their accusations, Jesus remains silent—to the fury of the high priest (**v 60-61**). This is a fulfillment of Isaiah 53:7:

"He was oppressed, and he was afflicted,
  yet he opened not his mouth;
 like a lamb that is led to the slaughter,
  and like a sheep that before its shearers is silent,
  so he opened not his mouth."

Then the high priest asks, "Are you the Christ, the Son of the Blessed?" (Mark **14:61**). Jesus says, "I am, and you will see the Son of Man seated at the right hand of Power, and coming with the clouds of heaven" (**v 62**). The title "Son of Man," the "right hand of Power," and the "clouds of heaven" are all references to Daniel 7:13-14, a prophecy about the Messiah. Jesus could hardly make his claim clearer.

This passage goes right to the heart of the gospel as it lays out the identity of Jesus as both Isaiah's Suffering Servant and Daniel's son of man in power. Jesus is judged by humanity while at the same time being the authoritative Judge over humanity.

The high priest thinks Jesus has just uttered blasphemy (Mark **14:63-64**). Rather than tear his clothes in repentance, he tears them in outrage.

> Jesus, the Judge, is judged by humanity.

The irony is that *he* has just committed blasphemy. The eternal God is standing before them, and here he is claiming to be who he is, and they deny that it is him. The reader knows that Jesus is who he says he is. The priests think they are the judge over him, but he says that the next time they see him, the roles will be reversed: he will be at the right hand of God, coming on the clouds to judge and punish them.

The dynamics of this text are still on display today. People look at Jesus and pronounce a judgment over him. They act like the judge of Jesus. Some people even irreverently say that when they die, they will have questions to ask God. But this passage reminds us that we should be more concerned about the questions he will have for us.

Jesus (as the Judge) will question us about our sin; at the same time, Jesus (as the Savior) died for our sins. If you are not a Christian, justice speaks against you—it rightly and justly calls for your condemnation. But if you are in Christ, then Christ has taken your condemnation. The debt has been paid. The sentence of justice has been served. That is why 1 John 1:9 can say, "If we confess our sins, he is faithful *and just* to forgive us our sins and to cleanse us from all unrighteousness" (my italics).

Why is it just for God to forgive sinners instead of judge them? Because justice has already been served at the cross. The punishment has happened. Justice now calls for forgiveness. God is faithful to provide it when we confess.

As the trial closes, they insult Jesus and treat him with mockery; they cover his face, strike him, and tell him to prophesy (Mark **14:65**). But the reader gets a glimpse of a great irony because we can see what is happening in the courtyard at this same moment. Jesus' prophecy from the previous chapter is about to come true.

The Denial ("Trial") of Peter

We have been on the lookout for the coming of the Son of Man in power. Will he come in the evening or at midnight or when the rooster crows or in the morning? We come now to the rooster crowing.

While Jesus stands trial before the chief priest, Peter stands on trial before the servant girl of the high priest. "You also were with the Nazarene, Jesus," she accuses him (**v 67**).

Peter denies the fact that he knows Jesus three times—twice to the servant girl and a third time to the other bystanders (**v 68, 70, 71**). Peter, the disciple who swore with the most bravado that he would not fall away (v 31), now denies Jesus in the most detailed, repeated way. He even invokes a curse on himself—he's saying, *Let me be cursed if I'm lying* (**v 71**). "I do not know this man of whom you speak," he insists.

How can you really know him and yet turn around and deny him? Has Peter ever really known Jesus? No; he has never really understood Jesus and his mission. All along, he has been thinking the things of man, not the things of God.

But at last Peter realizes the mistake he has made. "Immediately the rooster crowed a second time … And he broke down and wept" (**v 72**). He has failed to be awake at the time when it mattered.

Questions for reflection

1. What words would you use to describe Jesus in these scenes?

2. In what ways can we end up acting as the judge of Jesus instead of recognizing that Jesus is the Judge of us?

3. What message from this chapter do you need to share with someone this week?

14. THE DIVINE KING

Chapter 14 showed Jesus being forsaken by the Jews. Chapter 15 now highlights how Jesus is forsaken by the Gentiles. The chapter has three scenes: Jesus and Pilate (**v 1-15**), Jesus and the soldiers (**v 16-20**), and Jesus on the cross (**v 21-37**). There is rejection on the surface, but there is something much deeper happening beneath the surface. Mark keeps highlighting this undercurrent. Will the reader reject Jesus, too, like everyone in the narrative? Or do we have eyes to see and believe what is happening beneath the surface?

Jesus and Pilate

It's now morning, and the Jewish leaders bring Jesus to Pilate, the Roman governor. Pilate asks Jesus if he is the King of the Jews, and Jesus calmly answers, "You have said so" (**v 2**). The Jewish leaders accuse him of many things (**v 3**), and Pilate tries to force Jesus to respond to their accusations (**v 4**), but he will not. Pilate is amazed (**v 5**).

There are two deeper meanings here. First, Jesus' answer to Pilate points to the absurdity of the moment: "You have said so" (**v 2**). This is not an evasive answer. It is meant to provoke deeper reflection. He is a king, but not in the way Pilate is using the term. Pilate is thinking of a merely earthly, political ruler—one who might pose a threat to the rule of Rome. But Jesus is God and Lord over all—Pilate, Caesar, and everything that has breath. He will not simply say yes and allow a web of false connotations to define him. Pilate simply cannot fathom who he is. A simplistic summary like "King of the Jews" is so elementary that Jesus states the obvious: *That is all you know, so that is all you can say.*

The other deeper meaning is Jesus' silence (**v 5**). Jesus is silent, but that does not mean that he is not communicating. His silence is speaking volumes as the fulfillment of Isaiah 53:7.

The Deepest Injustice

The charge has shifted from the religious sphere (blasphemy, 14:64) to the political sphere (King of the Jews, **15:2**). But Pilate seems to realize that Jesus is not guilty; it is only out of envy that the chief priests have handed him over to him (**v 10**). He wants to find a way of freeing Jesus without offending the chief priests. He decides to take advantage of the tradition of releasing one prisoner at the Passover feast (**v 6**). When the crowds gather and demand their prisoner (**v 7**), Pilate offers them the innocent Jesus. But the chief priests stir up the crowds to choose Barabbas—a notoriously guilty murderer (**v 7, 11**). When Pilate asks them what they want him to do with Jesus, they cry out for his crucifixion (**v 12-14**). "What evil has he done?" asks Pilate—but the crowd refuses to produce any evidence. They simply shout more for his death. This is the clearest evidence against *them*: they, like the chief priests, are the guilty ones.

The crowd's choice of Barabbas is supposed to be shocking. Barabbas is guilty of insurrection and murder. He is really guilty. Jesus is really innocent. But the crowd chooses to release the guilty one and condemn the innocent one. Barabbas is what they think of when they think of a Messiah figure—someone who will murder the Romans and cause an insurrection. But Jesus is not that kind of Messiah. The crowd chooses the wrong Messiah figure.

At a deeper level, this is a picture of substitutionary **atonement**. The innocent one gets punished and the guilty one goes free. That is also true for everyone who is in Christ. We were guilty, and Jesus took our place. Imagine you were Barabbas. You were just released, and you know that you do not have to go through torture, scourging, and crucifixion. How would you react? I can picture Barabbas there with his thug friends, rejoicing that he got to go free. But he surely didn't understand. When he saw Jesus getting condemned, scourged, mocked, beaten, and murdered, did he ever think, *That should be me and should not be him*?

Pilate's actions are shocking too. This pagan Gentile is the only one to come to Jesus' defense: "What evil has he done?" he cries in **verse 14**. With the judge of the trial as Jesus' advocate, you would think that the verdict would be favorable! However, in a spineless perversion of justice, Pilate orders Jesus to be scourged and then releases him to the crowd to satisfy their bloodthirsty cries for crucifixion (**v 15**). Jesus' one-time advocate rejects him because he cares more about the reign of Caesar and its demands on him to keep the peace than he cares about the reign of "the King of the Jews."

Now injustice meets brutality—intense violence as Jesus is scourged (**v 15**). The leather whip has weights to tenderize the flesh and something sharp to catch the skin and tear it into ribbons. Jesus has red stripes up and down his back. But these wounds or stripes are our healing (Isaiah 53:5).

A growing number of people in our culture feel so weighed down with guilt and shame that they feel the need to punish or harm themselves. Cutting themselves feels somehow right or good, or like a relief. It is a horrible thing to be so weighed down with guilt and shame that self-harm feels like a helpful step. But the gospel gives us another way. Guilt and shame are real. Sins and failures lead to inner wounds. But giving yourself wounds cannot heal your wounds. Shedding your own blood cannot truly relieve you. It is in the shedding of Jesus' blood that there is healing.

Jesus and the Soldiers

The Roman soldiers lead Jesus away (Mark **15:16**). They seem to take special pains to ensure that Jesus is mocked to the maximum degree. Imagine a crown of thorns pressed into your skull like a series of nails hammered into place. The manifold disgrace that the soldiers heap upon Jesus probably exceeds the way in which they would carry out the punishment of common criminals.

The irony is unmistakable. The purple robe, the crown of thorns, the chanting and acclaiming as "King of the Jews," the reed, the kneeling and bowing—it all bears royal connotations. They are clearly mocking him, but just as clearly, the reader recognizes the truth hidden behind the scorn. Jesus is royalty; he should be dressed in royal robes with a crown and a reed (or scepter). They should anoint him, hail him as King, and bow before him. The truth of Jesus' deity is suppressed, but at the same time they almost can't help expressing it, even in a twisted and perverted way.

All eternity hinges on this question: do you see what everyone else in the story missed? Jesus is the divine King, who should be received and worshiped by the Jews and Gentiles, but instead he was rejected and condemned by the Jews and Gentiles in fulfillment of the Father's plan to save the Jews and the Gentiles.

Seeing this truth means that you can no longer live as the king of your life or try to save yourself—your King came from heaven to earth to take your place and bring you salvation. Embrace him as Savior. Hail him as Lord. Worship him as God.

The Cross of Christ

At the start of C.S. Lewis's *The Voyage of the Dawn Treader*, the three main characters, Lucy, Edmund, and Eustace, are looking at a painting of a ship. They cannot help but stare at the beauty of the painting—and before they know it, the picture comes to life, and they find themselves entering the story.

In the same way, the cross can become to us like a painting that we hang on our walls. We believe it, but if we are honest, it has simply blended into the background. We rarely notice it anymore.

My prayer is that as we gaze at the cross in Mark **15:21-39**, we will enter the story and experience it as if we were there. My hope is that you will hear the music playing softly in the background: "Were you there when they crucified my Lord?" May we be able to say, "I was there." And perhaps we will join the refrain, "Oh, sometimes it causes me to tremble, tremble, tremble."

Mark's account of the cross has three movements: (1) the reality of the cross (**v 21-37**), (2) the result of the cross (**v 38**), and (3) the response to the cross (**v 39**).

The Reality of the Cross

Verses 21-27 set the stage for the drama of the crucifixion. Mark calls attention to five background details that he does not want us to miss.

First, the camera zooms in on Simon of Cyrene being forced to carry the cross (**v 21**). This background detail is suggestive and illuminating in a few different ways.

Standard practice for crucifixion was that "every criminal condemned to death bears his cross on his back" (Plutarch, *Moralia* 554 A/B). This was the horizontal crossbeam, which would then be tied or nailed to the upright post at the site of crucifixion. The fact that Simon had to carry the crossbeam bears testimony to the gory truth that Jesus had been beaten so mercilessly that he was unable to carry his own crossbeam.

But there is more happening here than meets the eye. Why give Simon's name—and that of his two sons? Alexander and Rufus must have been known to Mark's readers. In fact, we learn in Romans 16:13 that someone called Rufus was a member in the church of Rome—perhaps the same Rufus. It could be that Simon's participation in carrying the cross was a moment that was so defining for these two brothers that one or both of them became believers.

More to the point in terms of Mark's thematic focus, the language Mark uses in Mark **15:21** is the language of discipleship: to take up one's cross and follow Jesus (see 8:34). Simon becomes the first one to obey Jesus' command—in a hauntingly literal sense. The cost of discipleship stands out. This verse will not permit us to maintain a shallow, sentimental view of what it means to carry our cross to follow Jesus.

Second, Mark draws our gaze to the wine mixed with **myrrh** (**v 23**). Why does he want us to catch this detail? Because Jesus is fulfilling a picture of the suffering of the righteous one in Psalm 69:19-21. In this psalm, the righteous one meets with pitiless reproach, shame, and dishonor (v 19). Part of the dishonor was to be offered poison for food and sour wine as a drink (v 21). Sour wine mixed with myrrh was a narcotic, so its purpose was to deaden the pain of crucifixion; but it probably was also offered as part of the mockery—since a cup of wine would be offered to a victorious king.

Jesus refuses this drink, but we are not explicitly told why. Surely, he wants his final act of obedience to be done in a state that is fully conscious and alert to the will of his Father. But it may also be in fulfillment of his earlier vow at the Passover meal that he would not drink of the fruit of the vine until the time when he will drink it new in the kingdom of God (Mark 14:25).

> Jesus has been shamed to the full extent that the soldiers can achieve.

Third, Mark points out that the soldiers divided Jesus' garments (**15:24**). This detail matters because it is part of the picture prophesied in the psalms. The psalmist tells the gruesome story of being encircled by evildoers who pierce his hands and feet, and gloat over him as they divide his garments and cast lots for them (Psalm 22:16-18). Jesus is stripped naked in shame and reproach, and all that is left of his possessions is taken. He has been shamed to the full extent that the soldiers can achieve.

Fourth, Mark wants his readers to see when the crucifixion began: at the third hour (Mark **15:25**). The Jewish way of counting time started with sunrise at around 6 a.m. The third hour is therefore 9 a.m.

Fifth, Mark highlights the inscription that contains the charge against Jesus: "The King of the Jews" (**v 26**). The irony, of course, is that his accusers are saying more than they understand. The charge is true. He really is the King of the Jews—and the eternal King of the universe.

Sixth, Mark directs our gaze to the right and left of Jesus, where we see two others nailed to crosses. The irony here is that James and John had asked to sit at Jesus' right and left for his coronation when he entered Jerusalem (Mark 10:37). Jesus told them that they did not really understand what they were asking. Now we see why. The two on his left and right are not disciples but convicted criminals. Once again this is a fulfillment of Scripture, which promised that he would be "numbered with the transgressors" (Isaiah 53:12).

Mark wants us to understand that these events are incredibly painful but completely purposeful. The people involved do not see the full picture and the larger story. God's prophesied plan is unfolding before their eyes, but they do not have eyes to see it. Do we?

Questions for reflection

1. Why is indifference an inappropriate response to Jesus? What would you say to someone who is indifferent to him?

2. Do you ever find that you have become numb to the glories of the cross because the story is so familiar? How can you help yourself to experience the story afresh?

3. What comfort does Mark's account of the lead-up to the cross give us in times when we ourselves are suffering?

PART TWO

Circles of Rejection

Now the story takes the reader through a series of concentric circles of rejection, leading to a climax at the center (Mark **15:29-37**). We begin at the edges of the scene and keep moving closer to the cross.

In the first circle, we stand on the outskirts and see people passing by on the road (**v 29-30**). They do not draw near to look more closely; they merely mock from a distance. But they are still participants in the story. They play the part of the wicked in Psalm 22:7-8 as they wag their heads and taunt Jesus. If Twitter had been around, these people would have spread the hashtag #saveyourself.

There is dual irony here. They do not understand that he is not here to save himself. They are blind to what is really happening. They mock Jesus as the one who would destroy the temple and rebuild it in three days. They fail to see that Jesus was speaking of the temple of his body. They are witnessing the destruction of the temple. They are certainly blind to the fact that in three days it will rise again.

In the second circle, drawing nearer, we see the religious leaders (Mark **15:31-32**). All of the original accusers are there to eagerly hurl their abuse at him. But again these people say more than they know. They are right when they say, "He saved others, but he cannot save himself" (**v 31**). Jesus cannot save others and save himself. He can only save others by staying on the cross and not saving himself. He could come down. In fact, he could call down legions of angels (Matthew 26:53). "Let the Christ, the King of Israel, come down now from the cross that we may see and believe," they cry (Mark **15:32**). But if he does, there will be no gospel achieved and nothing to believe. They fail to grasp the fact that it is not the nails that hold him there on that cross.

In the third circle, we move one step closer. No longer do we stand beneath the cross with the religious leaders. Now we come to those on the other two crosses. Even they have joined the mockery: "Those who were crucified with him also reviled him" (**v 32**). Victims on the cross would die by suffocating. You would have to push up with your legs and suffer the pain of the nail in your feet in order to breathe. Knowing this makes it all the more amazing that these two criminals were using their dying breaths to revile Jesus.

But we have not yet arrived at the center: the cross of Christ. The innermost circle comes in **verses 33-37**. The scene changes as darkness descends on the land from noon until 3 p.m. (from the sixth to the ninth hour). It is an unnatural darkness at what should be the brightest time of the day. This is not a fluke of the weather but a sign of divine judgment. In Amos 8:9-10, God promised to punish his people by sending darkness at noon. The darkness would be "like the mourning for an only son." This darkness signals God's judgment— but also his own grief at the death of his only Son.

Suddenly the cry of the Son pierces the darkness.

"And at the ninth hour Jesus cried with a loud voice, 'Eloi, Eloi, lema sabachthani?' which means, 'My God, my God, why have you forsaken me?'" (Mark **15:34**)

This cry from the cross has been called "the cry of the condemned." It represents the deepest possible pain. The Father and the Son have enjoyed perfect, unbroken harmony and fellowship in the Trinity for all of eternity—until now. In this climactic moment, the Father places the sin of the world upon his Son as the Lamb of God. The Father, who has eyes too pure to behold sin, turns his face away from his Son for the first and only time. Jesus endures a moment of separation from God. This is far worse than the mocking, scourging, and crucifixion. This is the searing pain of separation from God and the damnation of God. Jesus drank the cup of condemnation to the dregs.

> The Father turns his face away from his Son for the first and only time.

What should we see in the agony of this moment? I once read the story of a family that had waited too long to abandon their home as wildfires spread around them. The blazing fires surrounded them, blocking every escape route. The desperate dad had an idea. He had recently burned some trash in the field behind their home. They went to that spot. The children lay down first, then the mother covered the children, and the father put his own body on top, over all of them. The fires raged around them. They felt the searing heat, but they were spared because the fire did not come to the spot where they lay. There was nothing left there to burn.

In the same way, the cross is the one safe place for sinners to run to. The fire of God's wrath fell there once, and it will never fall there again. Here we have the answer to the cry of the condemned. "Why have you forsaken me?" The answer is: so that we would never be forsaken. Jesus was forsaken so we could be accepted. The place where he was condemned becomes the very spot where we hear the words "There is therefore now no condemnation for those who are in Christ Jesus" (Romans 8:1). The cross is safe ground for us because it is singed ground. The fire fell there once and will never fall there again.

Someone ran to give Jesus a drink (Mark **15:36**). But it was too late. "Jesus uttered a loud cry and breathed his last" (**v 37**). The agony of the cross was complete.

The Result of the Cross

Immediately Mark moves the camera lens from the cross to the temple. The temple curtain separated off the Most Holy Place, which represented God's presence. No one but the high priest was able to enter behind the curtain. Now it is torn in two (**v 38**). This is obviously a supernatural sign, but what does it signify?

There is a linguistic clue in that the word for "torn" only occurs one other time in Mark: at Jesus' baptism. Jesus saw "the heavens being torn open" (Mark 1:10). It is the answer to the prayer of Isaiah 64:1: "Oh that you would rend [or tear] the heavens and come down." Isaiah pictures heaven and earth as being separated by a barrier. Only God can break that barrier.

At Jesus' baptism we saw that God had come from heaven to earth. Now we see why: it was so that we could go from earth to heaven. Sinful humanity could never enter God's presence. Access to God is now open to us because the barrier is broken. The veil is torn. We can enter by the new and living way that Jesus opened for us through the curtain (Hebrews 10:20).

The Response to the Cross

The Roman centurion was perhaps the least likely person to see the cross of Jesus as the victory of God's Son. He must have seen hundreds of executions, all of them showing the victory of Rome. But this one was unlike any other. He saw the way Jesus breathed his last (Mark **15:39**). What did he see? The centurion saw that Jesus died with a "loud cry" (**v 37**): a shout of victory, not a whimper of defeat. Imagine his confusion. Was that a victory shout? What was going on?

Then his eyes were opened, and the truth became clear: this is the Son of God! This explosive realization changed everything. *If he is not dying for his own sin or paying for his own crimes, then he must be paying for mine!*

This is the point of the whole passage: those who see what the cross is (**v 21-37**) and what it does (**v 38**) come to embrace who Jesus really is (**v 39**).

This confession of faith answers the cry of the cross. Jesus was forsaken so that the centurion could be accepted. The same dynamic occurs at the beginning and end of Psalm 22. The psalm opens with the question of why God has forsaken the Messiah. The end of the psalm answers that question: so that God can accept the nations (v 27). The psalm begins with the same words as Jesus' cry on the cross and ends with the nations worshiping the Lord.

The centurion came to know and confess what God the Father had already confessed and would confess one more time: Jesus is the Son of God. The Father confessed this at the baptism: "You are my beloved Son; with you I am well pleased" (Mark 1:11). He confessed it in the middle of Mark's Gospel at the Mount of Transfiguration: "This is my beloved Son; listen to him" (9:7). He would confess it again in three days at the resurrection by acting in such a way as to say, *Arise, my Son.*

The Women at a Distance

The centurion stands right in front of the cross. The women, by contrast, are "at a distance" (**15:40**). The three women are identified as Mary Magdalene, Mary the mother of James and Joses, and Salome. Mary Magdalene is a close follower. The second Mary is Jesus' mother—she was also identified as the mother of James and Joses in Mark 6:3. Salome is probably the wife of Zebedee and the mother of James and John (she is probably the same person as Mary in Matthew 27:56 and 28:1). Why is it significant that they are looking "from a distance"? This is an allusion to Psalm 38:11:

"My friends and companions stand aloof from my plague,
    and my nearest kin stand far off."

Mary Magdalene and Salome were Jesus' friends. His mother, Mary, was his nearest kin. They used to follow him and minister to him in Galilee (Mark **15:41**). Now, in Jerusalem, they look at him from a distance as he is considered a plague—condemned and cursed.

Joseph of Arimathea before Pilate

It is now Friday evening, and there is a rush to bury Jesus before the Sabbath day starts. This evening is full of surprises (**v 42-46**).

A Surprising Disciple

Joseph of Arimathea is like the centurion in being one of the least likely candidates for discipleship. He is a "respected member of the council" (**v 43**). We have not met anyone from the Jewish council that was an advocate for Jesus while he was alive. One commentator notes that perhaps we have side by side here the centurion (a commander of the Romans) and Joseph (a leader of the Jews) to show that Jesus is the Savior of both the Gentiles and the Jews (James R. Edwards, *The Gospel of Mark*, p 488).

A Surprising Request

The request for the body of Jesus is truly miraculous. Joseph "took courage and went to Pilate and asked for the body of Jesus" (**v 43**). I think we need to understand why this request required courage. Roman law made it clear that the penalty for capital crimes included the loss of all honor in death—even burial. The Roman writer Tacitus says, "People sentenced to death forfeited their property and were forbidden burial" (*Annals* 6.29). Part of the shame of crucifixion was to show that no one cared for you. You were left to rot on the cross or be eaten by animals or birds. So, it would require courage even for a family member to ask for the body of someone convicted of high treason. It required even more courage for someone who was not a family member.

So this is a surprising twist: an unrelated person from the group that universally condemned Jesus is the one who asks for his body. One commentator says it just right: "His request was daring because it amounted to a confession of his commitment to the condemned and crucified Jesus" (William Lane, *The Gospel of Mark*, p 579). The Jewish council sought Jesus' death when he was alive, but now one of them shows allegiance to him after his death.

A Surprisingly Quick Death

Pilate expresses surprise that Jesus has already died (**v 44**). He summons the centurion to make sure that Jesus is really dead, and the centurion confirms it.

We learn from the Gospel of John that this quick death was important to fulfill prophecy. Soldiers would hasten a crucified criminal's death by breaking their legs so they couldn't push up to get a breath. But when they came to break Jesus' legs, they discovered he was already dead. This fulfilled the prophecy that none of his bones would be broken (John 19:36; Psalm 34:20).

A Surprising Release

Then there's an even greater twist: even though Jesus has been crucified for claiming to be King of the Jews, the Roman governor, Pilate, allows Joseph to take his body for a decent burial (Mark **15:45**).

A Surprising Burial

Burial for a Jew would have involved washing the body before wrapping it tightly with linen. John's Gospel confirms that Jesus was buried according to Jewish tradition (John 19:40).

A tomb cut out of rock (Mark **15:46**) would have been very expensive. In fact, the detail of a stone being rolled against the entrance fits the picture of a very fine tomb indeed for this time period.

> "If the tomb was an exceptionally fine one, it may have had an elaborate disc-shaped stone, about a yard in diameter, like a millstone, which was placed in a wide slot cut into the rock. Since the groove into which the stone fitted sloped toward the doorway, it could be easily rolled into place; but to roll the stone aside would require the strength of several men. Only a few tombs with such rolling stones are known in Palestine, but all of them date from the period of Jesus."
>
> (William Lane, *The Gospel of Mark*, p 581)

Jesus died as a convicted criminal but was buried like a rich man. This matters because it was a fulfillment of Isaiah 53:9.

> "And they made his grave with the wicked
> and with a rich man in his death,
>   although he had done no violence,
>   and there was no deceit in his mouth."

Once again, there is a story of Scripture unfolding here that is bigger than anyone really realized—down to the detail and the timing of everything.

Questions for reflection

1. Are you ever discouraged by all the ways that people mock, slander, and slight the worth of Jesus today? In the midst of that mockery, what hope does this text give you personally?

2. Jesus cried, "Why have you forsaken me?" so that we don't have to. How does the truth that you are never forsaken by God impact your daily life?

3. Why is it so important that the story of the cross has so many links with the Old Testament?

PART THREE

The Women at the Tomb

Mark **15:47** is a transitional verse that goes with the scene on Friday night, but also moves us into the next section by re-introducing the women. It makes an important point: Mary Magdalene and Mary the mother of Jesus saw where Joseph had laid Jesus. This is a signal to us that the women got the identity of the tomb right—that is, they went to the right tomb on Sunday morning because they knew which one it was.

Mark **16:1** shows us that the Jewish women observed the Sabbath—and Jesus did too. He died on Passover (Friday) and rested in the grave on the Sabbath (Saturday). What would happen on the first day of the week (Sunday)?

Every detail in the following verses points us to the answer.

The Attempt to Anoint Jesus

In Jewish culture, spices were used to deal with or offset the odor that would come from decomposition. The women think Jesus' body will decay so they are going to deal with that. They bring spices to anoint him (**v 1**). There is irony at work here. Jesus said that he would be killed and then on the third day he would rise. But no one seems to believe that. No one comes to the tomb to check out his claim of resurrection. The women go to the tomb not to witness his resurrection but to delay his decomposition.

The Sun

The signal that it is now a new day is the rising of the sun (**v 2**). But the sun in the sky is not the only thing that has risen!

The Question

"Who will roll away the stone for us?" (**v 3**). That is exactly the right question to ask. The women identify a flaw in their plan. It would take several strong men to move the stone. They cannot do it. Who will? The answer comes in **verse 4**. The stone is very large, but it has been moved.

The Rebuke of the Angel

The empty tomb provides evidence that the body is not there but no evidence for what has happened to it. Has someone stolen it? Entering the tomb, the women meet a messenger from heaven who proclaims the right answer (**v 5**). The angel preaches the gospel and rebukes the misguided plans of the women all in the same message.

"You seek Jesus of Nazareth, who was crucified. He has risen; he
is not here. See the place where they laid him." (**v 6**)

All their preparations to deal with death have left them unprepared to deal with resurrected life!

The Passive Construction

"He has risen" (**v 6**). It doesn't come across in the ESV translation, but the Greek here is a passive construction: "he has been raised." We have seen Mark use passive constructions like this before to highlight what God is doing:

- ▧ The temple curtain "was torn" = God tore it (15:38)

- ▧ The stone "had been rolled back" = God rolled it back (**16:4**)

- ▧ Jesus was raised = God raised Jesus from the dead (**v 6**)

Why does this matter? Certainly Jesus himself was active in the resurrection. John 10:18 tells us that Jesus has authority to lay down his life and to take it up again. But the passive construction here highlights the fact that, supremely, God is the one who has done this. This is the Father's vindication of the Son. Jesus was tried unjustly by wicked people. Now heaven declares its verdict. Everything that Jesus said and everything that Jesus did was right. Arise!

That is why 1 Timothy 3:16 can say that Jesus was manifested in the flesh (the incarnation) and was vindicated (or justified) in the Spirit (the resurrection). Jesus "was declared to be the Son of God in power according to the Spirit of holiness by his resurrection from the dead" (Romans 1:4). God raised Jesus from the dead by the power of the Spirit, and in that moment Jesus was justified by the Father—that is, all his claims and deeds were declared to be true and right. That is why Scripture can say that Jesus was raised for our justification (Romans 4:25). Jesus' justification at his resurrection forms the basis of our justification or vindication before the judgment throne.

Peter and the Scattered Disciples

Peter denied Jesus to save himself. Jesus took up his cross to save Peter; now, Jesus will not deny Peter but will embrace him as one of his disciples. The word of the angel is a message of hope, not scorn, for Peter and the scattered disciples. "Tell his disciples and Peter that he is going before you to Galilee" (Mark **16:7**).

The angel also points to the vindication of Jesus' words. He will meet them in Galilee, just as he said (**v 7**; see 14:27-28). They had been together in Galilee; they were scattered in Jerusalem. But Jesus will gather them again in Galilee, where they will finally see him with new eyes.

The Testimony of the Women

Two of the women who had been present when Jesus died (15:40) were observers of his burial (15:47); all three were witnesses of the empty tomb (**16:1-8**). They are the witnesses of the essential facts of the gospel (see 1 Corinthians 15:3-4).

This fits the insider/outsider theme we have seen throughout Mark. Jewish culture did not place any value on the testimony of women

(*Mishnah Rosh Hashanah* 1.8)—it was not even admissible in court. But women are the ones who are given the testimony of the empty tomb.

This could have been embarrassing for the church. The testimony of women lacked value as evidence. But it is one reason why the resurrection account cannot be a fabrication. Why would the early Christians have invented this detail? It would have been better to record male witnesses. The reason the church recorded the experiences of the women is because they really happened.

A Surprising Ending

I do not believe Mark 16:9-20 is part of Scripture. In other words, I do not think Mark wrote it, but that others added it later. There are several reasons for thinking this:

- Mark 16:9-20 is not found in our oldest and most reliable Greek manuscripts of the New Testament (e.g., *Codex Sinaiticus; Codex Vaticanus*).

- It is also not mentioned in the writings of early Christians, such as Clement of Alexandria (d. 215), Origen (d. 253), Eusebius (d. 340), or Jerome (d. 420).

- The language is different from the rest of Mark. One of the longer endings introduces nine new words that are found nowhere in Mark, and the even longer ending has an additional 18 new words that are not found in Mark.

- The style of the writing is also different. Mark 16:19 names Jesus as the "Lord Jesus," a phrase which seems to come from later Christian worship.

- It does not flow well. Mary Magdalene is introduced in 16:9 as if she is being introduced for the first time—but she has been mentioned several times in the preceding verses (15:40, 47; **16:1**).

- It appears to include a random collection of signs drawn from the book of Acts.

One of the main arguments for including the long ending is that the ending in **verse 8** is strangely abrupt—it does not fit. I could not disagree more.

Every time Jesus does something to demonstrate his deity in Mark's Gospel, the response of the people is the same: fear (4:41; 5:15, 33, 36; 6:50; 9:6, 32). This gospel is no tame gospel. It cannot be domesticated. Fear here means something like shock and awe and sheer terror as your categories and presuppositions are blown to bits and your understanding of Jesus keeps growing and stretching and expanding.

So it is entirely fitting that Mark closes with fear. "They went out and fled from the tomb, for trembling and astonishment had seized them, and they said nothing to anyone, for they were afraid" (**16:8**). Mark is closing his account by saying, *The gospel of Jesus Christ, the Son of God, is an event that shatters all our categories and leaves us with shock and awe. It is both awesome and terrifying.*

Sunday's Children

Someone has called people living today "Saturday's children." So many people today live in despair and darkness, like the people in this story on dark Saturday. They don't know about the bright victory of Easter Sunday. But those who are Sunday's children look at the empty tomb in stunned silence, shock, and awe. And then they speak into the night of darkness and death.

My last high-school basketball game is a memory that is forever etched in my mind. One scene really stands out. It was the fourth quarter. We were playing defense, and the opposing team dribbled the ball to half court. Suddenly one of my teammates stole the ball and passed it to me. I had one guy to beat to our basket. I outran him and scored my one and only career slam dunk. Our fans went wild. For a moment, I felt like I was walking on air. It was one of the greatest feelings in the world.

But I was in for a rude awakening. The fans from the opposing team were cunning and calculated. They started a chant that shut down our whole cheering section: "Check-the-score, check-the-score, check-the-score." The trash talk hit home. We were still behind by sixteen points. For a brief moment it had felt like we were winning, but the crowd quickly brought us back to reality: we were losing, badly. It put everything into perspective.

Do you see? The resurrection is the great game-changer and the defining event for Sunday's children. We don't have a buried hope but a living hope. Like the crowd at the basketball game, we know how to check the score. Check the score, death. If you feel that you are losing but you have the resurrected Jesus as your Lord, then you are checking the wrong scoreboard. No one will be in heaven with him and say to themselves: "Look how much I lost!"

> The resurrection is the game-changer. We have a living hope!

The other side of that equation is true as well. If you are not a follower of Jesus and you feel like you are winning, then you are checking the wrong scoreboard. There is no one who will suffer eternal torment in hell and say, "Look how much I won!"

Suffering does not cancel our hope; it just clarifies it. It reminds us that ultimately we can't hope in health or relationships or children or money. Put your hope in the one hope that can't fail or die because he has already defeated death. Jesus is our living hope—and he has risen. We are Sunday's children.

Questions for reflection

1. "The gospel of Jesus Christ, the Son of God, is an event that shatters all our categories and leaves us with shock and awe. It is both awesome and terrifying." Is this true of you? How is God calling you to respond to this gospel?

2. What does it mean to you to be "Sunday's child"? How will you take this truth into your week?

3. Of everything you have learned in Mark's Gospel, what do you most want to remember? How will you make sure you remember it?

GLOSSARY

Adoption: the truth that Christians have been adopted as God's children and heirs (see Romans 8:14-17).

Analogy: a comparison between two things, usually using one of them to explain or clarify the other.

Ancient of Days: a name for God which refers to his eternal nature.

Atonement: a way of making people "at one" or enabling two parties to come back into relationship with one another, after wrong has been done by one of them. Jesus atones for our sin, which means he brings us back into relationship with God.

Baptism: a symbolic washing with water, usually to reflect someone coming to faith in Christ and having their sin washed clean.

Calvary: the place on the outskirts of Jerusalem where Jesus was crucified.

Church discipline: the practice of reprimanding church members when they are perceived to have sinned, in hope that the offender will repent and be reconciled to God and the church. It is also intended to protect other church members from the influence of sin.

Commentator: the author of a commentary, a book that explains parts of the Bible verse by verse.

Confirmation: in churches which baptize people as infants, confirmation is a ceremony in which someone (usually a teenager or adult) affirms their belief in Jesus.

Covenant: a binding agreement between two parties.

Cult: religion.

Cultic: to do with religion.

David: the second king of Israel, whose reign was the high point of

Israel's history. God promised that one of David's descendants would reign forever—the Messiah (see 2 Samuel 7).

Day of Atonement: the one day in the year when the high priest could enter the Most Holy Place to make a sacrifice on behalf of the people (Leviticus 16).

Decapolis: a group of ten cities to the east of Judea.

Deity: divine status.

Discipleship: being trained as a follower of Jesus.

Dissonance: clash between two things.

Doctrine: the study of what is true about God, or a statement about an aspect of that truth.

Elders: the teachers of Israel.

Elisha: an Old Testament prophet; Elijah's successor.

Eschatological: relating to death, judgment, and eternity.

Eunuch: a man who has been castrated.

Evangelicals: Christians who, broadly speaking, emphasize the importance of personal conversion through faith in Christ, and the authority of the Bible.

Exorcism: casting out an evil spirit from a person.

Exorcists: people who claim to be able to cast out evil spirits.

Fall: the moment when Eve and Adam disobeyed God and ate from the tree of the knowledge of good and evil (see Genesis 3), bringing sin into the world.

Fallen: affected by God's judgment, which was a consequence of the fall.

Flesh: the natural, sinful state of humanity, without the Spirit of God.

Forensic: to do with law courts.

Foreshadow: hint at something in advance.

Gentiles: people who are not ethnically Jewish.

Gospel: one of the four historical records of Jesus found in the New Testament—written by Matthew, Mark, Luke, and John.

Grace: undeserved favor. In the Bible "grace" is usually used to describe how God treats his people.

Great Awakening: a period of revival in the churches of Britain and the USA during the 18th and 19th centuries.

Groundhog Day: when events repeat themselves.

Hebrew: Jewish.

Hosanna: a cry asking for help from God, or an expression of praise for a savior.

I am: the name God uses for himself in Exodus 3:14 and elsewhere. This is sometimes translated "Yahweh" or "Lᴏʀᴅ" (using small capital letters).

Incarnation: the coming of the divine Son of God as a human, in the person of Jesus Christ.

Jewish Zealots: a political group which played a leading role in the revolt against Rome in AD 66–70.

Lay people: people who are involved in religious activity but who have not been formally trained as priests.

Liturgy: written words which can be used in a church service.

Lord's Supper: communion; sharing bread and wine together to remember the body and blood of Jesus.

Messiah: the Christ, literally "the anointed one." In the Old Testament, God promised that the Messiah would come to rescue and rule his people.

Metaphor: a word-image which is used to explain something, but is not to be taken literally. Metaphors describe one thing as being another thing (e.g. "The news was a dagger to his heart").

Methodist: the Methodist movement began in the 18th century as a reform movement within the Church of England. It eventually became its own denomination.

Ministry: work that is done in service of God, especially preaching and teaching about Jesus.

Myrrh: a type of tree gum or resin used as an ingredient in some perfumes and cosmetics.

Nard: a type of perfume.

New covenant: the new relationship with God which we can have as a result of the work of Jesus Christ.

Object: a person or thing to which something is done or to which a feeling is directed. If someone is an object of faith, it means that people place their faith in that person.

Omniscient: all-knowing.

Pagan: a word used in the Bible to refer to those who do not follow the true God.

Parable: a memorable story that illustrates a truth about Jesus and/or his kingdom.

Party spirit: devotion to a particular party, faction, or group, to the exclusion of others.

Passion: Jesus' death on the cross. ("Passion" comes from a word which means "suffering.")

Pharisees: a Jewish group who lived by strict observance of both God's Old Testament law and Jewish tradition.

Profane: disrespectful; unholy.

Promised land: the land on the eastern coast of the Mediterranean Sea that God promised Abraham he would give his descendants (Genesis 12:6-8; 13:14-18), and which the Israelites eventually took possession of under the leadership of Joshua.

Rabbi: a Jewish religious teacher.

Reckon: count as belonging to. If our sins are reckoned to Jesus, they are counted as his.

Redemption: freeing or releasing someone from slavery by buying them for a price. The word is used in the Bible to show how, by dying on the cross, Christ released us from slavery to sin and death.

Render: give.

Repentance: turning around in order to live the opposite way than you did before.

Sabbath: Saturday; the holy day when Jewish people were commanded not to work (see Exodus 20:8-11).

Sanctuary: a holy, safe place. The innermost part of the temple was sometimes called the sanctuary.

Saving faith: belief that Jesus is Lord, which guarantees salvation.

Serpent: here, the devil.

Substitutionary: involving a replacement, where someone or something stands in or is substituted for another.

Synagogue: a local place of worship, prayer, and teaching for Jewish people.

Tabernacle: a large tented area where the Israelites worshiped God from the time of Moses until the rule of Solomon. This was where his presence symbolically dwelled (see Exodus 26; 40).

The Christ: the Messiah, literally "the anointed one." In the Old Testament, God promised that the Messiah would come to rescue and rule his people.

Theologian: someone who studies and writes about God.

Took on flesh: became a human.

Torah: the five books of Moses in the Jewish Scriptures (i.e. Genesis, Exodus, Leviticus, Numbers, and Deuteronomy).

Trinity: a name for God, referring to the biblical doctrine that the one God is three Persons, distinct from one another, each fully God, of the same "essence" (or "God-ness"). We usually call these three Persons Father, Son, and Holy Spirit.

Transfigured: transformed into something more glorious and beautiful.

The destroyer: death.

Unclean: unholy.

Vice-regent: someone who rules on behalf of someone else.

Vindication: being cleared of suspicion and proved to have been right.

Wrath: God's settled, deserved hatred of and anger at sin.

Yahweh: the name by which God revealed himself to Moses (Exodus 3:13-14). Literally, it means, "I am who I am" or "I will be who I will be". Most English-language Bibles translate it as "LORD," using small capital letters.

Zion: another name for Jerusalem—or, more specifically, the mountain upon which it was built.

BIBLIOGRAPHY

- Augustine of Hippo, *The Harmony of the Gospels* (Christian Literature Company, 1888)

- James A. Brooks, *Mark*, in The New American Commentary series (B&H Press, 1991)

- D.A. Carson and Greg Beale, eds. Commentary on the New Testament Use of the Old Testament (Baker, 2007)

- Arthur Conan Doyle, "The Final Problem", in *Strand Magazine* (1893)

- James R. Edwards, *The Gospel of Mark*, in the Pillar New Testament Commentary series (Eerdmans, 2001)

- Jonathan Edwards, *Sermons and Discourses, 1743-1758* (Yale University Press, 2006)

- Donald English, *The Message of Mark*, in The Bible Speaks Today series (IVP, 1992)

- R.T. France, *The Gospel of Mark*, in the New International Greek Testament Commentary series (Eerdmans, 2002)

- David E. Garland, *The Gospel of Mark*, in the New International Version Application Commentary series (Zondervan, 1996)

- David E. Garland, *Zondervan Illustrated Bible Background Commentary*, vol. 1 (Zondervan, 2002)

- Morna D. Hooker, *The Gospel According to St. Mark*, in the Black's New Testament Commentary series (Hendrickson, 1992)

- R. Kent Hughes, *Mark: Jesus, Servant and Savior*, vol. 2, in the Preach the Word Commentaries series (Crossway, 1989)

- Timothy Keller, *King's Cross: The Story of the World in the Life of Jesus* (Dutton, 2011)

- William Lane, *The Gospel of Mark*, in the New International Commentary on the New Testament series (Eerdmans, 1974)

- C.S. Lewis, *Mere Christianity* (Simon & Schuster, 1996)

- C.S. Lewis, *The Chronicles of Narnia* (Harper Collins, 2001)

- Martyn Lloyd-Jones, *Great Doctrines of the Bible: God the Father, God the Son* (Crossway, 1996)

- Christopher Marshall, *Faith as a Theme in Mark's Narrative* (Cambridge University Press, 2009)

- Jason C. Meyer, *Preaching: A Biblical Theology* (Crossway, 2012)

- Paul Miller, *A Praying Life* (Navpress, 2017)

- Paul Minear, *The Gospel According to Mark* (John Knox Press, 1960)

- John Piper, *Desiring God: Meditations of a Christian Hedonist* (Multnomah, 2011)

- John Piper, *Future Grace: The Purifying Power of the Promises of God* (Multnomah, 2012)

- David Rhoads and Donald Michie, *Mark as Story: An Introduction to the Narrative of a Gospel* (Fortress Press, 1982)

- J.C. Ryle, *The Gospel of Mark*, in the Crossway Classic Commentaries series (Crossway, 1993)

- J.R.R. Tolkien, *The Hobbit* (Allen & Unwin, 1937)

- Paul Tripp, *Instruments in the Redeemer's Hands* (P&R Publishing, 2002)

- Rikk E. Watts, *Commentary on the New Testament use of the Old Testament* (Baker, 2007)

- Ben Witherington, *The Gospel of Mark: A Socio-Rhetorical Commentary* (Eerdmans, 2001)

- N.T. Wright, *Mark for Everyone* (Westminster John Knox Press, 2004)

Mark for...
Bible-study Groups

Jason Meyer's **Good Book Guide** to Mark is the companion to this resource, helping groups of Christians to explore, discuss, and apply the messages of this book together. Ten studies, each including investigation, application, Getting Personal, prayer and Explore More sections, take you through the book of Mark. Includes a concise Leader's Guide at the back.

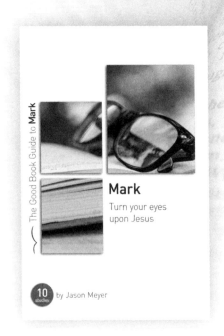

Find out more at:
www.thegoodbook.com/goodbookguides
www.thegoodbook.co.uk/goodbookguides

Daily Devotionals

Explore daily devotional helps you open up the Scriptures and will encourage and equip you in your walk with God. Available as a quarterly booklet, *Explore* is also available as an app, where you can download Jason's notes on Mark, alongside contributions from trusted Bible teachers including Tim Keller, Sam Allberry, Albert Mohler, and Tim Chester.

Find out more at:
www.thegoodbook.com/explore
www.thegoodbook.co.uk/explore

The Whole Series

- **Exodus For You** *Tim Chester*

- **Judges For You** *Timothy Keller*

- **Ruth For You** *Tony Merida*

- **1 Samuel For You** *Tim Chester*

- **2 Samuel For You** *Tim Chester*

- **Nehemiah For You** *Eric Mason*

- **Psalms For You** *Christopher Ash*

- **Proverbs For You** *Kathleen Nielson*

- **Isaiah For You** *Tim Chester*

- **Daniel For You** *David Helm*

- **Micah For You** *Stephen Um*

- **Mark For You** *Jason Meyer*

- **Luke 1-12 For You** *Mike McKinley*

- **Luke 12-24 For You** *Mike McKinley*

- **John 1-12 For You** *Josh Moody*

- **John 13-21 For You** *Josh Moody*

- **Acts 1-12 For You** *Albert Mohler*

- **Acts 13-28 For You** *Albert Mohler*

Find out more about these resources at:
www.thegoodbook.com/for-you
www.thegoodbook.co.uk/for-you

ISAIAH FOR YOU

"The book of Isaiah is full of good news—and it's news worth shouting about."

If you enjoyed *Mark For You*, try this expository guide to Isaiah by pastor and author Tim Chester. *Isaiah For You* will enrich your love for Christ, enlarge your view of God, and fuel your vision for the mission of the church.

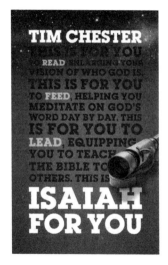

Isaiah For You is for you:

- *to read* as a book, mapping out the themes and challenges of Isaiah.
- *to feed,* using it as a daily devotional, complete with helpful reflection questions.
- *to lead,* equipping small-group leaders and Bible teachers and preachers to explain, illustrate and apply the Bible.

Find out more at:
thegoodbook.com/for-you
thegoodbook.co.uk/for-you

the good book

COMPANY

BIBLICAL | RELEVANT | ACCESSIBLE

At The Good Book Company, we are dedicated to helping Christians and local churches grow. We believe that God's growth process always starts with hearing clearly what he has said to us through his timeless word—the Bible.

Ever since we opened our doors in 1991, we have been striving to produce Bible-based resources that bring glory to God. We have grown to become an international provider of user-friendly resources to the Christian community, with believers of all backgrounds and denominations using our books, Bible studies, devotionals, evangelistic resources, and DVD-based courses.

We want to equip ordinary Christians to live for Christ day by day, and churches to grow in their knowledge of God, their love for one another, and the effectiveness of their outreach.

Call us for a discussion of your needs or visit one of our local websites for more information on the resources and services we provide.

Your friends at The Good Book Company

thegoodbook.com | thegoodbook.co.uk
thegoodbook.com.au | thegoodbook.co.nz
thegoodbook.co.in